Wings

SUNNY ANGEL

WITH PAUL KING

First published in 2017 by:

Red Admiral Press Ltd.
71-75 Shelton Street
Covent Garden
London
WC2H 9JQ
United Kingdom

www.sunny-angel.com
Facebook: Sunny Angel – Life story
Twitter: @777SunnyAngel

Paperback ISBN: 978-1-9997632-0-6
.ePub eBook ISBN: 978-1-9997632-1-3
.Mobi eBook ISBN: 978-1-9997632-2-0

Cover design by SpiffingCovers Ltd.

Printed in the UK

 **RED ADMIRAL PRESS**

For my loving daughter, Maya

Thank you for all our happy moments. When you're old enough to read this book, you'll understand why Mummy had the secret locked cupboard X

For my Mum & Dad

I love you both unconditionally. I understand you did the best you could. I have changed my name to save you any shame X

CONTENTS

RAY'S ASHES

I took my late husband, Ray's, ashes to Ireland in a plastic urn, which was in a small, maroon cardboard box provided by the funeral directors. Ray had Irish roots and wanted his ashes scattered in the River Shannon, but his family objected. I had considered creating a false set for them and began collecting twigs and dried leaves from near the flat, burning them to produce ash. I was doing this to keep my in-laws happy, but then thought better of it and decided I couldn't lie to them. As Ray's widow, I was determined to carry out his wishes even if it meant going alone.

Leaving home at 5 a.m. on a dark winter morning, I took a flight from London Stansted to Shannon Airport in the west of Ireland, then a bus to Limerick City. This was my second trip to Ireland – the first was with Ray to celebrate our wedding the previous year. Dressed in black, I had no change of clothes as I was flying back the same day, 10th December 2004. I carried just an urn of ashes – my Ray. Finding a florist in the town, I bought two roses – one red, one white, to represent love and peace. Limerick was overcast and cloudy as I walked from the bus station down towards the Shannon, and then past King John's Castle on the river bank. I had to squeeze through broken railings to get down by the water. The current was strong – so was the wind. I listened to our favourite song on my headphones – *I Knew I Loved You*, by Savage Garden. Unscrewing the top of the urn, I began tipping the ashes, Ray's remains, but also those of a shamrock-patterned baby-gro we'd bought the previous year. I'd miscarried three months before Ray died. The wind took a few of the ashes, the Shannon the rest. The flowers followed Ray into the water and I cried as my 'happily ever after' disappeared down the river. I stepped forward from the steps and let the river wash over my trainers. Overwhelmed with grief and despair, I considered jumping in and almost toppled over, but a gust of wind seemed to blow me back and I steadied myself. The sun peeked through the clouds as if to signal the end of the service. Sun rays. No more Ray. I stood motionless for a while, lost in thought. As I turned away and climbed back up towards the road, church bells chimed from the nearby cathedral. I promised myself I wouldn't rest until I knew the truth about Ray's death.

As was usual in the months following Ray's death, I needed a drink. So, before going back to the airport, I went to Ray's favourite pub. A middle-aged barman with a red face and two elderly male customers looked me up and down.

'Afternoon,' said one of the old men.

'What can I get you, love?' asked Redface.

'Double tequila, please.'

I went to the bathroom, washed the tears off my face, came back to the bar and lit a cigarette. Redface shook his head.

'You can't smoke here. It's illegal, so.' This was before the smoking ban in England. As I walked towards the door, he added, 'You can't take that outside, you're not allowed to drink in the street. How old are you anyway, like?'

'Twenty-six. Here's my passport.'

'No, that's OK. Hold the cigarette out the door.'

So, I stayed a while with my glass in my right hand and one foot inside the pub, and my cigarette in my left hand outside the door, along with my left foot.

Whilst I was drinking my second double, Redface came towards the door, having decided a table near me needed polishing. 'We don't get many like you here. I mean Asian girls, like. Smoking and drinking.' I ignored him. 'There was a black fella in here Tuesday,' he added helpfully.

'Oh, *really*?'

'I'm not being funny, like. There's not a racist bone in my body.' Redface spotted my wedding ring. 'So where's your husband then?'

'He's in the River Shannon.'

'What the fuck's he doing there, like? Swimming?'

'No, I've just scattered his ashes.'

* * *

Travelling back from Stansted Airport to Woking on the M25 around midnight, I was starting to sober up, driving carefully in the middle lane. A car flashed me, bright lights in the darkness, triggering memories of my stalker, my first 'husband' – Khan. Ever present. I got home to the flat I used to share with Ray, the flat where he was found hanged. Mentally and physically drained, I went to bed with a bottle of Jack Daniels.

My name is Sunny Angel and this is my story.

Chapter 1

TOWN CALLED MALICE

I'm Sunny, a single mum from Woking with one beautiful daughter, Maya, a cat called Mo and two snakes, Houdini and Jaya. People have often told me I should write a book about my life.

* * *

I was born on the 4th of July 1978 at St Peter's Hospital in Chertsey, Surrey. My family lived in a village on the outskirts of Woking, a commuter town twenty miles south-west of London. My parents are Indian – Hindu Punjabis – and we were the only Indians in the village.

At 16, I went to college to study A-levels, but my mother and older brother, Dilip, told me I wouldn't be allowed to go to university. Dilip was studying Maths at Oxford at the time. Traditionally, big brothers have considerable influence and responsibility in Indian families. This attitude was far from the norm in our community and both my brothers married university graduates. But the family envisioned an arranged marriage for me in the future, and higher education was not on the agenda. So, I didn't see the point in continuing in full-time education. I dropped out of college after a year and started working, aged 17. I also took up smoking and drinking in the pub, but only at lunchtimes – I wasn't allowed out at night, or allowed much of a social life, really, so I wasn't streetwise.

I got my first job in 1995 at Modo Merchants, a paper wholesaler in Weybridge. It was a warehouse on an industrial estate. My role involved making mock-ups of books and CD covers. The pay wasn't great, but I loved being able to buy my own clothes and run a car.

At work, I used to sign for the parcels that came to reception. There was an Asian delivery man who would take my signature and always gaze at me, unembarrassed, with a piercing stare. This was slightly creepy, although, he was quite good-looking, with a goatee beard, but I didn't pay too much attention at the time. In February 1997, I got a job at Galleon – BBC Magazine Subscriptions in Woking. It was a call centre within walking distance of my parents' home. The people were nice and I enjoyed the work.

Around this time, I began to sense that I was being watched. When I was driving, a car would flash me for no reason. Talking to a friend in the street, I would feel someone staring at me. But, when I looked around, no one stood out. I noticed camera flashes and believed I was being photographed. I became obsessed with the idea that I was being followed.

One Saturday morning – 15th March 1997 – I planned to go to Woking town centre to meet a boy to sort out a misunderstanding. Just childish stuff. Even though I was now 18, I wasn't allowed out on my own without good reason. As a diversion, I went to see a girlfriend, Naz. Mum dropped me off at Naz's house. I only had two hours to get to town and back. I did have my own car, but Mum didn't let me use it, except for work. I asked Naz to cover for me. She wasn't entirely happy, but agreed, urging me to 'Just get back in time.' I hurried to town on foot. It took about thirty minutes as I went the long way to avoid my parents' house. I wasn't used to going into Woking alone. I felt nervous – I wasn't comfortable lying and wondered whether I was doing the right thing. The sky was light grey, spring was still around the corner, and I remember feeling something wasn't right about the day.

I rang The Boy and arranged to meet him in the bandstand area, a slightly secluded place outside the back of the shopping centre. He arrived after me and we sat on a bench. It was early; not many people were out shopping yet. The Boy was Asian, of Pakistani origin. Like me, he wasn't supposed to hang out with the opposite sex and seemed worried about being seen in public with a female. While we were talking, The Boy suddenly looked up and stared at an Asian man in his thirties, about ten yards away, leaning against the bandstand, watching us intently. The Boy blurted out nervously, 'That man's a nutter!' and began telling a story about the man and a girl, but he was mumbling and not making sense. I don't think he wanted the stranger to hear what he was saying. The man continued to stare and, after about a minute, he walked towards us. The Boy seemed frightened as the stranger drew closer and hurriedly arranged to meet me somewhere else in five minutes. Whispering, 'Go quickly!' he stood up and disappeared swiftly into the shopping centre where he worked. The stranger approached, staring straight at me. As I stood to leave, he strode right up to me, blocking my path. I tried to walk around him, but he stepped sideways and held his arm out in front of me.

The stranger was only a little taller than me, but carried himself confidently. He had waxed, shiny hair and thick, black eyebrows that perched above dark brown eyes – bloodshot eyes – which bored into mine. I looked away, overpowered, then back at the stranger, who held my gaze like a cobra with its prey. The corners of his mouth pointed down slightly, like he knew pain.

'Excuse me!' I protested, trying to get past. My mouth was dry – there was no one else around.

'You shouldn't speak to that boy, Sunita.' I was stunned. How did he know my name? 'Your name is Sunita, isn't it? Stay away from that boy, I warn you. He might rape you. I've been looking out for you.'

A chill ran down my spine, but I felt I had to say something.

'Who are you? How do you know my name?'

'I've been watching you, Sunita, for a long time. Following you. You drive a white Nissan, don't you? You parked on the corner by the car park the other day, didn't you? You wore a skirt and boots on Friday. You smoke, don't you? And drink? Your family don't care about you much, do they?' This was scary – everything the stranger said was true. Then he added, 'I loved and lost a Sunita once. Tell me, could you be my Sunita?' He sounded disturbed.

'I'm sorry you lost a Sunita. No, I'm not her. I had a feeling someone was following me. Now I know I'm right. You're a nutter, please go away! Leave me alone!' As I tried to walk away, he grabbed my wrist and forcefully pulled me towards him.

'I know where you live. You will do what I say. My name is Raj. I'm Indian like you.' He seemed to make a point of saying that – *I'm one of you.* Raj is a popular Indian name that comes from the ancient Sanskrit for king. Still gripping tightly, Raj told me, 'I know about your family. I've been watching them, too. There's your mum and dad, and two brothers. I know what time they all leave and come back to the house.' I tried to twist my arm free but couldn't. Even my bones felt Raj's grip.

'Why are you doing this? I don't know you. Have I ever hurt you?' I asked.

Raj clarified his intentions. 'I always get what I want, and I *will* get you!' Then he let go of me. I laughed nervously and tried to walk on, but he stood in the way again and recited my number plate, Dad's number plate, and told me where Mum worked. When Raj explained that he used to work for a parcel delivery company, the penny dropped. He was the delivery man from my first workplace, now clean-shaven. 'I used to follow you on the train when you went to college.' I'd been on a day release course at my previous job. Raj seemed more proud than embarrassed by his revelation, adding, 'It was rude of you not to acknowledge me.' My chest felt heavy, I was breathless, but now knew I'd been right about being followed.

I'd forgotten to keep an eye on the time. My mobile phone rang. It was Naz, panicking. Mum had turned up at her house early, so Naz had to tell her I'd gone into town. Now I had to call Mum, who didn't even know I owned a mobile. My big brother, Dilip, had set up a phone contract for me in his name when I was 17, without my parents' knowledge as they wouldn't have approved. Mum shouted, 'Where the hell are you?' and arranged to come and pick me up. Raj listened to my conversation and teased me.

'I can't believe you lied, that's so bad! What are you gonna tell your mum now? Tell her you're with me!'

'What? No way! If my Mum sees me with a man, she'll kill me.'

Raj put his arm around me. I didn't try to stop him. He wasn't using force now, so it seemed safer that way. He whispered, 'Your mum doesn't care about you,' before adding, 'May God protect you from evil.' Then he wrote a landline number on a scrap of paper and put it in my pocket. I wanted to rip it up, but I was frightened of his response.

Raj stayed with me while I waited for Mum. When I saw her pulling up, I moved away quickly from Raj, who melted into the background, promising, 'I know where you are, you'll be seeing me.'

Chapter 2

BIG BAD WOLF

Mum shouted at me all the way home. She had a habit of making me feel worthless. '*Gandi goori* (dirty girl). Why you lying with me? Where you go?'

During the day, I just kept looking at Raj's number, like I was drawn to it. I rang The Boy, but there was no answer.

I called my friend, Adil. 'Look, I saw this man, Raj.' My description of Raj struck a chord with Adil, who warned, 'If it's Khan, stay away.'

'No, he told me he was a Hindu called Raj.'

I decided to ring Raj and tell him to stop stalking me. Dialling the number, I heard Dad coming up the stairs, so I hung up – Dad didn't know about the phone either. In my panic, I failed to realise that Raj would now have my number. A little later, I received a voice message – this was before texts. It sounded like Raj.

'How are you?'

The phone rang again – I ignored it. Raj left another message. 'I'm coming by your house in two minutes. Look out the window.' My parents' house was quite secluded, so I thought he couldn't possibly know where I lived. But a couple of minutes later, Raj was standing in the street right in front of our house. The realisation that Raj had been here before, hit me. Worried sick, I went downstairs to tell Mum and Dad, but wasn't quite sure how to tell them. Part of the problem was, I'd tricked Mum into believing I was going to Naz's house, but had been caught out sneaking secretly to town instead.

'There's this man been following me for months, flashing his lights at me in the car.'

Dad laughed. 'Don't worry about it. It's just someone having a joke, maybe. *Bewakoof!*' This is Punjabi for stupid.

'Why would anybody follow you?' added Mum. They didn't seem interested, so I went back upstairs and looked out of the window. Raj was still standing there in the street. He saw me, turned away and walked to the payphone up the road, and called me again.

'See? I told you. Now, next time I ring, you answer your phone. If you don't answer your phone, I'm going to burn the house down. Do you understand me?' Raj spoke very deliberately. He sounded like he meant every word. Terror struck me as I tried to digest what he'd said. I hoped Raj was joking, but I didn't really think he was. Peeking out of the window anxiously, I saw that Raj was now back in front of the house with a gas lighter, flashing it: *on – off – on – off.* The features on Raj's face lit up. He looked up at me, a look that said he meant business. I put my hand up as if to say, *please stop.*

I turned away briefly as Mum called me from downstairs to help with the cooking. When I looked back to the street, Raj had disappeared. Had he given up his little hoax? Or had he gone to get petrol? Was he already putting petrol around the house? My phone rang. 'If you don't do as I tell you, I will throw *acid* on your mum's face. I'll *stab* your dad. I'll *kill* your brothers. If you don't do what I tell you, *this* is what's going to happen. *These* are the consequences.'

Time seemed to stand still – I felt faint. I pleaded in

desperation. 'OK. Please don't hurt my family. Right, now, cards on the table. I've got a mobile phone, which my Dad doesn't know about. If you want to carry on talking to me on this number, you've got to know that I can't answer it every time you call, but I'll pick it up when I can. OK?'

Twenty minutes passed. Raj called me once more from a payphone. He said he wanted to see me again. He wanted me to come outside the house. I begged him not to, telling him, truthfully, that I wouldn't be allowed out. Raj accepted this, but told me he would come back on Monday morning and walk me to work. He dictated which route I was to take and at what time. Of course, he already knew where I worked and what time I started.

I realised I was in trouble and out of my depth. I tried to tell my parents about Raj again. It was difficult. We just didn't discuss things. 'Someone stopped me in town. He's been following me for months.'

But I couldn't get through to them. Dad was in a world of his own, watching television and drinking beer. He looked at me, then back at the telly. Mum had followed me into the room. '*Tsoh!* No one following you!'

Sunday was nerve wracking. I wondered what would happen on Monday. Should I do as Raj asked? Or should I call the police? It's hard to explain now. I feared for my safety and that of my family, but I couldn't talk to them about it. I didn't know what to do. I was young and inexperienced, very naïve, and felt I had no choice but to deal with Raj myself.

Monday 17th March 1997. I took big, deep breaths as I got ready for work that morning. Mum had caught me lending my car to my friend, Moonie, the week before, so I wasn't allowed to drive to work and had to walk. As soon as I left the house, I spotted Raj at the end of the road, waiting for me. *Damn! Call in sick,* I thought. But then I realised I would be home alone. Better to be in public should Raj turn violent. Warily approaching the end of my road where Raj stood, I looked back at the house. When I turned around, Raj had disappeared. I looked left and right at the junction but couldn't see him anywhere, so I continued walking. When I crossed the road, Raj appeared suddenly from a footpath and grabbed me, covering my mouth so I couldn't scream. I struggled, but Raj tightened his grip. I was helpless, but I tried to pull his hand away from my mouth and nose so I could breathe. He whispered slowly in my ear, a sinister sound that haunts me still.

'Stop struggling. I will let you go. Don't scream, OK? Just smile and I will walk you to work.' *I will* – not *I'll* – Raj spoke like this when emphasising a point. His voice was slightly high pitched, almost like a buzzing sound. With Raj's hand still over my mouth, and his other arm gripping me tightly, I nodded my head in submission. It all happened so quickly, I couldn't think straight. Raj let go of me but stayed close, like a shadow. He kept bumping into me and pushing me. I couldn't understand why, but he was like a dog with a new toy. As we went past *The Bridge Barn* pub, Raj shoved me hard and his mood turned nasty. 'Recognise this place? This pub? This is where I've seen you having a drink with a white man. What do you think you're doing? Indian girls don't do this. How dare you!' He then changed his tone and laughed. 'You must be very special and strong. You have guts. I admire you.' We were nearing my workplace, which wasn't far. Raj kept looking me up and down, examining me. He said he wasn't happy with the office suit I was wearing. I told him it was none of his business. Raj replied, speaking very deliberately. 'I am here to help you. I care for you. Your family don't, Sunita. It's a cruel world out there. You are so special.'

No one had ever called me 'special' before. Raj told me

he would meet me for lunch so we could talk more without my family knowing. Just before lunchtime, I looked out of the window. Raj was already waiting for me. I felt uneasy, but didn't say anything to anyone. I went downstairs, where Raj greeted me at the entrance. He asked what I normally did at lunchtime.

'I go to the petrol station for a sandwich and a drink.'

'You may do that today,' he replied, as if giving me permission. So, we went to the Jet Petrol Station, a minute's walk away. The Asian cashier looked oddly at us, as if he knew Raj, who approached the counter without leaving my side. The cashier greeted him with a Muslim greeting, '*Salaam Sahib*', which seemed strange as Raj claimed he was Hindu, like me. After lunch, Raj walked me back to work. He called later to say he would be waiting to walk me home and dictated the route. When home time arrived, Raj was outside as promised. He accompanied me to the end of my road and watched me until I entered the house. It felt like I was in a strange dream. Was I imagining all this? I went to help Mum in the kitchen. I wanted to tell her what happened, but couldn't. We didn't have that type of relationship. I went upstairs to my room, confused and isolated, and I cried, hugging my teddy bear.

The next day, Raj took me to a pub car park at lunchtime, pretending he was taking me for a drink. He shouted at me and pushed me into his car, where we just sat. He wouldn't let me eat my sandwich from the petrol station, so I spent the afternoon hungry. He was controlling me, testing me. I was angry, but, again, I was too scared to protest. On Wednesday, I made sandwiches to eat at my desk, which made Mum ask why. I told her I was working through lunch.

On Thursday, I still had a caller on the phone at midday, when I was supposed to meet Raj. He didn't have a mobile phone and I wasn't near the window, so couldn't warn him. My team had all gone to lunch. It was five past twelve when my call ended and I put away my headphones. I could hear a commotion in the hallway. Moving to the window to look for Raj, I couldn't see him outside. As I approached the stairs, my manager called me into her office.

'Sunita, we have a situation. Your boyfriend is very angry. He's threatened staff members. He's asking for you. He just tried to break the door down.'

'I'm so sorry! He's not my boyfriend. He keeps following me. He won't leave me alone.' My manager asked if I wanted the police called. I said that wouldn't help, that it would create problems with my family. If not my boyfriend, what was he? A stalker, who had become my companion because I didn't know how to shake him off? Now that Raj was escorting me to and from work, it would have been even harder to discuss things with my parents.

Walking out, I tried to remain calm. Raj was furious. 'Why were you late?' he screamed – we spoke only English at this stage. My colleagues watched on uncomfortably, but didn't know what to do. Raj grabbed my wrist – no one intervened. I managed to jerk free and move away, heading quickly towards the town centre. Raj followed me and stuck close. I quickened my pace but he grabbed my arm and stopped me just outside the petrol station. Raj twisted my arm behind my back until it hurt. I felt angry, but it was a powerless anger, impotent in the face of Raj's superior strength. *When I was a little girl, I felt the same powerless anger as V controlled me, abused me.* Now Raj was controlling me. 'You will say sorry, or I won't let go! LOOK AT ME!' I continued to stare at the floor. Raj turned my arm further, like a corkscrew. I whispered the word '*Sorry*', but I didn't know what I was sorry for. Raj let go of my arm and herded me back towards my office, pulling and prodding. He ordered me to tell my boss I was unwell so I could go home sick. She reluctantly accepted my story as I hadn't been off sick before. I tidied my desk and left feeling slightly ashamed, and even more alone.

Raj was waiting outside, but his mood had changed completely. He smiled and walked me to his car in *The Bridge Barn* car park, where he opened the door for me, almost like a gentleman. He looked me in the eyes and quietly apologised for his behaviour. 'I love you. I can't bear to be away from you. I'm afraid of losing you.' Raj now seemed vulnerable and promised he wouldn't use force any more. He wanted to know more about me. Why didn't my family love me? Raj now seemed caring and thoughtful, but I was guarded with my answers.

I needed to use the bathroom. 'I'm going to the ladies. I'll go to the pub toilets. Don't panic! I'm not having a drink.' As Raj's mood seemed better, I was trying to assert a little independence but I made eye contact as I opened the car door, wary of his reaction. When I put my foot out, he grabbed my hand, roughly. My heart sank as Raj's mood darkened again.

'I will come with you to the pub. Leave your bag and phone in the car.' In the ladies, I looked in the mirror and psyched myself up to stand up to Raj. Then he called me from just outside the door. There was no escaping him.

At the bar, I ordered a drink and cheekily asked Raj if he wanted one.

'What are you doing?' he asked, pretending to be shocked.

'Ordering a drink! What does it look like? I changed my mind, too, just like you! Oh dear, my handbag is in your car. Are you paying? Or can I have your keys, please?' I suppose I was trying to show myself I could deal with him. I asked for half a Stella – that's what Dad drinks – while Raj ordered himself a pint. We sat outside and Raj lit a cigarette. I asked if I could smoke, too. He agreed. I teased him for telling me off a few days ago for drinking and smoking in the pub.

'Yes, but you did that with white men, not me!' The pub was close to both my parents' house and work. I was concerned about being spotted by Mum or my work colleagues, especially as I was supposed to be sick.

As lunchtime went past, Raj wanted to cuddle me more and talk less. Sometimes, Raj made me feel *special*. I suffered from low self-esteem and had never felt particularly special before. Astonishing as it may seem, I began to grow fond of Raj, who slowly, but surely, took control of me. Although, every time he tried to touch me inappropriately, or kiss me, I would edge away.

Once, he asked, 'Why do you move away from me? Most girls would drop their clothes and jump at the chance of something happening.'

'I'm not "most" girls. I don't do that. Please don't keep trying. The cuddling is nice, but I'm not having sex with you. I'm not the type of girl who has sex with everyone and anyone. I'm saving myself for marriage.'

'I have great respect for you,' replied Raj.

* * *

In 1947, India gained independence from Britain, but was split into two nations – India, with a Hindu majority, and Pakistan, a state for Muslims. Most of West Punjab became part of Pakistan, including Lahore, the old capital of the Sikh Empire, whilst East Punjab lay within India's new borders. But Partition awakened old hatreds, tearing apart communities as The Punjab went up in flames. In West Punjab, Hindus and

Sikhs were slaughtered by the thousands, whilst Muslims, in turn, were ethnically cleansed from East Punjab. Millions fled their homes on both sides of the new border, including Dad's family, Hindus, who had to run for their lives when he was a baby. Gandhi and the other leaders pleaded in vain for an end to the violence, but the genie of religious bigotry was out of the bottle. Hindus, Sikhs and Muslims were gang raped or murdered, their bodies mutilated in the name of religion. The same happened in Bengal and elsewhere in India. Hundreds of thousands died, and an estimated 12-14 million people were displaced; the largest mass migration in history. Since independence, India and Pakistan have fought several wars.

At college, my best friends were British Pakistanis, fellow Asians from a similar background. We were the children of immigrants who came to the UK for a better life. Although, we practised different religions – they were Muslim, I was Hindu. As well as Naz and Adil, there was Moonie. He was my first boyfriend. A shy boy, softly spoken with a sweet smile, who was my height, about five foot two. I broke the ice by calling him 'Little Guy'. He pretended to take offence and we kind of dated for a year. I was the Sun, he was the Moon. Moonie gave me a sense of belonging, something I hadn't always had. Sometimes, we would go into the woods next to the college, but we only held hands – I wasn't ready for anything else. Other times, during free periods, we would go and play pool in *The Planets,* an amusement arcade in Woking. On my seventeenth birthday, Moonie told me that his parents had arranged a marriage for him with a bride from Pakistan. I was heartbroken, although, I knew my family would have objected as much as his to us being together.

* * *

Sometimes, Raj spoke kindly to me, but in a controlling way. At other times, he was bullying. He would take my mobile phone, call my friends and threaten them, warning them to stay away from me. Seeing so many Pakistani names on my phone, Raj asked, 'Why have you got Paki friends, anyway?'

'What does it matter?' I asked. I couldn't understand why he was so racist. Raj just smirked.

Raj asked me about Moonie and threatened to hurt him. Maybe he'd heard something about us, but I played dumb, pretending I hardly knew him. Oddly, Raj never called Moonie, but he threatened Naz, who was trying to keep in contact with me. I learnt the full story whilst writing this book. Raj lived near Naz. One day, he approached her near her flat and told her, 'I don't want to see you again. Stay away from her.' Naz is very feisty and stood up to Raj. A few days later, she came home to see Raj by some bins, where he'd set fire to some cardboard. 'You see this fire?' he warned her, 'It's nothing. If you try and cross me, that will be your house.'

For some reason, Raj asked me about my work skills. I told him I could do some stuff on Word and Excel, and I mentioned that we had a computer at home. Raj decided I would help him with his CV, and we would do it at my parents' house while they were in. At first, I thought he was joking. Then, I hoped he was. As we walked towards the family home, Raj was wearing his best shirt with a waistcoat and shiny shoes, which went *clip clop* on the ground. I had butterflies in my stomach. I'd never brought a boy back before, and, at 26 – which he claimed to be – Raj was hardly a boy. At least he's Indian, I thought. I would just tell Mum and Dad that I was helping him with his CV. At the front door, I took out my door key.

'No. Use the doorbell.' Raj wanted to be welcomed personally. Dad answered the door, beer in hand, and a puzzled expression. Then Mum appeared. I introduced Raj and explained about the CV. It all felt so weird bringing the stalker home to meet my parents. I found it hard to blink.

'Sunita! Go make Raj a cup of tea! *Jaldi, jaldi* (hurry)!' clucked Mum, inviting Raj into the lounge. Dad disappeared back to his TV room. Indians boil tea with milk, sugar and spices in a saucepan, but Raj took his tea the English way, kettle and teabag. As the kettle boiled, I could hear Mum chatting away and Raj using his best posh voice. I brought Raj his tea and we stayed with Mum while he drank it.

* * *

'So, Sunita help you with CV, Raj?'

'Yeah. I need to update it.'

'So, you Indian, Raj?'

'Yeah, I'm Indian. Like you. Hindu.' *I'm one of you.*

'Where family from in India?'

'Er, Delhi. New Delhi. I'm from New Delhi. Where are you from, Aunty Ji?'

For a moment, Mum looked like she'd swallowed a wasp, but she recovered. 'Yamuna Nagar. It's north of *Dilli*,' – that's how Indians pronounced it. 'So, how you know my daughter, Raj?'

'She's helping me with my CV. Woking. I met her in Woking.'

Mum tried another tack. 'So, where you working?'

'Yeah, Woking.'

'No, where you *working*?' Mum persisted.

'Ah, um, business. I'm a businessman.'

'Businessman? So, why you need CV?'

'Well, I'm just starting up. Import export. So I'm working as a van driver to get some money while I'm starting up, Aunty Ji.'

'Oh, really?' There was a pause before Mum produced her best fake smile and asked, 'What part of Dilli you from, Raj?'

'The north part. North New Delhi,' replied Raj. New Delhi is India's capital, but a relatively small part of Delhi. Mum beamed – the perfect hostess. She obviously knew Raj was lying. I wanted the ground to swallow me up.

We left Mum to go and work on Raj's CV. After returning his cup to the kitchen, like a well brought up young man, Raj shoved me in the back in the corridor. We passed Dad's TV room, which has a door frame but no door. Raj marched in, introduced himself and seemed to linger while he surveyed the room and my brothers, who were watching something with Dad. Raj seemed pleased as punch being in the house with my family; an honoured guest.

We were now alone in Dad's study where the computer was. Raj kissed the back of my neck. 'No, please! Not here,' I whispered. I opened a new Word document on the computer and Raj dictated what to type. After a few minutes, I reviewed our work. At the top it said, *Name: Raj.*

'Raj, we haven't put your surname. What is it?'

'We can put that later. I'm bored with this now.' Raj now made his excuses and left, waving at Dad and my brothers as he swaggered past the TV room, before popping his head around the door of the lounge to exchange a cheery, 'Bye,' with Mum. Looking back, it's clearly odd that Raj dictated a CV with no surname. Of course, he wasn't really there for the CV. In the context of Indian and Pakistani culture, Raj's behaviour in coming around was quite shocking. In fairly traditional families like mine, unmarried girls of 18 just didn't bring boys home like that. Raj knew this. He'd been watching the family and figured he wouldn't be in any physical danger, but he would have known his visit might create difficulties for me. I now see that Raj would have been happy to undermine me in the eyes of my parents. I think he also wanted to suss out my family and the house at close quarters. When Raj had gone, Mum exploded.

'Who the hell is he? Why you bring that Paki around here? Calling me Aunty Ji! Make me sick.'

'Paki' is a racist term, short for Pakistani, but often used by some white people when referring to South Asians, including Indians – I've been called a Paki many times. Though, some Indians use the term specifically for Pakistanis.

'No, he's Indian. His name's Raj. He's 26,' I protested. I wanted to say that he was the man who'd been stalking me, but Mum shouted over me.

'I know all Indians in Woking. He never Indian, he not called Raj. And he never 26! And *you*! You nothing special. Why he like *you*? Now you in trouble,' Mum warned, calling for Dad. After ranting at Dad in Punjabi for a while, she asked in English, 'Why she bring him here?'

'How do I know? She's your daughter,' shrugged Dad, passing the problem back to Mum and returning to his TV and beer.

That evening, Raj called me on the phone and played me. 'See? Your family don't care about you. If a daughter of mine brought a man home, I'd kill him! And I'd slap my daughter! Your big brother is a big girl!' Raj paused before adding, 'Don't worry, I'm here for you.'

The next day, Raj phoned to say he was sending me a pizza at home. I begged him not to.

'Please don't. Mum's downstairs and Dad will be back soon.'

'Nonsense. Anyway, it's too late, I've ordered it. I want you to eat it.' The doorbell rang. I hurtled down the stairs, but only in time to see Mum open the door.

'It's for Sunita, from Raj,' announced the delivery boy.

'Why he sending you pizza?' shouted Mum. She didn't like people doing favours for me and was especially unhappy with a present from Raj, whom she took to be Muslim and Pakistani. Conspiratorially, she added, 'We better not tell Dad.'

Rather than throw the pizza away, Mum hid it in its box in the oven – Asians tend to cook on the hob. Two days later, I'd forgotten to perform a chore for Mum in the kitchen. As punishment, Mum produced the pizza and showed Dad, triumphantly.

'Look what he send her! *This!*' hissed Mum, brandishing the offending box. 'Why is he sending her pizza?' Dad asked Mum, before grabbing a bottle of beer from the fridge and wandering back to the TV.

Disappointed at Dad's apparent lack of interest in Raj's gift, Mum slammed the pizza onto the kitchen table, snapping, 'Go on! Eat your bloody pizza!'

I ate one slice to prove some kind of point, I suppose. It was cold and stale, the topping a soggy mess.

Raj would ring me on my mobile phone, which Mum now knew about, although Dad still didn't. Sometimes, I didn't have it with me because it was hidden in my room. So, he would ring on the landline. If Mum or Dad answered, he would put the phone down. Or he would hang up after two rings and I would go and call him. If he rang from his brother's house, where he lived, he would withhold the number so Mum and Dad couldn't trace the call. But, other times, he used payphones as he didn't have a mobile. I got to know all the payphone numbers nearby. If I reached the phone first and dialled 1471 to trace the call, I would know how far away he was, five or ten minutes, or whatever. Raj used this against my parents.

'Why don't they call the police? That's what I would do if someone kept calling and putting the phone down. They obviously don't care about you.'

Chapter 3

A ROCK AND A HARD PLACE

Lord Ganesh is the Hindu elephant deity, popular throughout India, associated with knowledge, prosperity and new beginnings. Also known as a protector, Lord Ganesh thwarts those with evil intent.

* * *

One day in April, we were walking towards Raj's car for lunch, which had become the norm, and had a disagreement on the way. Raj had asked me to take the afternoon off sick. I said I couldn't. Without warning, Raj grabbed my wrist and started pulling me in the direction of my parents' house. He was raging. I was just beginning to trust him and had forgotten what his temper was like. I tried to stop walking a couple of times but Raj strode on, his iron grip pulling me in his wake. I dreaded to imagine why Raj was taking me home. I feared he might hurt my parents. When we got there, he demanded I open the front door. I was shaking with fear, but complied. Not feeling I had much choice, I hoped for the best. No one was in.

In the hallway, Raj made a speech. 'I can't take the frustration any more. Do you hear me? I want to know if you can cook, and clean and iron. Well? Can you?' There's no answer to that, is there? I was dumbfounded, but I thought I was safe – the questions seemed so innocent. But then, Raj grabbed me, threw me to the side and removed his tracksuit bottoms to reveal his grey boxer shorts. My heart pounded in my head and I felt a panic attack coming as Raj blocked my exit. He asked me what was upstairs – I didn't reply. With his tracksuit bottoms in one hand and my wrist in the other, he hauled me up the stairs. I tried to resist, but Raj was stronger and pulled me up and along the corridor. *This triggered a flashback – I'm helpless, V on top of me.* I prayed in my mind to the Hindu gods for help.

'What are you doing?' I stammered, although I had a pretty good idea. Raj dragged me into my bedroom. He knew where it was as he'd seen me at the window often enough. Lying back, Raj pulled me towards him on the bed. I struggled but ended up on top of him. He started undressing me. I gripped his hand to stop him, but I was too weak. Suddenly, he changed tack and pushed me to the end of the bed, away from him.

'I really love you! I'm mad about you. I really want to make love to you. If the only way is through marriage, let's get married. God will be our witness. You will bring a picture of your god and I have something from the mosque. What? You hadn't guessed? My name is Khan. I'm a Muslim.'

I couldn't take it in. It's an understatement to say I experienced a range of emotions that day. One minute Raj – or rather Khan – appeared to be trying to rape me, the next, he was expressing his love and proposing marriage. He'd also revealed that he wasn't a Hindu like me after all, but a Muslim. At first, I wondered if it was another trick, but then I realised he was serious. The danger of rape seemed to have passed. Khan held me gently and saw the fear in my eyes. He led me towards the window, where there were photos and small statues of Hindu gods, incense sticks and *sindoor*, red powder, which is used for prayer rituals, but also by Indian brides in wedding ceremonies.

'It's OK, trust me. I love you. Here is a picture of your Hindu god, Ganesh.' Khan placed the sindoor in the parting of my hair, the Indian way. Then, he held both my hands softly, looked into my eyes and we said the word, *Qubool* – I agree – three times, the Muslim way. Whatever the legality, I now believed I was married. It was Monday 14th April 1997. I went along with the wedding only because I was scared. A few moments earlier, I believed Khan was going to rape me. I wasn't expecting marriage today, but I was backed into a corner, just stalling for time. I felt trapped and could see no way out.

Standing in his grey boxer shorts, Khan chucked his tracksuit bottoms at me, saying, 'Go and show me your ironing skills, Wifey!'

So, after a kind of makeshift Hindu-Muslim ceremony, I ironed Khan's tracksuit bottoms before my new 'husband' escorted me back to work. There was plenty to ponder that afternoon. For my family, marriage to a Muslim was unthinkable. His religion didn't bother me – my biggest fear was sex. We were now married and Khan would want to sleep with me, but I wasn't ready. Because of my childhood experiences, I associated sex with abuse. Khan met me after work and promised he would bring me a gift that night. True to his word, he turned up at my house at nine with a signed photo of himself, addressed to Mrs Khan – Khan was not a generous husband. This was poster size – A1 I think, like he was a pop star. I lowered some yarn through the window, which Khan tied through the rolled-up poster so I could haul it up to my bedroom. I was hardly going to put a poster of Khan on my wall, so I hid it under the mattress.

The next day, Tuesday, Khan made me change my name to Sunita Khan at work. No one asked me why, but I could see the worry in my colleagues' faces. At lunchtime, Khan took me to his car and made to undo the buttons on my blouse. I resisted.

'No, not like this! I don't want my first time to be this way. Can we go somewhere special? When can I move in with you? Where do you live? I can't be married to you and stay at my parents' house, can I? I'm not stupid! You're not having sex with me until I'm out of my parents' house!' I was bluffing and hoped Khan wouldn't find a solution to the problem, but he called my bluff.

'OK! I've waited this long. I'll see what I can do. I'll get you out of that house. Then will you sleep with me? After all, I am your husband now. You have to do as I say.'

I forced a smile. 'Get me out of the house and then we can talk.' But I'd already talked myself into a corner.

Walking home from work on Wednesday, I was intercepted at the end of our road by Mum, who greeted me sarcastically. 'Oh! Hello, Mrs Khan!' Mum had found Khan's poster, which I'd hidden under my mattress. At first, she smirked. 'Ha! That's old picture. He never look like that now.' The poster showed a younger Khan wearing a purple shirt and black waistcoat. It was taken outside a court building after Khan had been acquitted of some offence – rightly, according to him. Mum snarled. 'Anyway, if you married, why you still here? You must have had wedding night.' Then she added. 'We better not tell Dad.' Back home, the poster was missing. Later, on the phone, I told Khan she'd found the poster.

'What was she doing looking under your mattress in the first place?' he asked. He began telling me how I couldn't trust my family but suddenly stopped, mid-sentence.

'I don't believe it. Your mum and stupid brother are walking up to the house!' I thought he was playing games, but he opened the window and held the phone out. I heard Mum laughing. This could have been at Khan, or possibly, knowing Mum, at the fact that Khan's brother lived in a council house.

'What do you want?' Khan asked.

'Come downstairs! We want talk to you!' barked Mum.

'Go away. We don't want your sort round here,' replied Khan.

A little later, I saw Mum walking back towards our house with Dilip, which was unusual. I politely asked them where they'd been.

'Nowhere,' lied Dilip.

Later the same evening, on the phone, Khan said, 'See? You can't trust them. They lie.' He was slowly gaining my trust as he poisoned me against my family.

One lunchtime in April, Khan talked about my family. 'They don't care about you, or they wouldn't let me come near you.' Khan held out his left hand and, touching each finger in turn with his right forefinger, proceeded to sum up each family member. 'There's Billy, right. Well … he's just a boy. And Dilip? He's scared of his own shadow. If I blow in his face, he wets himself. And your mum? Ha!' Khan just smiled and shook his head. 'Huh, your mum.' Reaching his little finger, Khan turned his attention to Dad. 'And your dad? He might as well just stay home and wear bangles. But you? You're the only one who stands up to me. I really admire you.'

Chillingly, he then added, 'You can save them, but they can't save you.' I felt I had to protect my family from whatever was coming.

* * *

Indians and Pakistanis are cricket mad. For Dad, cricket fixtures don't come bigger than India versus Pakistan. When they play, Dad settles in front of the television with a beer to watch the match. At moments of tension or excitement, he joins in with the Indian cricket fans' chant:

'*Hindustan Zindabad! Pakistan Murdabad!*' – Long live India! Death to Pakistan!

* * *

On the Wednesday lunchtime, Khan had told me, 'Did you know your dad's a Paki, just like me?'

'What do you mean? He's Indian.' I didn't know what Khan was on about, but he'd come prepared and presented me with a fold-up map of the Indian subcontinent.

'Ask him to show you where he was born. If he loves you, he'll tell you the truth.'

That evening, I waited until Dad had finished eating before I asked him. He saw me hovering with the map. I didn't really feel comfortable asking Dad this, but I was curious, and I knew Khan would ask me for the result. I hesitated.

'What do you want?' asked Dad.

'Dad, where were you born? Can you show me on the map, please?'

Dad rolled his eyes and walked off just as Mum came in. 'What you doing?' Mum generally liked to know what was going on.

'I was asking Dad where he was from. Raj said he's Pakistani.' I still referred to Khan as Raj, not wanting to admit to Mum and Dad that he was really a Muslim.

'Give it to me.' Mum took the map and we followed Dad to the kitchen.

'Where you born? You never tell me,' Mum now asked Dad. 'Show me on map.' Dad pointed to the town of Nankana Sahib, the birthplace of Guru Nanak, the founder of Sikhism, just west of Lahore in present day Pakistan. 'Ha, you never tell me. You Paki,' snorted Mum. Dad protested that he was Indian and that his family had to leave when Pakistan was created.

'How can I be Pakistani? I'm Hindu.'

Dilip and my younger brother, Billy, came into the kitchen and saw the three of us poring over the map. Dilip asked what was going on.

'Dad's a Paki,' explained Mum. Dilip smirked. 'Why you smiling?' asked Mum. 'You half Paki!'

The next day at work, I looked out of the first-floor window just before five. Mum was waiting with Dilip. I don't know why Dilip was there, but they were both smiling about something. Home time at Galleon was marked by a bell that went off dead on five, so everyone left at the same time. When I got downstairs, an argument was in flow between Mum and Khan, who'd also turned up to collect me. My heart was pounding. I didn't know who to turn to. As I approached, Mum grabbed my arm as if to show Khan who was boss. Khan shouted at her to leave me alone. It was now Khan's turn to tug at my arm.

'Look! You doing it now!' shouted Mum triumphantly. They were like children squabbling over a toy. A group of about 20, mostly white, colleagues were standing, watching, not knowing quite what to do whilst Mum and Khan continued bickering. The pair of them shared the ability to wind each other up and the confrontation descended to playground level as Khan played his trump card.

'You married a Paki!'

Mum's face was thunderous. My supervisor pulled up beside us in her car. 'Quick, Sunita, get in. I'll drop you up the road.'

Khan ordered, 'Don't you dare go with no honky!' Indians and Pakistanis use the word *gora* to describe white people. It may or may not be derogatory, depending on how it's said. But Khan had chosen to racially abuse my supervisor in English. I now decided to walk away from both Khan and my family. I headed towards Woking town centre. I'd only taken a few steps when I heard Mum taunting Khan.

'Ha! What you gonna do?'

I turned around to see Khan walk up to Mum menacingly. He wagged his finger in her face. 'You will *see* what I will do!'

I stood still, terrified Khan would attack Mum or my brother. Dilip was something of a spare part during the confrontation, skulking behind Mum. I think he was scared of Khan, who had now followed and ran up to me. He grabbed me, promising, 'I'll get you out of there.' Khan told me to go with them. As I re-joined Mum and Dilip, Khan shouted, 'Get your bags packed. I'm coming for you.'

Back home, Mum shouted, 'You never see Khan again.' I heard her talk on the phone about marrying me off in India. Mum's great hobby was gossiping on the phone to her friends. I was terrified at the prospect – sex with a stranger and out of England for good, perhaps.

I decided to break off with Khan. He was tearing the family apart, and I'd had enough. When I thought I was alone, I rang him at his brother's house and nervously begged him to leave me be. There was a brief silence before Mum and Dad barged into the room. Mum slapped me across the face, snatched my phone and shouted at Khan, 'Ha! I caught her now!'

Mum told Dad to hit me, which he did for the first time in my life. She'd decided to tell Dad about Khan after all. While Dad punched my back and kidneys, Mum goaded Khan down the phone and wandered out onto the landing. 'She getting beaten now. Ha! Can you hear her crying? You won't take her now.'

'God is punishing you for going with a Muslim man,' sobbed Dad.

Mum hung up on Khan and came back into the room. 'Why you hitting her? Hitting girl is sin!'

'*You told me to!*'

Dad was crying as he and Mum left me lying on the floor. In the early hours, I sensed Khan by the window and our neighbours' security light came on. He asked if I was OK, so I told him about the beating. I apologised to Khan for trying to end our relationship and felt pathetic for doing so. He showed concern, saying, 'You must go to the police.' Khan was worried Mum and Dad would marry me off in India, and warned me to keep my passport close. Then he told me he loved me, before disappearing into the night. On the Friday morning, after peeing blood, I went to the police station as instructed. A police officer came to the house and questioned Dad, who cried again. I felt awful, didn't press charges and withdrew my complaint. That afternoon at work, Khan called me and asked if I'd made the complaint. He told me he'd had enough of my mother. What I really needed was for my family to rescue me from Khan, but he slowly convinced me that he was rescuing me from them.

On Saturday 20th April, Khan came for me as promised. He'd called me just ten minutes earlier and ordered me to pack a bag and act normal. This was my 'go bag', essentials for a quick getaway. As arranged, Khan signalled by beeping his horn. I opened the front door and ran out to his car with my plastic bag. My heart was beating so fast. I was swept along by the events; sad about leaving home. But I'd been backed into a corner, written off as 'dirty'. I was young, easy for Khan to manipulate and scared of resisting him. I believed he would harm my family if I didn't go with him.

Khan told me to lie low in his car as he drove through town. He seemed cross, put out, as though he were doing me a favour. He wouldn't tell me where we were going. We arrived at the *Maybury Hotel* in Woking and checked in. I was anxious, fearful of what lay ahead. I wanted to call my family to say I was safe, but Khan had taken my mobile phone. Realising the magnitude of what I'd done, I broke down and cried. There seemed to be no going back now. Khan held me in his arms and comforted me. 'Shh. Listen, everything's gonna be fine.'

Khan went out for the evening without me and returned in the early hours. He was dressed for a night out in shiny shoes, a crisp, white shirt and black trousers; wearing *Hugo Boss* aftershave. He was a little drunk and giggly. He kissed my forehead gently and hugged me. Then, he went into the toilet and returned, wearing only his black boxer shorts. I was horrified and, assuming the worst, made for the door. Khan gently took my hand. 'Woah! Silly girl. I promise you, I won't do anything.' Khan smiled at my innocence. 'Did you think I slept in trousers then?' I hadn't really thought that far and looked away embarrassed.

Khan got into bed and under the covers. I sat in a chair in my jeans and t-shirt and tried to fall asleep, frightened of joining Khan. As I began to doze off, Khan walked over to me and gently stroked my tear-stained cheek. I opened my eyes as Khan lifted me up gently and carried me over to the bed while reassuring me. 'It's OK. I promise you, I won't touch you tonight. Just sleep, OK?' As I joined Khan warily under the duvet, he cuddled me. The room was cold so he lent me his Aston Villa top to wear, which, I remember, carried the aroma of his aftershave. Staying awake, I watched Khan fall asleep and then snuggled up to him for comfort and warmth, relieved that nothing had happened. We spent Saturday and Sunday night in the hotel. Khan was mainly out and about while I remained in the room, alone. He kept his word and, apart from cuddling, made no advances towards me. We didn't even kiss. Khan told me, 'One day, me and you will be in *Jannat* (Paradise) together. You're special.'

My family contacted Khan's older brother, asking for my whereabouts and return. His brother was angry with him and shouted down the phone. They spoke the Mirpuri dialect of Punjabi, which I just about understood. Khan promised his brother that I was still 'pure'. My parents claimed Khan had taken £400 from me. Shortly before this, he'd asked to borrow £400, which, being gullible, I'd given him. Mum used to open my post sometimes, so she may have read a bank statement and guessed this. Khan explained to his brother that it was just a loan and promised to pay me back, although he never did. He became angry with my parents. 'You have to go back. They've caused me problems! Just you wait and see what I do to them! I *will* get you out of there. I promise you. Just wait until I have enough money.'

Khan called my parents. Mum answered and called him a dog (*kuta*). Contemptuously, Khan ordered her, 'Put the man on.' Mum carried on shouting, but Khan brushed her aside. 'You listen to me! *Put the man on!*'

Dad came to the phone and Khan spelt out his demands. My parents weren't to hurt me, and they weren't to send me to India. Khan assured Dad that I was still a virgin. They were discussing me as if I were an object.

While Mum continued to shout abuse at Khan in the

background, Dad's approach was more conciliatory. 'No problem, *baadshah* (king of kings). No problem.'

Khan knew how hard it was for me to do what he now asked. I was an unmarried Indian girl returning to her parents after spending two nights with a man, although nothing had happened sexually. I now suspect that Khan's plan was to make my family believe he'd slept with me so they would disown me, whilst gaining my trust by not doing so.

Khan dropped me off at my parents' driveway and watched me from a distance to make sure I went in. I lowered my head in shame. I didn't want to go back after running off with Khan. I just wanted to be on my own.

Mum didn't believe I was a virgin, so I arrived home to a hostile reception. I was back in the family fold, but it didn't feel like it. When I helped Mum in the kitchen, she would call me *gandi goori* – dirty girl. It was assumed that I'd slept with Khan and, at meal times, I was generally ignored. But, one day, Dilip spoke to me when we were both in the kitchen.

'Our family is like a hand.' Dilip held up a clenched fist, then opened it to show five fingers, although I already knew what a hand was. 'Each of us is a finger, but you're the infected finger that needs to be cut off.' Smiling, he added, 'And Billy and I won't have to share the deeds to the house with you.' Billy was my younger brother. I've never been money oriented and, unlike Dilip, I hadn't given any thought as to how my parents might eventually leave their money. I always craved my family's love, not their property.

A policewoman, Gemma, called me at home. My parents had previously reported me missing. Gemma asked how I was. She knew of Khan from previous dealings. I said I was scared and needed help, but I didn't know what kind of help. I explained that my parents didn't believe me about

Khan, and that I didn't want to sleep with him. Gemma replied, 'I can tell from your voice you're not at the end of your tether yet.' She didn't think I'd had enough of Khan. My actions in leaving with him had made it difficult for me to explain my dilemma.

Life went on. Dad would look at me with disgust, telling me God was punishing me. Mum called me 'dirty' and 'useless' on the phone to her friends and moaned how hard life was for her. I couldn't talk to anyone and felt I had no one to turn to. Khan continued to come at night and throw tiny stones at the window. He would ask if I was OK and promised to get me out. But, at other times, when I saw Khan for lunch, he would threaten me or grab my throat. At night, I hugged my teddy bear for comfort and soaked it in tears.

Emotionally, I now plunged into the depths. I had no self-worth. I'd 'married' a man to stop him raping me but I believed that, inevitably, he would. Mum and my brothers despised me for supposedly sleeping with him. I could see no way forward and, on Tuesday 22nd April, I tried to end my life. Taking an afternoon off work, I bought a packet of paracetamol from a chemist. I chewed and swallowed the tablets in big mouthfuls, thirty pills in all. Wandering the streets, I expected to fall down when the time was up. A stranger stopped in his car. At first I thought he was lost but he offered me a lift. Naïvely, I replied, 'That's kind of you, but no thank you. I don't know where I'm going.' The stranger eyed me oddly before driving off – another 'adventure' I missed out on, no doubt.

I decided to tell Khan to his face that I'd had enough, that I was ending my life. Becoming dizzy, I walked slowly to Khan's brother's house. Khan's Capri wasn't there. I sat on the kerb. His young nephew, who was about eight, was playing outside and called me, '*Chachi Ji*', which means auntie, but more specifically, paternal uncle's wife. This was surprising as I'd never seen him before. Maybe Khan had shown him a photo. I asked him whether Khan was in. He said he'd been gone for hours.

A passer-by asked if I was alright. I explained I'd taken tablets and wanted to die. An ambulance was called. At the hospital, I was given a horrible black tar-like substance to take and threw up. The doctor in A&E asked if I wanted my parents notified.

'No, they don't care.' I tried calling Khan to tell him not to pick me up from work. There was no answer. I walked part of the way home, then took a bus. When I arrived home, Mum shouted at me.

'Stupid girl! Hospital call me. You can't even kill yourself! We won't tell Dad. Our secret.' Like much else, the matter was brushed under the carpet. In the end, I didn't tell Khan about my suicide bid and nothing was resolved.

The struggle for control over me intensified. Mum was now escorting me to work, but Khan continued to meet me for lunch. He was also now coming to the house most nights. Our house was two semis knocked into one. Neither of my parents ever earned mega bucks, but I think Dad bought the property at auction after a house price crash. My bedroom was at the front of the house, on the left-hand side near the bathroom, toilet and a spare bedroom. My parents' and brothers' rooms were in the right-hand half of the house, so I was a little secluded. In the early hours, Khan would throw small stones at my window from the neighbour's driveway. I would creep downstairs and let him in through the window of Dad's study, which was at the back of the house. He would stay for a couple of hours in the study or even upstairs in my room. We didn't have sex, or even kiss, but would cuddle, fully-clothed, before he crept out. Or, we'd wait until everyone had gone in the morning and leave together. Other times, Khan would tell me to sneak out at night to meet him in his car. I would climb back into the house through a window. I came to see Khan as my protector. Once, he asked, 'What would you do if your family saw me and came to stab me with a knife?'

'I would protect you by being your shield,' I replied.

Another time, we were tiptoeing upstairs, trying to synchronise our footsteps on the creaky floorboards. Near the top of the staircase, Khan stumbled slightly. Mum called from her bedroom.

'Who there?'

'Only me,' I replied. Khan joked later that he should have answered.

On another occasion, Khan came in through a downstairs window around 3 a.m. We were in the lounge under my parents' bedroom, just cuddling. Khan liked me to wear a *hijab*, a Muslim headdress, which I'd kept hidden from my parents. Khan said he would give me a present and began biting my neck like a vampire. I'd never really kissed boys before, and Khan didn't really kiss. So, I was shocked, but managed to push Khan off me. He banged against the wall, making a noise. I started to take the hijab off and Khan slapped me. We heard Dad's footsteps and saw a light come on. Khan escaped via the window, but wasn't able to close it before Dad appeared. I'm pretty sure Dad saw me hiding the hijab when he came in. I wasn't in pyjamas, I was dressed as if I was going on a date.

'What are you doing here at this time?' asked Dad.

'I couldn't sleep, Dad,' I lied. Dad knew I was lying and looked around for Khan. Back in my bedroom, I could see Khan from the window. He was standing under the street lights, not unduly concerned about Dad or my brothers seeing him. The next morning, I hid Khan's love bite. Mum asked me what the noise was last night. I brushed it off. 'If I told you, you wouldn't believe me.'

In late April, I was admitted to hospital with a kidney infection. Back at home, after being discharged, Dilip told me about a telephone conversation he'd had with Khan. 'Your mate, Khan, rang. He said you're on drugs. You're pathetic! He said he's helping you come off them, like an uncle. He seems like quite a nice guy. We were having a laugh. About you. Apparently, he's married with kids.' In fact, Khan was prescribed methadone, the heroin substitute, which he had to take daily. Dilip may have been pretending to believe the drugs story out of spite. I also think that, unlike Mum, who enjoyed a good row with Khan, Dilip lacked the stomach to confront him. Khan began openly ringing on the home number, asking to speak to me. Dilip would happily pass me the phone. One day, I heard him say to Khan, 'You can have my sister – we don't want her.'

Khan exploited this. 'See how stupid they are? They don't care for you. *Now*, you must listen to *me*.'

Word of Khan and me spread. A Sikh friend visited Mum at the card shop where she worked and told her I'd brought shame on the family for going with a Muslim man. She helpfully suggested that Mum should consider committing suicide. This was all my fault.

Mum's hostility was relentless. Once I was helping her with the dishes when she tore into me. '*Pero ho marja* (Go away and die). You bring shame on family. No one will want you. You dirty.' I ran out of the kitchen, unable to cope with Mum's disgust. Mum screamed for Dad. 'Help, she giving me too much stress. My heart can't take it.' I followed Dad back into the kitchen where Mum was clutching her chest, theatrically. Dad looked worried.

I picked up the phone. 'I'll call an ambulance.' I dialled 999.

'No!' shouted Mum. 'I'm going to die. It's *your* fault, *kuti* (bitch)!' Mum asked Dad to fetch her some cushions, which she lay on. When Dad wasn't looking, Mum alternated between smirking at me and giving me evil looks. I'd called the ambulance, anyway, and it arrived within minutes.

'Bitch!' screamed Dilip, as I followed the paramedics taking Mum to the ambulance. Dilip and Billy believed I'd caused Mum's self-diagnosed 'heart attack'. At hospital, Mum was put on ECG heart monitors and various tests were conducted, which she passed with flying colours before being discharged in less than an hour.

In the hospital, Dad gave me an ultimatum. 'Stay at home and don't see Khan any more, or give me your keys now and never return.' I agreed to come home with Dad and stop seeing Khan, which is what I wanted, anyway. But, when we arrived home, Dilip had taken a baseball bat to my room, smashing a cupboard and destroying my sound system. He threatened it would be my face next time. Despite his Oxford degree, he lacked the common sense to realise that heart attack victims are generally not released within the hour. Mum was able to manipulate the rest of the family. Although Dad wanted me there, no one else seemed to.

Chapter 4

THE WRATH OF KHAN

I needed police assistance to break with Khan, but I had to do this alone. I informed Surrey Police that he'd threatened me and my family. The police must have spoken to Khan, whose response was immediate. He turned up at the card shop in the shopping centre where Mum worked and threatened her. 'I will *throw* you off the *fucking balcony*.' The police were called and escorted Mum home safely. I was home with Dad when she returned. Mum was visibly shaken.

'Your bloody Paki boyfriend threaten me. He come my work, threaten throw me over balcony – three floors down. Long way! He say he throw acid on my face!' I felt awful. My attempt to get out of this mess had failed. I went to comfort Mum but she pushed me away. 'Don't touch me. *Don't touch me! Gandi goori* (dirty girl)!'

A detective constable was assigned to the case. He followed Khan for a while and kept an eye on Mum at the shopping centre. Khan was well known to Surrey Police as a small-time heroin dealer with a history of violence. A panic alarm was installed by the police in my bedroom, linked to the police station, which we were to use if Khan appeared, and our house was earmarked for police protection. Mum now knew Khan was dangerous. In a later sworn statement, Mum noted that Khan had threatened to kill me and to throw acid in her face. But the atmosphere at home was now toxic. Meanwhile, Khan told police that my parents were being violent towards his wife – me!

One Saturday, Mum came into my bedroom. She pushed me and demanded my passport. I took the passport from under my pillow to prevent her from taking it, but she tried to snatch it and then grabbed my arms. I wouldn't let go, so there was a struggle, but she managed to grab the passport as I didn't want to fight her.

Dad appeared in the doorway. 'Leave her. Give it back. Why do you need it?' I'm not sure why Mum wanted my passport, but I figured she wasn't taking me on a cruise. I broke free and pressed the panic alarm. Within minutes, there were blue flashing lights and the police were in the house.

'Where is he?' They meant Khan. A policeman asked why I'd raised the alarm. They ushered Mum and Dad to the end of the corridor and told them to stop speaking in any language. I apologised for pushing the button, explaining that Mum had taken my passport against my will. I told them I wanted to leave, although I didn't have anywhere to go. The police ordered my parents to return my passport. Dad started crying and begged me to stay. The policewoman asked if I wanted to take any clothes.

'No, she's not allowed,' said Dad – he didn't want me to leave. The policewoman asked if I had anywhere to go.

'Car parks, maybe?' I replied, not really having a plan.

'Be careful. I don't want to be called out for your rape or murder. Go to a friend's house.' But I had no one to turn to. I was escorted from the house feeling frightened and sad. I hated seeing Dad cry and didn't really want to leave, but Mum had forced me into a corner. I walked aimlessly until I no longer recognised the streets. Over the next twenty minutes, I had five missed calls from Khan on my mobile. Not strong enough to resist, I answered the sixth. Khan was angry.

'Where are you? Your mother has called me! Why did you leave? Where are you going? I'm coming to get you!'

Mum must have got his brother's number somehow. Perhaps she rang to taunt him – I don't know – but, she didn't know when to leave well alone.

I shuddered with fear, crying. 'I don't know where I am. I've had enough. I belong to no one.' Khan screamed more abuse at me. Then he apologised and asked me nicely where I was. He told me he loved me and claimed my parents had said I was dead to them. I found the name of the road. In a few minutes, Khan's Capri pulled up and I got in. Khan grabbed my hair and slammed my head on the dashboard as punishment for Mum calling him. I couldn't understand why she'd called Khan, especially after being threatened by him. She'd obviously succeeded in winding him up.

We drove a short way and parked up near his brother's house on the Goldsworth Park Estate. As evening approached, Khan went back to his brother's place, leaving me alone in the car. He gave me a jacket to keep me warm but I shivered all night. I had my phone with me. I was hoping things might calm down and they might call me, but they didn't. I looked at their number on the phone and cried. Khan had told me he was locking me in, so I didn't try to get out. It didn't occur to me that he was lying and that, of course, I could open the doors. I just believed him. My kidneys were hurting. The pain was awful. It starts off burning, like cystitis, then feels like peeing out razor blades whilst being punched in the kidneys.

The stillness of the black night was eerie. I was cold, frightened and alone. I felt I could never go home. I'd brought shame on the family, although I hadn't, in fact, slept with Khan.

Khan came to see me around eight in the morning. He was surprised I was still there. 'I thought you'd have gone back. I'm sorry I couldn't stay with you. I'll be back in ten minutes.' Khan gave me a hug. Warmth. I held on to him tightly and he smiled back at me before leaving. He returned with a blanket and two plates of hot food and ate with me in the car. I was overwhelmed by his kindness. He explained that he wasn't sure where he could have me as his brother wouldn't allow a Hindu Indian girl in his house. Khan didn't have any money, so we couldn't rent straight away as we needed a deposit. He would ask some friends about accommodation.

I looked into Khan's eyes. 'Do you really love me? Last night was horrible in the car alone. Can you stay with me, please?'

Khan paused before answering. 'Don't be so fucking stupid! You're my wife, of course I love you. I'm here, aren't I? I'll try and stay with you tonight, but my brother will start asking questions if I'm not home.'

I spent another few nights alone in the car. Khan would visit, but didn't spend long with me. It was cold and uncomfortable. Worse still, I was on my period, and therefore bleeding. I was still working at Galleon at the time and Khan drove me to the leisure centre to shower. I remember it was a 25 pence admission each time. I didn't have any clothes to change into, so Khan asked his sister-in-law to make me some *shalwar kameez*, Asian trouser suits. People at work gave me funny looks as I'd previously dressed in western clothes. I was too ashamed to tell anyone what was happening.

Khan's car had no road tax. An official knocked on the window one night and said the car had been reported as being parked there for several days. I pretended I couldn't speak English. Later, a group of Asian men approached the car, looking at me. They were speaking Urdu. Then, in English, one suggested, 'I think he needs to be taught a lesson. Let's take her.' I was petrified. Someone knocked on the window.

'Why are you in the car?' he asked. 'Are you from Southall? Has he kidnapped you?' He offered to bring me some food. His friends hovered by the car. I didn't know them, or whether they could be trusted. Although they seemed hostile towards Khan, in my confused state, I wondered if he'd sent them to test me. I was fearful of them, and of getting a beating from Khan if he saw us talking. I ignored the men and eventually they drifted away. I thought I'd better tell Khan about my visitors. He went crazy and swore. Starting the car violently, he hammered the gears and drove the car to a place I didn't know, where I spent the next night.

Staying in Khan's car, I became ill, bleeding from urine and kidney infections. Khan didn't know what to do with me and hadn't resolved where we would live, so he called my parents and explained that I was ill. He made out he was doing me a big favour and dropped me back at my parents' house, where I received a frosty reception. Mum pronounced that the bleeding must have been due to, 'rough sex.' I told her that I hadn't slept with Khan, but she didn't believe me. Mum and Dad took me to St Peter's Hospital, where I was admitted. I was a very child-like 18-year-old, worried about my health. In hospital, though, I was safe from Khan for a few days, safe from the possibility of sex. I was also temporarily free of my family's disgust. Initially, the hospital planned to remove my appendix. I called Mum on the hospital pay phone. She told me to get lost – *dava ho*. I was distraught. My ward nurse of the last ten days was walking past and gave me a hug. I cried on this stranger's shoulders.

Dad was visiting every day, but he was shouting at me.

He told me that Khan was already married. Dad said Khan had phoned to say that *I* was hassling *him*, and that I was on drugs. Dad seemed to believe Khan – a man who'd threatened his wife – over me. The hospital notes state that family visits were causing me distress. I told Khan what Dad had said. He laughed in my face and boasted that my family believed every word he said. Khan made me ban Dad from coming to see me – perhaps he had something else to hide.

My friend Adil came to visit me. I was surprised to see him. I knew Adil from college. In those days, he was like a caring brother to me, the big brother I should have had. What is strange is that Mum, who wasn't visiting herself, had contacted him. Adil is from a Muslim Pakistani background like Khan. Perhaps she wanted to cause trouble for me, or maybe just wind Khan up. Adil made fun of my pyjamas – I smiled weakly. He could see I wasn't the same girl and asked if I was OK, but I was worried Khan would find out he'd visited.

'Please, you've got to go. If he finds you here, I'll be in trouble.'

Khan came to collect me from hospital, hugged me, then drove me to a spot near his brother's house. I slept alone in his car one more night. Then we moved into a flat in Sheerwater, belonging to a friend of Khan's who was away. Why did I go with Khan? I felt unwanted at home, as if I was being allowed there grudgingly. It seemed that, in my family's eyes, I would never escape the fact that I'd run off with Khan and supposedly slept with him. Khan hadn't touched me at this stage, so had gained my trust to some extent. Although, I knew he could be violent. We were there for a week, living together, shopping together. I bought some new clothes of Khan's choice and performed at least some of my wifely duties, cooking and cleaning the flat, which was filthy. The first evening, Khan looked meaningfully towards the bed. I panicked. 'I'm not ready. I'm not on the pill. If I get pregnant, we'll have no money to feed our baby. Please let's just wait. I'd like it to be special. What's the rush?' I was trying to buy more time. I still had nightmares of being raped as a little girl and couldn't bear the thought of someone touching me sexually. I wasn't able to tell Khan about my abuse – I felt too frightened and ashamed. Khan agreed to wait until I was ready, so we would just cuddle on the bed. Khan was out mostly, while I stayed home in the flat, waiting for him since he'd made me take time off work, sick. Khan brought over some of his stuff from his brother's house, so it seemed like we were setting up home properly. He seemed to be giving me hope that everything would be OK.

Khan decided to host a drink and drugs night for a few friends. I wasn't invited to the party. I was made to stay on the double bed, which was hidden from the lounge area by a net curtain and beads. This happened a few nights running, with me under orders not to move or make a sound. On Wednesday 28th May 1997, Khan had about eight friends over, some Asian, some white, including a woman whose cackling I remember vividly. The small studio flat was full. I was desperate to go to the toilet and my kidneys hurt. I got up and moved the curtain beads slowly, trying to get Khan's attention, but couldn't. There was a thick fog of marijuana and cigarette smoke. Khan looked totally stoned. I managed to sneak out to the bathroom without being noticed. On the way back, Khan spotted me. I felt a knot in my stomach.

His friends saw me too. 'Wow, who is she? She's so beautiful! Can't believe you've been hiding her away.' I saw anger in Khan's eyes; he saw fear in mine. Grabbing my wrist, he screamed for everyone to get out. No one challenged him and the party ended abruptly. I froze.

Once we were alone, Khan shoved me onto the bed and then went off to the bathroom. I got up and followed him. When he came out, I pleaded with him.

'Please don't be cross, I'm sorry. Please don't get mad at me. I really needed the toilet.' His eyes threatened violence. I looked down. Suddenly, Khan grabbed my jaw tightly and rammed me up against the wall so my feet weren't touching the floor. I squeezed my eyes shut so he couldn't see the terror in them.

'Open your eyes! LOOK AT ME!' he screamed.

I opened my eyes. Gently, but firmly, I tried, 'Please put me down … now.' The whites of Khan's eyes were bloodshot red. His face was different, too – I'll never forget the hatred.

Khan's demons seemed to pause for breath. He actually put me down, hugged me and said, 'Sorry.' But I sensed this wasn't over. The switch in Khan's head clicked back to *Violent*. He lifted me by the armpits and threw me. I banged my head on the cold, hard wall. He tore at my clothes. I fought back with all my might. He punched me hard on the jaw. I kicked him as he got on top of me. He sat on my legs to constrain me. I struggled, but he laughed at my attempts to break free. I was begging.

'Please stop, please! I'm sorry, please stop.' He carried on laughing, almost bitterly. He punched me in the face, almost knocking me out. I saw bright lights. I wanted to hit back but he was much stronger than me, and he was going to get what he wanted. I was terrified. I didn't want to have sex with him yet. Not like this. I wanted it to be special. It didn't have to be candles and flowers special. I just didn't want my first time to be like this. I always dreamt it would be with someone who would love me enough to make it gentle and caring. Khan was now on top of me. I pleaded with him to get off. He was hurting me all over. The window was still open. I felt the cold air and the cold wall on my back. I tried to break free, but lacked the strength. Eventually, exhausted, my efforts fizzled out. He began undressing while sitting on top of me, throwing punches at me all the while. I was now crying. 'Please stop!'

Khan covered my mouth with his hand. Then, putting his mouth next to my ear, he whispered slowly. 'Sssh. Just do as I say.' I was trapped. I closed my eyes and froze. I felt his fingers going up my top, reaching to undo my bra. He then reached under my long, ankle length skirt and pulled down my pants, slowly. I tried to stop him, grabbing his hand and then my pants.

This had happened when I was a three-year-old. Now 18, I was just as helpless and started to shake and fit. *Why isn't God helping me?* I thought. *Why won't Khan stop? This can't be love.* Khan wedged his knee in between my legs so I couldn't close them. I tried to push upwards. I managed to sit up by the wall, but he pulled me down by my legs. I couldn't understand what he was saying anymore. He was so drunk and drugged up. I felt something very hard by my leg. He grabbed my face, stared at me, wanting to see fear. He kept opening my legs. I struggled and grabbed my pants briefly, but Khan was too strong for me. He slapped me hard across the face and punched me in the chest. Khan moved towards my ear, as if to whisper again. Instead, he sunk his teeth into my ear. The pain was excruciating. I put both hands up to protect the ear, letting go of my pants, which Khan now pulled down completely. I screamed as he brutally raped me.

The whole ordeal lasted over two hours and I've spared much of the detail. After he'd finished with me, he threw me off the bed. I crawled, naked and in agony, to the bathroom, where I saw the wounds on my body in the mirror. I lay on the floor for the rest of the night with a sheet, too frightened to get into the bed. I felt sore everywhere.

In the morning, daylight streamed through the window and showed what the darkness had done. The Big Bad Wolf had a hangover. Sheepishly, Khan made eye contact. I quickly looked away. He asked, 'What happened? Who's beaten you up? Tell me, please?' Khan grabbed my jaw, gently by his standards.

'You did this!' I yelled. I moved away and removed the sheet showing him my naked, scarred body.

Khan wrapped me up quickly in the sheet. 'I am so sorry. Please forgive me. I did too much fuckin' drink and drugs last night.' That was it. Sorry. I couldn't believe he didn't know what he'd done. My body was burning in pain. I couldn't forgive him. Khan had broken my body, my trust and me.

Khan went to work. Strangely, I was still scared to be alone, although his scent was all over me and images of my ordeal were playing over and over in my mind. There was no one to turn to. Curling up on the floor, I cried myself to exhaustion. Then I cleaned up the mess – the blood smears on the wall and bed.

Khan came home for lunch and to have sex with me, but in a 'nice' way this time. I was so sore already. He asked me if I'd bled as it was my first time. My mother hadn't consented to sex education at school, so I didn't understand the question. Instead, I shouted at him. 'You should know, you were there. I bled from everywhere else, my face, and my ear where you bit me.' I didn't bleed in the way Khan meant.

Khan said that, since he hadn't worn a condom, I might now be pregnant, but it would take a few weeks to show on a pregnancy test. He promised to make up for raping me by having 'good sex', and not hitting me. I was still scared of undressing in front of him, or even seeing him naked, which was awkward. We were supposed to be married and loved up. Well, really, he was some nut job stalker psycho freak and I was damaged goods, a runaway suicidal victim. He saw me coming a mile off.

Khan ordered me to make him lunch and to clean his shoes, which then had to be placed in a particular way, Khan's way. Afterwards, I had to take his clothes off and massage him. I was then forced to perform various acts before having sex with him. He didn't hit me so much this time. I pleaded with Khan in vain to stop, but he wouldn't.

'Just relax. If you relax it won't hurt. Relax, or I'll hit you in the face.' Unsurprisingly, I couldn't relax, so he hit me in the face, and it was all my fault. It was also my fault that, not only did I ruin the 'experience' for him, but I made him feel bad for hitting me. He made me apologise.

Once he'd raped me the first time, he thought he could do it whenever he wanted. Over a period of days, my attitude changed from defiance and outrage to acceptance, and the desire to minimise the violence. When Khan raped me, he would threaten to do so again, immediately, to keep me scared. I didn't realise that he would need to have an erection first, so I was on constant alert. Fearful. He was now doing what he wanted, when he wanted: sexually, mentally, physically and emotionally. The real me didn't exist. I was lifeless.

* * *

People on both sides of my family in India dabble in Indian Black Magic – *Jadoo* – which is something many Indians and Pakistanis believe in. Khan told me my parents were using black magic to prevent me from having his children. But, Dad was in fact trying to protect me from Khan, although I didn't realise this at the time. As well as magic, Hindus believe in *havans,* a ritual carried out by a priest using consecrated fire. Havans can be used to promote good health, bring prosperity and celebrate an important event … or to counter black magic.

* * *

Khan wasn't using contraception and claimed that I was pregnant, although there was no evidence. This became something of an obsession for him. He asked if my family would accept our baby. Dad contacted Khan's older brother. They wanted to perform a havan in my name. Khan claimed that he also did black magic, but he gave me permission to attend the havan, maybe influenced by his brother.

'Just remember, you have our baby in you.'

But I didn't go. I couldn't face my parents, especially after being raped.

Khan took me out for a walk one night and suddenly raised his voice. 'Your parents are causing a lot of trouble for me! They have reported you missing! Surrey Police looked for your dead body under my brother's fucking floorboards. He is angry! I am angry! Why would they do that? They know where you are. They don't care about you, anyway!'

Khan forced me into a public phone box and demanded I call the police and tell them I wasn't missing. He held the phone, listening and whispering how I should respond to the female officer's questions. I was unhappy that my parents were antagonising Khan, because he would take it out on me. I also felt that by making this call, an opportunity for the police to rescue me from Khan had gone.

Chapter 5

METHADONE IN HIS MADNESS

One night in June, Khan broke the news that we had to move out. He would return to his brother's house for now, and I would have to go back to my parents' home once more. It turned out that we were only staying in the flat while his friend was on holiday. There was no forewarning, and it was late as Khan walked me to the end of my parents' street. He waited until Dad opened the door. I felt ashamed as Dad let me in and told me, coldly, to sit down in the lounge. I went to hug him but he backed away. Dad informed me that I wasn't welcome unless I went to the police station and withdrew a complaint I'd made against a police officer.

Some weeks earlier, a policeman had warned me not to carry any bags for Khan, claiming he was a drug dealer. When I'd challenged Khan about this, he grabbed my throat and forced me to reveal the name of the officer before marching me down to the police station. Khan was outraged that the police had broken data protection laws by divulging his activities and ordered me to make a complaint.

Mum woke up and came downstairs. 'What the hell she doing here?' she asked Dad before hissing at me, '*Koon beniya* – (bloodsucker)!'

I agreed to go to the police station and we arrived there about 2 a.m. I explained the reason for our visit to the policewoman at the counter. I was beaten and bruised by Khan, so had to explain that Mum and Dad weren't responsible. She led me towards an interview room. Mum now produced a letter from the hospital and screamed, 'She pregnant. *Dirty* girl!' This was news to me. I'm not sure why she saved this for the police station.

I couldn't live with Mum's hatred and asked if I could have some helpline numbers and clothes from my parents' house so I could go alone. Dad claimed he had paid for my clothes and that I couldn't have them. He didn't want me to leave. 'Dad, you know that's not true,' I protested. 'I've worked since I was 17. I paid for them.' My parents were asked to leave. Dad suggested they arrest me for the night and detain me until I withdrew my complaint. The officer sighed wearily. This wasn't possible – the police station wasn't a hotel. Meanwhile, stupidly, I asked the officer to call Khan at his older brother's house. It's hard to explain why I did this, but I had nowhere else to go.

Khan turned up at the police station with his brother. Khan's big brother was much older than him, more like Dad's age. It turned out that Dad knew him from the pub, but hadn't realised he was Khan's brother. This might explain how Khan knew about Dad's place of birth. Asians of their generation gravitated towards each other, even Hindus and Muslims. At the sight of Khan, Mum resumed her performance.

'She pregnant! *Kuti* (bitch)! Look! Here's your letter'. Mum waved the letter again. I wasn't pregnant and couldn't work out who would send these letters. I found out through hospital records in 2014 that Khan was calling the doctor requesting scans for me, *before* he raped me. So maybe he wanted to play games with my parents. I did have a kidney scan while I was in hospital, so it's also possible that Mum misinterpreted a letter regarding that.

Khan looked furious, a look I was familiar with. He walked up to Mum and screamed, 'Shut up!'

Dad tried to placate Khan. 'No problem, *baadshah*. No problem.'

Mum was unimpressed with Dad's craven behaviour. 'Ha! *Him! He no baadshah. Bewakoof!*'

As I walked out of the police station in tears, Khan's older brother spoke to me for the first time.

'Please go back to your parents. I will speak to them. If they hurt you, I will take you to my home. I promise.'

Khan now pleaded with his big brother, 'I want to keep this one, *Lala. Bhaijaan*. Please!' Khan sounded like a child.

Bhaijaan told Khan to shut up and took control of the situation. Turning to Dad, he urged, 'Please stop this, sahib! Take your daughter home. Don't hurt her or you will have me to answer to.'

With four older adults standing over me, I felt like a child. I walked away from everyone, away from the street lights and into the darkness, heading towards the train station. Khan followed and grabbed me.

'You heard my brother. Go with your parents.'

'Leave me alone! All of you!'

'Ssh! I will get you out of there, I promise,' whispered Khan, before bending down and kissing my tummy dramatically. 'Do it for our baby,' he added, before guiding me towards my parents' car. Like Mum, Khan obviously knew something I didn't. Back home, no one spoke to me. Now, I really was no longer 'pure', but I couldn't discuss it with anyone. The fact of having sex with Khan, which had been assumed before it happened, was more important to my family than the circumstances. The fact that I'd been violently raped. I felt as worthless and dirty as Mum told me I was.

A few days later, Mum came into my bedroom with a strange look in her eyes. She was carrying a kitchen knife and we were alone in the house. She spoke of honour killings and proposed a suicide pact. I had brought shame on the family.

'I stab you first, then you stab me. They find us both dead on floor.'

I was petrified – this was my mother. There was no way I could stab Mum, but I thought about letting her stab me. I moved to the window and shouted for help. Our neighbour was in the front garden and looked up. Smiling sweetly, Mum shouted, 'Everything is OK!' We heard Dad's key in the front door. Mum left my room, taking the kitchen knife with her.

One evening, Dad collapsed; he was unwell. Mum knew where to apportion blame. 'If he have stroke, I never look after him. Your fault.' The next day Mum had another 'heart attack', although apparently not the kind that needed a doctor or an ambulance. Even I now blamed myself for my parents' health deteriorating. I was low and vulnerable.

Dad took me to Croydon to see a black magic man. Black Magic Man's services were much in demand, so we waited in a queue before being ushered into his room at the top of the stairs. There was a powerful aroma of incense as we entered. The sorcerer was about 70, with a beard and prayer hat, like a devout Muslim. Black Magic Man asked me all sorts of questions in Urdu, including questions about Khan and sex. I pretended not to understand. I wasn't going to discuss S–E–X in front of Dad. He gave me a *taweez*, a small paper scroll with magic words to ward off evil spells. Mum sewed this into a black piece of cotton, which I wore like a belt under my clothes. This was to remove the magic, which Dad believed Khan had applied to me. I was given some healing water and shown how to smear a lemon on my arms, leg and face after bathing. The lemon then had to be buried and something else burnt – I forget what – as part of the ritual. I also had to eat ash from incense sticks.

Khan came in the night, stood below my bedroom window and asked how I was. I told him about the knife incident and how I couldn't bear the atmosphere at home. He told me he loved me and would rescue me. He promised he wouldn't hurt me anymore. I wanted to believe him and agreed to go. But, I was still scared of what Khan might do to me or my family. As a precaution, I updated his CV on Dad's PC with his correct details. I was leaving a trail in case the worst happened. I didn't hear from Khan for three days, but then he came for me and beeped his horn twice. I ran out with my 'go bag' – essentials. Emotionally, I was in turmoil. I thought I'd escaped from Khan, but I couldn't live with my family's disgust, so I went back to Khan, hoping against hope that things would be better this time.

* * *

Khan decided we would stay somewhere away from Woking. We found a place called *Tumbledown Dick* near Farnborough – a bed and breakfast above a pub – and spent the night there. I can't remember how much it cost – Khan just took my money. It was just a basic bedroom with a shared bathroom. In the evening, Khan went out, came back drunk and saw I was upset, so he gave me a beating. 'Stop being so fucking miserable.' In the morning, as I brushed my teeth, Khan was watching me. 'That's not how you brush your teeth. You do it like this.' He demonstrated the 'correct' way to brush teeth, grabbed my hair, pulling my head back in the process. 'You will *do* as you're told. Brush your teeth like I've shown you.'

Of course, there was nothing wrong with how I brushed my teeth. It was just another excuse for bullying. I always tried my best not to give him an opportunity, but he'd found another reason. Trying not to cry, I carried on brushing, but this time doing it the Khan way. Khan continued to supervise my work but my tooth brushing apparently failed to impress. 'You're brushing your teeth the way white people brush their teeth.'

Something snapped. I thought that, if he was going to beat me up anyway, I might as well stick up for myself. 'Why are you being so racist about it? You know, you're living among white people. If you don't like it, why don't you just fuck off back to Pakistan?'

Khan looked at me, slightly amused, before slapping my face.

'You've still got that fire in you, haven't you?'

'I'm not going to do this. You promised me you wouldn't hurt me. How can you say that you love me? How can you say that? You've just hit me because you say I don't brush my teeth properly. What's wrong with you?'

Khan followed me as I backed towards the door. Grabbing my wrist, he pulled me onto the bed and we struggled. 'What are you doing now?' I asked him.

I closed my eyes but Khan ordered me to open them. He wanted to see the fear. At first, I refused, so he bit my neck. Khan carried on biting until he drew blood, like a wild animal. I gave in almost immediately, but he carried on biting – the pain was unbearable. When he'd finished, he looked at me and I saw madness in his eyes, his constricted pupils like pinpoints. The toothbrush beating was particularly frightening, there being no drink or drugs involved – just Khan.

Eventually, I covered myself up and we went downstairs for breakfast. The owner asked what we wanted to eat. Khan replied, 'She'll just have toast.'

I wasn't allowed to speak to him because he was a white man.

'Are you OK there, love?' He could see that I'd been whacked about a bit. In Punjabi, Khan commanded me not to look at the owner and began talking about himself.

'Yeah, I'm here with the army.'

Believing I was relatively safe in public, I blurted, 'No, you're not,' in English.

Khan was furious and shouted at me in Punjabi for daring to answer back. The owner clearly didn't believe Khan, but decided to have some fun.

'We get a lot of army boys here, what regiment are you in? What's your rank?'

This was near Aldershot, which is an army town. Khan had no answer because he was lying, so he flipped and threw the salt and pepper cellars at me. No one intervened – they didn't know what was going on. Khan yanked me up by the arm and we left without knowing our next stop.

We ended up in Aldershot in Hampshire, out of Surrey Police's area, where we rented a room in a shared house. Khan took my money and filled out all the forms on my behalf. When we first entered the room, I had mixed emotions. Despite Khan's violence, I was trying to convince myself things would work out. I regarded myself as his wife now, for better or worse. But things went from bad to worse. And from worse to even worse.

After a couple of days, we had to go back to my parents' house for my belongings because I'd left most of my clothes behind. Khan was wearing a smart orange shirt and a black bandana on his head; he meant business. He called the police from the end of the road to warn them that there was likely to be a 'breach of the peace'. We waited at the end of the road until the police arrived and followed them after a couple of minutes. Mum was standing in the neighbour's front garden filming proceedings on her camcorder. Khan told me to get my ID – this was so I could secure a bank loan. When I entered the house, Dad was there. I felt a lump in my throat. Dad told me God was punishing me and predicted that I would be back when my money ran out. It was never about money for me – just love and kindness. I collected three bags of clothes and other possessions. As if uncertain of my loyalty, Khan hissed at me as I carried them to the car through our police escort. 'You can never go back to them now.' For his final trick, he shouted loud enough for Dad to hear. 'Bring your baby cradle. We'll need it for our baby.' I'd made the baby cradle at school when I was 15. Khan patted my stomach, although I wasn't pregnant. He wanted Mum and Dad to believe I was carrying his child. Perhaps he wanted to believe it himself.

* * *

Within a few weeks of moving to Aldershot, it was my 19th birthday – 4th July 1997. My mobile phone rang – Khan answered. It was Surrey Police, who told me that one of my grandparents in India had died. 'We don't really know, but I think it's your grandma on your dad's side. Yeah, I think it's your grandma. By the way, your dad wants to wish you a happy birthday.'

My grandmother, Mata Ji, had suffered a stroke a few years before. Dad was very close to his mother, but she was mistreated by her husband, Pita Ji, and Auntie Anita. I was trying to do a silent prayer for her spirit to pass over and do my last blessing for her. Khan looked at me and punched me right in the face.

'See? They don't care about you.' Snatching my mobile phone, Khan added, 'I don't want you calling your family.'

'Look, please let me ring my dad. He'll be very upset.' Khan refused.

I needed to go to the bathroom. This was one of Khan's favourite games. 'You're not allowed to go … actually you can go. Go on, I'll let you. Go on, go!' As I moved towards the door, Khan had second thoughts. 'No, you can't, I've changed my mind.' I carried on anyway. What was the worst he could do? Khan followed me closely. I walked through the main room in the house, where there were two white men. Would he hit me in front of them? As I reached the bathroom, he pushed me aside and blocked the door. 'I told you, you can't go.' At this point I was desperate for a pee. I closed my legs. Khan held me right in the bladder and squeezed hard. 'You've got to wait now, until I say you can go. And if you wet yourself, I'm going to hit you.' The pain was immense. I looked Khan in the eye.

'Why are you doing this to me?' I asked.

Khan's face changed suddenly. Something had struck a chord and he looked guilt-stricken, just like the morning after he'd raped me the first time.

'I'm so sorry. I'm sorry. I really love you.'

'But this isn't the way to treat people you love.'

Khan hugged me and let me go to the toilet. I stayed a couple of minutes to compose myself and thought about Mata Ji and Dad. Back in our room, I was crying, upset about Mata Ji's passing. Khan tugged at my arm and started undressing me.

'Please don't. Please, just leave me alone.'

But Khan wouldn't listen. He raped me again. Later, he

came to me as I lay curled up in a ball on the floor, bleeding. He said he loved me and was sorry. He wouldn't hurt me like that anymore. But then he added, 'That'll be a birthday you won't forget.' The next morning, I could hardly walk.

I went to the doctor – Khan came with me. I was diagnosed with polycystic ovaries and a problem with my uterus, which meant it would be very difficult for me to have children.

Outside the surgery, Khan went berserk and punched me in the face. 'It's your parents. They've done black magic on you.' Back home, he threw the baby cradle across the room, yelling, 'You'll *never* be a mother!'

* * *

Bollywood is the principal home of Indian cinema – Hindi-language films produced in Mumbai, India's second city. Romance or tragedy, comedy or gangster flicks, Bollywood movies sometimes combined all four genres. Productions are lavish and the scenery magnificent, but no Bollywood classic is complete without extravagant song and dance numbers. Soundtracks – *filmi music* – are at the heart of Indian popular culture. Pakistanis also watch Bollywood films and listen to the songs, Hindi being very close to Urdu, the official language of Pakistan. Khan would play Bollywood hits in his car or van. Sometimes he would sing along.

* * *

In Aldershot, we kept some Bollywood cassettes, which I'd bought in India, in the baby cradle. I wanted to feel like part of a normal Asian couple. Some of these songs form the soundtrack to my life with Khan, especially the soundtrack from the 1992 epic film *Khudah Gawah* – God Is My Witness – a tale of love and intrigue set in Afghanistan and India. There was also a song I stumbled across from the film *Himalaya Putra* called *Kaga Sab Tun Khaiyo* – Crow, Feed On My Body. *'Choon choon kai yoo maas, do naina maat kaiyoo more piya milan ki aise,'* which translates roughly as, 'Sieve through my flesh, choose with a fine-tooth comb and pick what you want to eat of me, eat it all … take what you want, but please don't take my eyes, as I'm still hoping to see my loved ones once more.' Sometimes, when I heard this song, I would beg to see my family.

After a month's tenancy, we had to leave the house because the beatings were upsetting the other residents, who'd threatened to call the police. Our next stop was truly awful – a small room in a filthy house on Morland Road in Aldershot. I remember the walls were magnolia and heavily stained with nicotine and dirt. Our room was just a double bed, a cupboard and a bulky box TV in one of three upstairs bedrooms, which all had locks on. The other people in the house were Asian, which Khan preferred, although I wasn't allowed to talk to them. Khan made me leave work. He was now working for an Indian takeaway, having been sacked by the parcel delivery company for concealing his criminal record. Someone had tipped them off.

My life descended, literally, into darkness when Khan placed flattened cardboard boxes in front of the bedroom windows and kept the curtains drawn shut. He would lock me in when he went out and turn the electricity off, so I couldn't switch on the light. A full-size mirror was placed on the window sill, which Khan would take down from time to time to conduct full inspections of the damage he'd inflicted on my body. The bed was moved up against the wall, adding to my sense of imprisonment. I was cold, alone, locked in without heat or light and unable to use the bathroom. Embarrassing to admit, but I wet myself several times.

Khan continued to beat me black and blue. He would ring my friends, whose details were in my mobile, and threaten and abuse them, often making me listen. He frightened them all away. He rang Mum, who told him she would do a funeral for me, which is an Indian way of saying I was dead to her.

Dilip had a lovely Muslim girlfriend called Mubina, who'd met our family. Khan rang her family trying to stir up trouble for Dilip. He asked why she was going out with a Hindu. And he asked me, not unreasonably, why it was OK for Dilip to go out with a Muslim, but not me. He wondered, 'What kind of man is your brother? He can't even look after his sister.'

Dilip told Khan, 'My sister is dead. I don't care what you do to her.'

Another time, Khan pushed me to the floor, held me down and rang Dad. He put the phone on loudspeaker so I could hear the receptionist, and then Dad's voice. Khan asked Dad, 'Can you hear her? I've got your daughter here. I've just hit her. Can you hear her? There's nothing you can do. I'm raping your daughter now. There's nothing you can do.'

Dad pleaded with Khan, 'Why don't you just leave her alone? Please, leave her alone.'

I also begged Khan, 'Please, please don't let my dad listen to this, please. I'll do whatever it is you want me to do. Please don't hurt my family like this.'

Khan was a chameleon. A violent, sadistic bully. He could appear kind and caring, although this was usually done to suit his purposes, especially in the early days when he was grooming me. He sported different appearances – goatee, clean-shaven or devout long beard. He wore his hair long or completely shaved off. He also adopted funny voices, could do accents and mimicked people. A couple of times at my parents' house, they said there was a girl on the phone – it was Khan. Particularly when he was trying to sound sincere, Khan spoke English very properly, like a character from an old British film. But, he also urinated in the street when he'd been drinking. At first, Khan told me he was 26, but later showed me a passport saying he was born in June 1966 – 666, the Mark of the Beast. This would have made him 31 in 1997. However, he hinted the passport was forged and he may have been older. Khan made me wear traditional Asian trouser suits, *shalwar kameez,* no makeup and a hijab to cover my hair. Although, he sometimes wore my mascara. He took care with his own appearance, always wearing scent or aftershave.

Khan came from Mirpur in Kashmir. In 1948, India and Pakistan went to war over Kashmir, which is now divided between the two nations. Mirpur is on the Pakistani side of the border.

When I first met Khan, we spoke English. Later, we spoke Punjabi sometimes, before he forced me to learn his Mirpuri dialect and beat me if I got it wrong. Once, I was seeing him off and he nearly got run over in the street outside the house. I ran outside to see if he was alright. He shouted, 'How dare you leave the house with your head uncovered?' Khan would assault me if his football team, Aston Villa, lost. Driving along, a red traffic light would earn me a punch, right there in the car. Feeding time was interesting because Khan ate meat and I'm a vegetarian. To begin with, he accepted this, but, after a while, he forced me to eat meat. When I refused, he would open my jaw, push meat down my mouth and slap and punch me until I ate it. On one memorable occasion, Khan went to the trouble of buying a pig's trotter, which he forced me to eat while he watched. As a Muslim, Khan didn't eat pork himself. His motive was pure, insane cruelty. Khan also invented a novel game with fizzy drinks. He would fill his mouth with cola, force my mouth open with his hand, spit the drink into my mouth and make me swallow it. Once, Khan decided to conduct an experiment. There were fresh wounds on my arm where he'd cut me. He took the salt cellar and grabbed my wrist. 'Keep still, right.' He wanted to test the saying *rubbing salt into the wound,* so he poured salt onto my cuts, where it seemed to sizzle in my blood. It hurt like hell. Khan looked into my eyes, like a scientist waiting for the results. Despite the excruciating pain, I managed to compose myself and reported, as calmly as I could, that it didn't hurt at all. He seemed disappointed and didn't repeat the exercise.

Khan made me watch pornography, porn videos and cable channels so I could learn to please him. Apparently, me just lying there wasn't good enough. He wanted me to learn different positions and do different things. I didn't realise there was a completely different side to sex. I mean, I do now, but I didn't realise at the time that you were supposed to enjoy it! I thought you just got up and tidied up the aftermath. Now, I could write the book, but back in those days, I was unworldly, very naïve. Khan would mimic the people in the films and ask, 'I hope you're learning.' Once, after watching porn, Khan got excited. He moved towards me and whispered softly, 'Blow me.' I had no idea what he was talking about, so he grew impatient. 'I said, blow me!' I was confused but knew I had to do something, so, without further ado, I blew in Khan's face as if he were a set of candles. Khan was exasperated and stood up. 'That's the trouble with you virgins, you're too innocent.'

Khan took my money and made me take out loans, so he

effectively had two wages when I was working, but I couldn't even buy food for myself. Khan told me he was a heroin addict and that he was on methadone, the heroin substitute. This may have explained his often strangely constricted pupils. Khan also told me about his drug dealing. I suspect this was mainly in the past as I didn't see any evidence of Khan dealing in drugs or using them, apart from the parties those first few days I lived with him, the time he first raped me. When I lived with Khan, he worked mainly as a van or delivery driver. I administered Khan's methadone, which he was taking in gradually reduced quantities. On a good day, Khan would give me credit for helping him beat his addiction, and said I was good for him.

When I had my periods, I would have to beg Khan to buy me some sanitary towels because I was bleeding everywhere. He would whack me even harder, saying, 'Why aren't you pregnant? There's something wrong with you. I'm having sex with you. I've come in you so many times. There's nothing wrong with me – there's something wrong with you.'

Chapter 6

STARGAZING

The most important festival in the Hindu calendar is Diwali, the festival of light, which celebrates the triumph of light over darkness, good over evil. Diwali also commemorates Lakshmi, the Hindu goddess of wealth and prosperity, born from a cosmic ocean of milk.

* * *

Khan was interested in true crime stories. Early on in our relationship, before we lived together, Khan took me by train on a trip to London. He made me buy a child's ticket to save money. We went to look at the *The Blind Beggar*, a pub in Bethnal Green frequented by the Kray twins, where Ronnie Kray shot dead rival gangster George Cornell. Khan also took me to a house, another former crime scene where people had been killed and body parts found – I can't remember the details. On the train back to Woking, Khan told me a story about some gangsters who dismembered a body. He joked that he would do that to me if I ever left him.

On another train outing in June 1997, Khan was fascinated by a newspaper headline and told me the story. 'There's this boxer, right. Mike Tyson. He's bitten the other guy's ear off! Evander Holyfield. Tyson bit his ear off!' Then,

Khan moved his mouth towards my ear and whispered, 'I wonder what that would be like. What if I bit your ear off?'

Sometimes Khan would pace up and down, mumbling to himself. One day, there was a story in the news about an honour killing. A girl was murdered by her family for running off with a man from a different religion. A short while after this, Khan was pacing and mumbling. He was concentrating, like he was working something out. Then he seemed to come to a conclusion. 'They marked the girl up, cut her into pieces and put her body parts in different places.' Khan's violence was one thing, but this was terrifying.

'What are you on about?' I asked. Khan produced a black marker pen.

'They cut her into pieces.' Khan grabbed my arm, slung me onto the bed and pulled my clothes off. For once, I hoped it was only rape and I wasn't resisting. My clothes were torn anyway; I would only have to sew them up. Khan went to the window and adjusted the curtains to let in a little sunlight. Goose pimples shuddered on my flesh. I dared not make eye contact while Khan continued to mumble, as if he were either on drugs or doing black magic. Then he began to draw on me with the marker pen. The felt tip was cold as ice.

'What the hell are you doing?' I asked fearfully. Khan punched my jaw, pushed me onto my back and put his left hand over my mouth. Bit by bit, with his right hand, Khan divided my body into sections with his marker pen. He outlined my neck, my chest, my stomach, my private parts, thighs, knees and ankles. Once again, Khan looked for the fear in my eyes, and once again, he found it. Was he going to carve me up? I tried to see if he had any tools. Khan ran his fingers over the pen markings on my body and, with a look in his eye I'd not seen before, began to speak.

'This part, I'll give to your mum. This piece here, I'm

going to leave in their shed. And this part,' he grabbed my hand, 'I'll give them for Diwali.' He pointed at my ankle. 'This part here, I'll give them for New Year.'

I was cold, naked and scared as I asked, 'Why are you doing this to me?'

Khan's eyes were bloodshot. He clasped my jaw so I couldn't speak, his hand like a vice on my cheeks. Suddenly, he let go.

'I could do this to you, but I won't because I love you. I *really* love you.'

* * *

Dud Chacha, Dad's brother, came with him to England in the 1960s. Sent by their father to provide money for the family in India, they no doubt hoped for a better life for themselves, too. Like many Punjabi Hindus, they lived in Hounslow in West London. After Dad wed Mum, Dud Chacha fell in love with an Indian woman, but my family didn't approve of her – I'm not sure why. Dud Chacha married her in secret, but things turned sour. He stopped sending money to India, giving it all to his wife instead. Rumour has it that Grandad and Anita, Dad's sister, placed a curse to make Dud Chacha leave his wife. In the event, *she* left *him* and aborted their child. Dud Chacha was heartbroken, descended into alcoholism and spent some time in prison, as well as a psychiatric hospital. He also suffered from epilepsy and was unable to work.

For a few years in the 1980s, Dud Chacha lived with us in Woking, when I was a child. He was softly spoken, kind and always had time for me. I still have a miniature plastic tea set that he bought me. Dud Chacha never raised his voice or said a bad word about anyone. He was generous and handsome, although he had scars on his neck and hand, resulting from drink-fuelled incidents. In rehab for his drinking, Dud Chacha became involved with a Scotswoman. I remember they showered together, which was a bit racy for my family! Dad wasn't comfortable with this arrangement. He wouldn't let us watch kissing on TV. 'Gordon Bennett!' Dad would yell – that was an English expression he used – before switching channels with the remote.

Grandad – *Pita Ji* – was unimpressed with Dud Chacha's lack of financial contribution and flew to England to sort matters out. Pita Ji means Dad, but my grandfather didn't like being called Grandad, so he was Pita Ji, and my grandmother was *Mata Ji*. I remember the family taking him to Madam Tussaud's in London to look at the waxwork of Mahatma Gandhi – Father of the Indian nation. I think I was about eight years old at the time. In Punjabi, Pita Ji considered his options. 'If I cursed a plane with Dud on it, the plane crashes and 300 people die, but that bastard would survive.' So instead of trying black magic to bring down an aeroplane, Pita Ji took Dud Chacha back to India with him. Why did Dud Chacha comply? Indian families are close-knit, respect for elders is ingrained in Asian culture, and Pita Ji was the head of our family. He was also a hard man, and Dud Chacha a broken one who never returned to the UK.

We would see Dud Chacha in the summer holidays when we visited India. His deterioration in health was noticeable – he no longer received medication for epilepsy, nor treatment for his addiction to alcohol. But he always had a smile or a kind word for me. I remember one time when we were teenagers, Billy and I went shopping in Ambala – Dad's home town. We realised we didn't have enough rupees left to take a rickshaw back to the family house. Luckily, we saw Dud Chacha, who gave us money to get home and made sure we were taken by a particular driver, whom he trusted. Back at the family home, I tried to pay Dud Chacha back but he refused.

'No! I can't take money from you. You're a child.'

On another occasion, the family were walking in Ambala and I saw Dud Chacha lying in the gutter.

'Look! It's Dud Chacha!' I shouted, pleased to see him but also concerned. Auntie Anita snapped at me to ignore him and we continued on our way.

When he was still in England, Dud Chacha would show me the moon and the stars. He taught me about Sirius, the dog star, which shines brightest around my birthday on 4th July. Later, when we visited Ambala, Dud Chacha would take me up to the roof terrace at night and show me the constellations. When we parted, Dud Chacha would remind me that we weren't so far away as we shared the same sky. All I had to do was look up. A few years ago, a friend first showed me Saturn through a telescope on Albury Heath in Surrey. It was amazing, the colour and the ring! Now I love watching the stars and planets through binoculars. My favourite stars are the Pleiades, the Seven Sisters. It's funny, I was always scared of the dark and this intensified when Khan kept me locked up for days in that cold room. But it doesn't feel like darkness when you're looking at the heavens through a lens.

* * *

Locked alone in the room in the dark for days on end, my eyes became unused to the light. But my other senses seemed to sharpen, and sounds and smells took on a greater significance. Khan's van pulling up, or his key in the door, would trigger a reaction, instinctive fear. I particularly remember certain smells from this time, too – the metallic tang of keys, or the aroma of rubber-soled shoes. Then, when we were together, there was Khan's personal scent. This wasn't body odour – Khan kept himself clean – but he had this distinctive, overpowering scent, which I can recall clearly.

After a while, Khan started to let me out occasionally at night, like a dog on a lead being given a run around. At first, I struggled to walk downstairs because he didn't feed me every day, so I'd lost a lot of weight and felt weak. I remember vividly feeling fresh air on my face at four in the morning for the first time after weeks of captivity. I'd almost forgotten how it felt. The noises of the outdoors and the sound of leaves rustling in the wind seemed different, more alive, almost like lost friends.

I felt as if I'd been freed from a dungeon, although, not quite, because Khan was with me. He would tie an old rope around me, or his leather belt, so he could pull me along, or he would grab the back of my neck and push me forward. This wasn't every night, just an occasional treat when Khan would say I'd been a 'good girl', but really, it was just when he was around and felt like some fun. I had to go barefoot so Khan could smash bottles and make me walk on the glass. Once, I tried to sit down, fatigued and hungry, but Khan kicked me in the leg and yanked me up by the rope. But it wasn't all bad. If I saw coins in the street, I was allowed to pick them up. Sometimes, I was allowed to keep these few pennies as a 'reward', although he often took them off me later, anyway. These walks were like a game of snakes and ladders, but without the ladders. I was resigned to my fate. There was no fight left in me.

With my feet bleeding in the early hours and my tormentor prodding me along the streets of Aldershot, I would sometimes gaze up at the stars and think of Dud Chacha, and his unconditional love for me.

Chapter 7

POSTER BOY

One day in the Autumn, Khan was in a tender mood. He'd brought a box over from his brother's house and we sat on the floor while he showed me the contents. These included his stalking trophies. He'd already told me he was the parcel delivery man who'd followed me for months before making his move, but now he showed me his spoils. There were photos of me shopping in Woking, me entering and leaving my parents' house, me driving and me outside the pub. I was shocked to see one snap of me with friends taken almost two years ago. I took a closer look whilst Khan continued emptying the box. In the pictures, I wore Western clothes, whereas I now dressed in *shalwaar kameez* and *hijab*. Khan produced my GCSE certificates and national insurance card – which I thought I'd lost – presumably taken from my parents' home. Khan had stalked other women, too, and had lots of photos of them as well as their possessions – a used lipstick, a make-up mirror and a set of car keys. I felt angry inside. So many victims. He spoke of their different body scents and the perfumes they wore. He told me I was the best, proudly adding that I was his ninth virgin. This was like a thunderbolt. I felt dizzy. Despite his cruelty, Khan had made me feel special before. But now I was just another victim. His ninth virgin.

And then, Khan calmly boasted that he'd raped a twelve-year-old girl. He claimed the incident occurred when he was at school in Birmingham. Khan felt the girl 'thought she was something special. She needed taking down a peg or two.' He described how he got on top of her, how seeing the fear in her eyes gave him a buzz.

I felt physically sick. I felt hatred for this monster. *He raped a twelve-year-old.* Khan proceeded to catalogue a list of stalking victims, droning on about the artefacts he'd collected from them. All I could think was, *he raped a twelve-year-old.* I thought about smothering him with a pillow, putting an end to his miserable life right there and then. I wasn't strong enough, so I decided to wait till he was asleep. That night, after a characteristically brutal 'love making' session, Khan fell asleep and began to snore gently. I looked at Khan, my stalker, my abuser, my torturer … my lover. *He raped a twelve-year-old.* I picked up the pillow and raised it above my head to suffocate him. But I couldn't do it. Maybe I lacked the courage, but I wasn't able to take a human life. And, for a part of me, Khan was the man who gave me cuddles. I felt sick, and I felt torn.

Life with Khan was not a barrel of laughs, but one amusing incident stands out. Khan's hair was turning white and he kept dying it black, but once he stopped for a while and white roots appeared, making him look older. We went into a takeaway where he ordered some chips. I think the man in there was Bangladeshi. Khan didn't like Bangladeshis. They were 'too dark' and he couldn't understand their language. Typically, Khan had ordered nothing for me. The man serving us asked, 'Would your daughter like something?' I burst out laughing – I'd almost forgotten how to. Khan's face was like thunder. 'She … not … my … daughter. She's my WIFE!' I looked young for my age and was under-weight with my hair covered. The man behind the counter made matters worse.

'But she looks about ten!' I couldn't stop myself. I tried laughing silently and had to walk outside.

Khan's violence deteriorated. Sometimes he was knocking me unconscious. But there would be moments of tenderness, and those cuddles – my weakness. Once, Khan came home from work at a factory in Ash, near Aldershot. He had chased a colleague with a hammer after being racially abused. Instead of venting his anger by beating the crap out of me like any self-respecting sadist, on this occasion, Khan cried like a baby while I cradled him in my arms. Khan bragged that he'd been a member of a gang in Birmingham. His left hand and forearm were scarred, he claimed, from petrol bombing houses. He told me his best friend died in his arms from stab wounds.

Indian and Pakistani women wear a wide variety of fashions. When I was at home, Mum and I usually wore western clothes. Only on special family occasions would we wear Indian clothes, brightly coloured suits. Some Pakistani women dress the same way, particularly in the big cities, Lahore and Karachi. But many, especially in rural areas, dress more conservatively with plainer, pale colours and baggier cuts. Khan made me dress this way, with a *hijab* – headdress – covering my hair, although no face covering. When I was 16 and at Brooklands College, sort of seeing Moonie, he visited the card shop in town and asked Mum's permission to date me. Needless to say, she refused, laughing in Moonie's face. Dilip got involved and tried to play big brother, coming down to the college and warning Moonie off. Then, as a kind of punishment, Mum and Dilip made me wear Indian suits to college for a couple of days, while my Muslim friends all wore western clothes.

* * *

The Shah Jahan Mosque in Woking was built in 1889, the first purpose built mosque in England, named after a female ruler, the Begum of Bhopal in India, who financed its construction. Because of this connection, Muslim soldiers fighting for Britain in the two World Wars, who died of wounds in English hospitals, were buried on Horsell Common in Woking.

* * *

One time, while we were living in Aldershot, Khan evidently decided the Muslims back in Woking were in need of some guidance. He produced his black marker pen and some paper and dictated what I was to write. We were going to make posters to 'teach them a lesson'. I can't remember the exact words. I was concussed much of the time but it was along the following lines:

'To Whom It May Concern: these Muslim girls ... they aren't what you think; they are no better than the white girls.'

I didn't want anything to do with this. 'You can't write this? You're a Muslim, why are you doing this? I can't do this!'

Khan punched me on the ear. 'Fucking write it!'

I was wearing a headdress which kept slipping and, with my ears ringing from the punch, I was losing Khan's thread, making him angrier still. It seems there were some teenage Muslim girls hanging around the Peacocks Centre in Woking, wearing tight jeans and t-shirts, smoking and chatting to boys. In the poster's text, Khan alleged that these girls were sleeping around and complained that they didn't cover their heads. The poster warned that this was just the beginning. There would be further revelations, giving the names and addresses of people in the Muslim community having affairs.

So, Khan's rant was in capitals in my handwriting, which I hadn't thought to disguise. Khan drove me to Woking and we went to the library where we made A3 copies of the posters, about 20 I think. Using sellotape, we put the posters up all around Woking, near the mosque, by the train station where the Pakistani taxi drivers congregated, in phone boxes and in the town centre. While we were doing this, Mum walked past on her lunch break and saw me. Although I could have died of embarrassment, I wanted to hug Mum, but she gave me a look of disgust – at me in my 'Paki' clothes as she later called them. Khan glared at her and she scurried away.

Khan made me do this under CCTV cameras. I didn't always know what he was up to, but this time I did. He was trying to get me arrested, but it backfired. Perhaps as a joke, Khan gave a few posters to some Muslim guys in a minicab office. They agreed to distribute the posters, but when they read the content they were horrified and complained to the police. Khan was asked to attend the police station and took me with him. 'Look, I'm getting called in about this. It's your fucking mother! If they try and take you into the side room, you say "No comment". If they keep pushing you, say you don't speak English.'

'But they know I speak English.'

'Just say that two black men gave you twenty quid to put them up. That's all you say. If you say anything else, I'm going to beat the shit out of you.' Khan had a problem with black people, something to do with gang violence in Birmingham.

The police informed Khan that they were arresting him for literature and public disorder, or something like that. They took me into a side room. The senior officer asked, 'Sunita, how are you doing?' They could see I was completely smashed up.

'Hi, how are you?' I replied. 'He's told me not to say anything about anything. What's this about? I'm sorry. He doesn't like me talking to anyone.' I looked at the floor.

'Do you recognise this?' He showed me one of the posters. I looked away.

'Two black guys gave it to me to put up.' I figured Khan would find out if I didn't follow the script. His hare-brained alibi was designed to get him off the hook, but not me.

'Have you actually read it?'

'Bits of it.'

'That's funny, because we've been to your parents' house and your Mum happily gave us this.' He pulled out some psychology course work, noting, 'It absolutely matches your handwriting.' *If only I'd finished my psychology 'A' level!* I thought I was in trouble.

The police officers looked for my reaction. I was young, naïve, very much controlled by Khan, and I didn't want to get him into trouble because he always said that I had to protect him like a shield. I was also scared he'd beat the crap out of me. I could have blamed Khan, told the police he made me do it and they would have believed me, but I didn't.

'Oh, they do look similar, don't they?' I suppose I was scared and trying to be cocky.

The policeman was confused and scratched his head like Oliver Hardy. 'I don't know why he's written about Muslims, because he's a Muslim.'

'I don't know either.'

'Why didn't he write it himself?'

'He can't write or spell,' I muttered quickly.

'Oh! So you're like the Dangerous Duo – he's streetwise and you're the intelligent one. When's the next lot coming out, Sunita? Is there more to come?'

'No, there isn't. Not to my knowledge.'

'Is there more already done?'

'I don't know what you're talking about. No comment. I'm not under arrest.' The interview continued in this vein for some time, with me being uncooperative, but they were after Khan, not me. After a couple more hours, the police released Khan. I think they let him go on bail 'pending further investigation.' Two police vans turned up at his brother's house, where Khan was supposed to be living, with a warrant looking for a printing press. Khan's older brother wasn't happy at all, but Khan found it hilarious. He thought he was invincible and could do what he wanted. I must have had an adrenalin rush after the interrogation because I asked Khan, 'What the fuck is wrong with you? You're a Muslim and you've just kicked up a hornet's nest in the Mosque. How can you find that funny?' He didn't assault me on this occasion, being in a good mood after a job well done.

Khan discovered from the police that it wasn't Mum who'd reported him. 'It was the fucking Pakis,' he snarled, and took me with him to the cab office where he swore at the driver responsible and threatened him. On this occasion, I managed to calm him down. After a few days, Khan came home and announced, 'I'm taking you to Woking.' I asked him what had happened, wondering if he was going to bait me in front of Mum and Dad. It even occurred to me he might burn their house down for a laugh. I grabbed a coat and shoes, my heart racing. Khan was excited. 'You won't believe this. There's something I need to show you.'

We drove to Woking and into the Peacock's car park on the top level. Below us, a group of Asian girls all wore headscarves. Not one wore jeans or a t–shirt. 'Look, this is the power that you and I had on the Woking girls. See? See what fear does to people? No one calls me a creep.'

* * *

Six years later, I applied for a bank loan when my husband Ray ran up serious debts with cocaine dealers. The Asian cashier arranging my appointment recognised my name. 'Aren't you the girl who put those posters up? I was at college and had to change the way I dressed because of you.'

Chapter 8

WINGS

Whenever Khan was home during daylight hours, he would open the curtains in our room and move the mirror away from the window to let some light in. He didn't like the darkness himself. One day, Khan was lying on the bed talking to his mother on my mobile phone, when a beautiful butterfly appeared, as if from nowhere. It was black and red with white spots – a red admiral I think. Perhaps it came to our room as a caterpillar and matured into a butterfly right there under our noses. The poor creature flapped its wings, frantically trying to find a way out into the world. It seemed in a bad way. I thought it was suffocating and wanted to help it escape. I managed to cup my hands around the butterfly, hoping to let it out, but I needed Khan to open the window. Knowing I wasn't supposed to make a sound, I stood in front of Khan to gain his attention but he frowned at me and put his finger to his mouth. I thought I'd probably get a beating now anyway, so I pleaded with him. 'Please! Open the window.' Khan glared at me and kicked me hard on the back of the leg with his steel toe caps. I tried not to wince, not wanting to harm the butterfly.

'Who's that?' asked Khan's mother. They spoke Mirpuri, which is related to Punjabi.

'No one, *Amma* (Mum). It's just the maid, cleaning,'

replied Khan. He worked as a delivery driver and his mother clearly didn't believe he employed domestic servants.

'She sounds nice. When do I get to meet her?' Khan didn't reply but Amma persisted. 'Does she make you happy, *beta* (child)?'

'*Ji, Amma,*' – Yes, Mum – said Khan reluctantly.

'Well, she asked you to do something. You'd better do what she asked.'

'*Ji, Amma.*' I now feared for the creature in my care. In the previous house, where we'd stayed in Aldershot, Khan had booted a kitten across the living room, so he wasn't exactly an animal lover. I turned away from Khan, instinctively protective. But Khan opened the window and the butterfly flew to freedom. When Khan had finished his call, I hugged him tightly in gratitude.

* * *

Some people claim that cats and dogs know when their owners are coming home. Khan seemed to radiate a kind of toxic power and, often, I could feel it when he was approaching the house. He owned me totally.

On Sunday 31st August 1997, in the early hours, Khan was making deliveries for the takeaway and I was locked in our room as usual. I sensed Khan's presence, my stomach tightened and I began to shake. Khan's car pulled up. I braced myself as I heard his key in the front door. Khan unlocked the room, took me downstairs to cook him a meal and watch TV in the living room. Normally, we avoided the other residents, but there was no one around. Khan's programme was interrupted by a news flash. 'Fucking watching that …' His eyes fixed on me. I sensed trouble brewing in his troubled mind.

A solemn voice announced that Princess Diana had been involved in a car crash in Paris. Dodi Fayed had been killed – the Princess was fighting for her life in a French hospital. Princess Diana was my idol. The Queen of Hearts. She visited the sick – AIDS sufferers and lepers – and performed random acts of kindness. When I was a little girl, I had her poster on my bedroom wall. Khan liked her, too. '*Fucking* hell! Lady Di. She was one of the good people in the world.' Well, he would know. The switch in Khan's head flicked again and he went berserk. He threw his china bowl of food against the wall, smashing it. Noodles everywhere. Khan's glass followed and he began howling abuse at me. 'Clean it up! NOW!! Fucking bitch!' I moved towards the wreckage and started picking up the pieces. Khan walked over and trod my hand into a shard of glass. 'PICK IT UP!' As I carried on picking up the pieces, Khan beat my back. First he used his fists, punching again and again, punching and screaming. Then he whacked me with something sharp, which cut and sliced my skin. I think it was the edge of a piece of broken china. Khan cut me properly that night and I still bear the scars. Tears in my eyes meant I couldn't focus on the china and glass I was picking up, so I cut my fingers and hands as well. The beating over, I hauled myself upstairs to our room. Khan followed and raped me while I still had glass sticking out of my hand.

* * *

Being a single mum is hard at times, but at other times, so joyful. I have often hidden much of my past, but my scars were something I couldn't always hide. Covered in hundreds of scars, each had their own story: cuts, burns or whip marks from Khan's leather belt. In January 2014, when my daughter was five, she came into the bathroom to sing me a song whilst I was having a bath, *Twinkle, Twinkle Little Star*. Maya started counting. She reached over a hundred and I saw her lean in closer to the bath.

'What are you doing, Beautiful? Water is hot, be careful,'

'Mummy, I'm counting those marks on your back. What are they?' Maya asked with innocence and curiosity. I froze, a single tear ran down my cheek. 'Mummy, what's the matter?' Maya showed concern.

'It's something Mummy doesn't like to show, these are called scars, marks from ouchies. They don't hurt anymore'. I ended my bath and gave my girl a cuddle.

'Is that why you don't wear that lovely dress, Mummy?' asked Maya. The dress was backless and elegant, but didn't go with my scars. I kept it in my wardrobe wishing I could wear it one day. That evening, I decided I wanted to be stronger and I was ready to be. I wanted my daughter to see my strength. I began designing a back tattoo. Maya saw my plans in the morning. She loved the design and gave me more ideas. Her input was amazing.

'It's time Mummy makes those scars go away with new happy memories'. The tattoo shows a butterfly for new life, a dragonfly for hope and angel wings for the times I've fallen and been carried, as well as a tribute to all the ones I've lost to heaven. After the tattoo healed, I wore my backless dress and celebrated with Maya.

Chapter 9

BIG BROTHER

The *Raksha Bandhan* festival, or *rakhi,* celebrates the bond of love between brothers and sisters. Various mythological and historical events are associated with the festival. Growing up, I would tie a red thread, the rakhi, around Dilip and Billy's wrists, and they would make me a small gift and vow to protect me.

* * *

On birthdays, Dilip would often give me a present, only to take it back later on a whim. Once, he did it with a cuddly toy. Other times, he would give me a completely useless gift. When I was back in my parents' house, just after Dilip had smashed up my bedroom, he gave me an early birthday present, a pair of navy blue tracksuit bottoms. It was almost as if he was feeling guilty and was making a peace offering, but as usual there was a twist. The tracksuit bottoms were a couple of sizes too big, so it seemed like a wind up as well. Since tracksuits weren't really my style and I wasn't allowed out to do any sport, I asked Dilip if he could exchange them for me. That might sound strange, but it's just that I was very inexperienced still and didn't know how to do stuff like that. Instead, Dilip handed me the receipt. 'Just go back and get a cash refund.' Then he laughed strangely, like he was in on a joke that I didn't get.

By an odd twist of fate, I was wearing the tracksuit bottoms the night I left home and slept in the car. Khan's sister-in-law had made a *shalwaar kameez* for me to wear. He told me not to wear the tracksuit bottoms. I mentioned that I still had the receipt and could get a refund. We went to the Peacocks Shopping Centre and Khan decided to kill two birds with one stone while we were there. First of all, he tied a rope around me and tugged me past the card shop where Mum worked, to wind her up – *your daughter belongs to me*. Khan laughed as Mum disappeared to the back of the card shop, ashamed. Then he took me down to the sports shop, untied the rope and sent me in to get the cash refund. But it was a credit card purchase, so, of course, the shop would only make a refund to Dilip's credit card account. Now I understood why Dilip had laughed – he knew I couldn't get cash back.

Khan wasn't happy, but then he had a brainwave. 'Right, we'll see how funny he finds it when I use his credit card.' In those days, the credit card receipt showed the full number and the expiry date. I tried to screw up the receipt, but Khan punched me in the shoulder in full public view and snatched it. I begged Khan not to use Dilip's credit card details, but he did. He used it to pay his brother's bills, including his British Telecom bill, three or four hundred pounds, and he bought hi-fi equipment off the QVC Shopping Channel.

When we were living in Sheerwater, Khan asked me about my job at Galleon, realised I had access to customers' credit card details and saw a further opportunity. He instructed me to get the credit card numbers and expiry dates – there were fewer security checks on card purchases in those days. At first I refused, but Khan wasn't taking no for an answer.

He threw cigarette ash on me, threatened to burn me and threatened me with knives. Then he cut me on the back with broken glass, basically torturing me for the card details. He threatened to hurt my family and went into the card shop where Mum worked.

'Your mum's here right now.' I could hear Mum's voice. Khan described what she was wearing. 'I've got a cup of acid. I'm going to throw it on her face. *Now,* are you going to get me those credit card details?' I think Mum probably didn't recognise him as he now had a shaven head and beard.

Under duress, I gave Khan the information he wanted. I was able to memorise the credit card numbers, but I avoided debit cards where the money comes straight from someone's bank account. Khan was using the credit card details to book hire cars – he also used Dilip's card for that. The first time was an eight-seater Galaxy for a family event. When we lived in Aldershot, he would get me to book cars over the phone using false names, which he would collect using stolen credit cards he'd acquired elsewhere. Being under 21, I wasn't allowed to drive the cars, so Khan would collect them using his own passport and driving licence as ID. Needless to say, I didn't have a choice. What Khan did with the cars, I don't know. He'd tried to repair his brown Ford Capri with money from a loan I'd taken out, but it was now clapped out. He'd also ruined the bonnet by spilling battery acid on it. I think he was planning to throw acid in someone's face, or at least threaten to.

* * *

As time went on, Khan carried on raping me and coming with me to the doctor to see if I was pregnant. I'd transferred to a GP's surgery in Aldershot. One time, he was supposed to meet me there but missed the appointment for some reason. The woman doctor could see I was malnourished, battered and bruised.

'He's an absolute bastard. Look what he's done to you. What if you had a daughter and someone did that to her?'

'But I can't have kids.'

'You wouldn't want kids with this man. Why don't you escape?'

'But where to? Nobody will have me, I'm damaged goods. I'm better off dead.' This poor doctor just looked at me with tears in her eyes.

'No, love, you've got a life. You need to go and live it. This isn't a life you're living.'

On the way home from the doctor, I found a twenty pence piece on the floor and called my parents from a phone box. Dilip answered.

'It's me, Sunita. I miss you all.'

Dilip now surprised me.

'Why don't you come home, Sunny? We don't care if you're pregnant. We want you back.' My money ran out.

Sometimes, I was locked in the house for a couple of days, with no food or access to the bathroom. Too scared to call for the other residents, I wondered what would happen if Khan had an accident or just didn't come back. Would I just die there? The silence was sometimes deafening. One morning, Khan came home in a cold sweat – he'd forgotten to take his methadone. He was helpless as I administered his drug and gently held him. When he'd recovered his strength, Khan punched me in the mouth and went out. Perhaps he didn't like me seeing him weak, not that he needed a reason to batter me.

On my own in the house, I started cutting, self-harming. This wasn't the first time – I'd cut myself as a child. Now I cut myself with a shard of glass or razors. I did this because I was in pain and I wanted the pain to end. The physical pain took over from the emotional pain, which flowed out, but only for a short while. Self-harming solves nothing – it hurts and I wouldn't recommend it, but it's what I did at the time. After doing this a few times, I decided that I'd either kill myself, or he'd have to do it, because I'd had enough. I cut my arms with broken glass and bangles. I wrote Khan's name on my forearm. I didn't have any tablets or anything around. I thought about taking his methadone, but I'd done that once before and he'd almost knocked me out. Also, I didn't want to deprive him of his medicine because I did care for him.

Khan came into the house and saw blood on my arms. He seemed frightened at violence not of his making and punched me in the head. I stood up and looked in his eyes. 'Go on. Hit me. Hit me really hard. But don't you dare ever say you love me, because this isn't love. I've had enough.' I showed Khan my arm and he saw the blood dripping. He also saw where I'd carved his name. I pleaded with him. 'This is how much I love you. Now show me how much you love me by finishing me off, because I can't take this torture any more. That's it, I've had it. I've had enough. If you really loved me, you'd finish me off right here, right now. That's my last dying wish. Let's see how strong you really are.' From my desperation came strength, which Khan saw in my eyes, and, for the first time, he started to cry.

'But I can't do that. I love you.'

'Come on, come on. Stand up. Be a man. Come on,' I shouted. 'You're always bullying me, come on and do it. Finish me off. I beg of you. Kill me, kill me. I can't carry on.' Khan broke down, sobbing, overwhelmed with guilt.

'No, I won't. I love you too much. I – I can't believe I've

done this to you. I'm so sorry. Sorry for all the times I've hit you. I can't do it anymore.' Then Khan gently kissed my wounds and bandaged them with tissue. He cuddled me, and we rocked backwards and forwards. 'What have I done? What have I done to you? I'm so, so … Why don't you go back to your parents?'

'After everything you've done to me? I can't go back.'

'Look, the door's open. You're free. Go!'

I was so close, just inches from the door. As I edged towards freedom, I turned back and saw Khan in the corner, sitting on the floor, weeping and rocking like a wounded animal. He was broken, perhaps seeing in my self-inflicted violence a mirror image of what he was doing to me. I cried, too, and felt the blood trickling down my arm and onto my hand. Seeing his vulnerability for the first time, I pitied Khan. I walked over to him, knelt down and cuddled him, as he'd just cuddled me. 'You can't do this to people. You just can't. It's not love. You can't just have me trapped here. But I can't escape. I can't leave you like this.' And I stayed with him – he was all I had.

* * *

Khan claimed that Dad and Dilip had been to see him, offering £7,000 to have me back. 'I told them I can make more money sending you out to work. And when I've had my fill with you, I can sell you to the Arabs.' According to Dilip, some months later, the meeting was with Khan's brother at the Woking Liberal Club, where he and Dad drank. In Dilip's version of events, Khan didn't turn up. It's quite possible that Khan's brother wanted nothing to do with such a transaction, but he informed Khan about the approach.

I'd stopped working at Galleon, but Khan decided I should

make myself useful by earning some money. He was feeding me a bit more now, and accompanied me to an employment agency where they sent me into a back room to do some computer tests. I'd almost finished the tests when I was asked to leave the premises. Khan had asked to join me in the test room and had been refused, so he'd punched a door. Outside in the street, Khan whacked me on the side of the head. I don't know why he wanted to come into the room with me – it's not as if he could use computers, or I needed his help with the tests. In those days, it was hard enough applying for an office job wearing Asian clothes and hijab without Psycho in tow. Eventually, I got a job with BT in Aldershot, working in the telephone exchange. Khan decreed, 'I forbid you to look at men, talk to men or sit with men.' Khan didn't like my Indian name, so I was now Shabana Khan. Because I couldn't lie to Khan, I asked the people at BT to call me Shabana, even though my application form stated: Sunita. I also requested permission to sit apart from men. Perhaps reasonably, they explained that I couldn't perform my job without dealing with men. Apart from colleagues, the job entailed speaking to the public. When I got home, I tried to take the initiative.

'They say I have to talk to men. Shall I leave?'

'No,' Khan replied. He obviously wanted my wages. The next day, when I left work, Khan was waiting at the security gate with his fists ready. He accused me, correctly, of speaking to men and gave me a pasting, punches and slaps, in public. No one intervened.

Khan would sometimes make me go home at lunchtime to cook him food, or be raped by him. We lived more than a mile away, so I would have to run some of the way there and back, which was especially difficult being malnourished. Khan sometimes drove past me on the way back, presumably as some kind of joke. I longed to talk to Dad, to hear his voice. One time, Khan was out somewhere and didn't need me at lunchtime, so I phoned Dad at work during my lunch break. 'Dad, I really miss you. I need you to know I love you so much. I'm sorry I've caused you all this pain, but I really love you.'

'If you love me, you'll do this for me.' Dad wanted me to visit the sorcerer in Croydon again, who had advised Dad that Khan was performing black magic on me. 'You don't have a brain – you're being controlled,' Dad explained. He said he was also casting spells to protect me from Khan. 'I know it's not your fault. I want to help you. I care about you. I want you to come home …' Dad's voice quivered, '… but you have to follow my rules. You must come and see the *jadoo* (magic) man. These are the conditions. If you love me, you will do as I ask.'

'Dad, I'd love to meet you. I'd love to give you a cuddle.'

'Never mind about cuddles. I'll pick you up and take you to Croydon. You'll have to wear something called a taweez.' A taweez is a locket containing sacred inscriptions.

'Dad, I can't wear anything like that. Khan will find it. He does things to me.' Dad became angry.

'You obviously like Khan beating you up, don't you? You don't love me if you don't do as I say.' But I couldn't explain to Dad about the rape and the torture. My break was over, so I had to end the call.

'Dad, can I call you again?'

'There's no point if you're not going to listen to me. You are stupid.'

I felt sad, but when I saw Khan waiting for me at the end of the day, I was glad I'd at least got to speak to Dad.

At the weekend, Khan went to a pub, the *Golden Lion* in Aldershot. He took me with him, but I had to stay out of sight, crouched on the floor of the car, which was parked outside. Khan was drinking for about three hours. I needed the toilet but I didn't dare go into the pub in my hijab with Khan in there. I could hear music from the jukebox – Toni Braxton's *Unbreak My Heart. Say you'll love me again. Undo the pain you caused when you walked out the door.* I thought about Dad.

Khan returned to the car, well-oiled, and drove home. Staggering into our room, Khan was drunk, but I threw up. Khan stared at me with wild, bloodshot eyes. 'If you're pregnant, I will strangle the baby in the delivery room with the umbilical cord.' I remembered these chilling words when I gave birth to my daughter, Maya, in 2008.

Usually, I had to crouch on the floor of Khan's car or work van in the car park when he went to the pub. But one day he made an exception and took me to *The Bridge Barn* in Woking, near my parents' house. This was the pub we'd frequented in those early weeks back in March, shortly after Khan had first barged into my life. He took me to the same outside table where we'd sat previously and told me to sit in exactly the same place as before, while he went inside to get a drink for himself. Needless to say, there was no drink for me. Whereas in March I'd worn my work clothes, a trouser suit, I now wore a *hijab* and *shalwar kameez*. Khan returned to the table, sat down and lit a cigarette, just like the first time. He looked at me thoughtfully as he sipped his lager slowly. Suspecting he had something spectacular planned, I shook with fear, like a dog used to being mistreated. After a while, Khan spoke. 'Do you remember when I first took you here? Do you remember when I told you I always get what I want? Well, I got you, didn't I? And look at you now!' Khan continued, his voice dripping with contempt. 'And where are your family now? Where are they? They're nowhere.

They don't care about you.' Khan had brought me on a trip down memory lane solely to demonstrate how low I'd fallen. A tear trickled down my cheek.

* * *

One morning, Khan was happy and excited. He'd made me leave BT after about three weeks – I can't remember why. Today, he was taking me on a trip in a hire car. 'You're going to meet my family.' He seemed proud, he was looking forward to it. I was surprised – I'd thought I was unacceptable to his mother, being a Hindu. Khan was making me feel special and began listing his family members. On the way there in the car, Khan shared his thoughts with me. 'Listen, right, Shabana,' – that's what he called me. 'If your family at home call you a bastard, the world will call you a bastard. But, if at home you are loved, no one will call you a bastard. Do you understand? The problem with you, Shabana, is that your family don't care about you. They don't love you. That's why the world's been cruel to you. My family know I'm bad, but they still have me back. They love me, anyway. But yours? Huh! Your family treat you like that and you still love them. You stupid bastard!' Khan laughed at the irony. At a red traffic light, Khan saw me shed a tear. He'd hit a raw nerve and stroked my face gently.

We reached Luton, where one of his sisters lived. She was away, as were her daughters, but we met Khan's nephew, who was about 25. He seemed nice, but I'd been warned not to talk to him. Khan introduced me as his wife. We went out to get some takeaway food. Khan stopped for petrol and briefly left me alone with his nephew. The nephew asked me in English how I was. He would have seen my scars and he looked concerned. I checked out the window for Khan before quickly replying, 'I'm not allowed to talk to you.' Khan appeared suddenly and opened the car door asking:

'What's happened?'

'Nothing, *Mamu*,' answered his nephew, who saw the look Khan gave me.

Back in the house, the three of us watched a family wedding video, which featured a long-haired Khan as one of the guests. I don't know what the nephew made of us. Khan cuddled me on the sofa, like we were a happy couple, as he told me who all the relations were. He was on his best behaviour, whilst I behaved as conditioned, replying, '*Hanji*,' – Yes, sir – when he ordered me to make tea, and asking permission to go to the toilet. Khan's nephew suggested we sleep on the double bed in his mother's room, but Khan declined. He would spend the night on the sofa and I would sleep in his niece's bed. Perhaps Khan felt his brand of rape as love making was a little noisy for his sister's house. He told me I wasn't allowed to sleep under the covers, so I just lay on the bed, cold but unmolested.

The next day, we drove to Birmingham. On the way, Khan spoke mainly in a Birmingham accent. He wasn't trying to be funny and I knew better than to laugh. It was as if he were an actor rehearsing a character. When we reached Birmingham, Khan took me to a house. He rarely explained why we were going anywhere, so I often feared the worst. We went upstairs and looked out of the front bedroom window. I heard a noise, flinched and waited for Khan's reaction. But he was being nice. He hugged me and explained that this was our house – his and mine. Apparently, I'd been paying the mortgage from what wages I'd earned and the bank loans he had me take out. Khan kissed me on the forehead, saying he had to go somewhere but couldn't take me. He suggested that I hide, in case someone came in. He liked to keep me in a state of fear.

After a while, Khan returned and we went to pick up his sister from hospital. This wasn't the sister from Luton. In the car, I asked, 'Am I gonna meet your sister, then?'

'No, you'll have to go in the boot.'

'Please, no. You know I don't like small dark places.'

Khan parked, ordered me out and manhandled me roughly into the boot of the car. Slam! Darkness. I was hyper-ventilating, my heart working overtime. I thought I might suffocate. Khan started the engine. I tried talking to him but he put some music on, pumped up the volume and sped off quickly. I felt every speed bump and corner turn as I was tossed about in the boot. Shutting my eyes, I tried to pretend I wasn't cooped up like an animal – it didn't work. I opened my eyes and it was just as dark. The car stopped and I heard Khan get out and shut the door. Fear gripped me. I had no idea where I was, nor whether or when Khan would return. Maybe there was oxygen in the car, but I started to feel faint. I was alone in the car and wondered if this was the end. Would I just die here in the boot? I thought about Mum and Dad. I kept still, fearing that, if I moved, I would set the car alarm off and earn a beating if Khan did come back.

After a while, Khan came back with a woman who turned out to be his sister. She sat almost on top of me. I could feel her weight but knew better than to make a sound. We drove for about an hour before parking. Khan and his sister left the car, leaving me in the boot. I was gasping for air, but also trying to breathe as little as possible.

Eventually, I heard Khan and his brother, the one from Woking, who asked in Mirpuri, 'Where is she? Have you left her in Birmingham?' I'm not sure where we were, presumably not far from Birmingham.

'No, *bhaijaan* (big brother), she's in the boot.'

Bhaijaan was appalled. 'How long has she been there?'

'Several hours,' Khan replied, puzzled that this was an issue.

Bhaijaan was frantic. 'Let her out, *pagal* (idiot)! She could be lying dead in there! She's someone's daughter! You can't treat people like that!'

'I'll just take her up the road ...'

'NO, LET HER OUT NOW!'

Khan's brother was much older, perhaps more like a father-figure. I was released from my captivity and nodded my appreciation to my rescuer.

I never fathomed why Khan told me I was going to meet his family but didn't follow through, apart from the nephew in Luton. Was he playing games, or did he just have second thoughts? Much of what Khan did and said is beyond understanding. Driving back down to Woking, Khan allowed me to sit in the front. He grinned at me. 'I can't believe you didn't wet yourself! What was it like?'

Chapter 10

A WALK IN THE PARK

My parents were friends with an Indian family in Croydon. When I was growing up, we would visit them sometimes at weekends, or they would come to us in Woking. The grown-ups would watch a three-hour Bollywood film, whilst my brothers and I would be sent off to play with their son, V. He was an only child, six or more years older than me. Between the ages of about three and eleven, I was sexually abused by V.

V kept a stock of Space Invader type games, which kept my brothers occupied while he focused his attention on me. He would take me to his room where he would lock the door and make a point of showing me he'd done so. A fragment of a memory – I'm lying still as a statue wearing a little green and white dress. V is on top of me, pinning my tiny arms down, touching my leg and trying to go inside with his hand. I would threaten to tell on him but he would laugh, telling me no one would believe me. He would slap me across the face or make his dog bark at me to instil fear, silence. V had this way of sliding his glasses up his nose before speaking. 'No one will believe you. I'll set the dog on you.' I was frightened of dogs for a long time afterwards.

At home, once, aged four I think, I was watching Dad doing some paperwork. He crossed something out with his pen. I asked him what he was doing. Dad explained that if something's wrong, you cross it out. I went upstairs, took a biro and scribbled on my thighs and my private parts. I didn't like what V had done to me there, so I crossed it out.

When I was about six, I remember that Dilip and Billy had finished playing their video games, so V offered to get them some more games, but there was a catch – I would have to come with him. Obviously, I didn't want to, but he grabbed me by the arm and hauled me up to his room. Inside his bedroom, he lifted me up. I asked, 'But why, brother?' He made me call him brother. Even at that age, I knew he didn't need me to reach the games. He had a big, mirrored wardrobe. I saw him looking up my dress in the mirror, looking at my pants. Tame by his standards, but I knew something wasn't right, so I threatened to tell on him. Again, he slapped my face hard.

'No one will believe you,' V warned, adding, 'You'll be back.' Downstairs, he told everyone I'd fallen over. They believed him and didn't ask any further questions.

That night, I cried so much in bed. V had made me feel bad. I also felt lonely, isolated, but I decided to tell on him. The following morning, I plucked up the courage and told Mum he'd been looking at my pants. Previously, I hadn't known the words to talk about the actual sexual abuse, but this time it was something I could describe. I remember Mum taking me into her bedroom, being quite cross with me, as if she didn't need the hassle. I said I didn't like going to V's house.

'If you don't go there, Daddy not love you anymore,' said Mum. Perhaps she just thought I was a child having a tantrum.

When I challenged her about this in 2012, she claims she asked me if I had sex with V and that I had denied it. This is quite possibly true. I doubt that I knew the word *sex* at that age, and I don't think V had penetrated me then, in any case.

For a while after that, we were supervised more closely. But then V's abuse intensified. When I was nine, V was lying on top of me, pulling my dress up and my pants down. His weight bore down on me, his clammy hands were all over me, inside me. I was crying – my vision was blurred from the tears. He made me touch his penis, although I didn't see it, and didn't know what it was. Then he penetrated me with something hard – I didn't know what at the time. I was frightened, too scared to tell anyone. After my previous attempt to tell Mum about V, I didn't think anyone would believe me.

V would play hide and seek with me and my brothers. V always chose to be the seeker first. When he'd finished counting he would shout, 'Ready or not, here I come,' and it was game on. Hide and seek for real, with consequences for me. I would hide, petrified, trying to keep quiet, hoping V wouldn't find me, but, of course, he always did. We played this game in V's house, where he would take me to his room with the lock, or at my parents' house, where he sexually abused me in my own bedroom. Dilip and Billy always 'won' the game, as V made no attempt to find them, but on one occasion in our house, when I was about nine, Dilip came in and saw V on top of me. V claimed that he was playing a game, me weighing him, although I must have been half his weight and was not a set of scales. Dilip would have been about eleven, V fifteen or sixteen. Dilip knew something wasn't right so he told Mum what he'd seen. Mum was concerned and examined me in private. She said that I didn't look right down below and took me to our next-door neighbour, a midwife, for a second opinion.

After this we didn't see V's family so often, although Mum kept in touch with them and V was invited to family parties.

Seeing him, I would feel defenceless and would panic. At Dilip's 18th birthday party, V tried to touch me, so I locked myself in the bathroom.

V's abuse cast a long shadow over my childhood. There was no counselling, no chance to speak out. As I became an adult, he was still there. Mum even invited him to my 18th birthday. I didn't bleed the first time Khan raped me. Well, actually, I bled all over, but not like a virgin. V's abuse gave me a fear of men, a fear of sex. I self-harmed for the first time as a child, and discovered alcohol as a teenager, but not in the usual way of fitting in; but to switch off. Ironically, I ended up with Khan partly because I feared an arranged marriage and sex with a stranger. With no self-worth, I hadn't healed from the previous abuse and, perhaps unknowingly, radiated my victim status to another abuser.

* * *

Khan continued to tug me along the streets of Aldershot at three or four in the morning using an old length of rope. Despite the degrading humiliation of Khan's version of power walking, we were talking a bit more now. One night, there was a full moon as we walked past the Church of St Michael the Archangel. Khan led me into Aldershot Manor Park, which is partly wooded, for a bit of variety. We sat down on a bench. Khan was unusually quiet so I spoke.

'Sometimes you frighten me and sometimes I feel loved by you. Why do you hurt me so much?'

Khan thought a few moments before replying.

'I hurt you because I love you.' I don't know whether this was meant to be profound or just something to say. I could hardly make out Khan's face in the darkness. He often shut me up when I was talking but he remained silent, so I continued.

'Surely, that's not love. When I was a little girl, a boy used to hurt me. This boy, he didn't love me, but he hurt me. So, what you're doing when you're hurting me, that can't be love.'

Khan asked me what this boy used to do. So I spoke about V. I could sense Khan becoming angry as I outlined V's abuse, so I was guarded with my replies. I explained how I told Mum I didn't want to go to their house, but she warned me Dad wouldn't love me if I didn't go. Mum always dragged Dad's name into things. *Daddy not love you anymore.* I was shaking and crying as I talked about V's abuse. At first, Khan tried to make sense of my revelation.

'*That's* why you didn't let me come near you. *That's* why you panicked. It all makes sense now.' Next, Khan thoughtfully considered his response before punching me on the shoulder and then the jaw, but his verbal abuse hurt more. 'You're *disgusting*. I don't want you. Someone abused you when you were a kid? You're fucking disgusting! No wonder you're the way you are. You're damaged. I don't want you. No, that *isn't* love. No wonder your family hate you so much. Why don't you just go and kill yourself. No one's going to want you now, are they? Why don't you do the world a favour and just go and kill yourself?'

Khan stood up and walked away, leaving me on the bench in tears with a rope around my waist. I felt ashamed, shunned by my family and now, even seemingly rejected by my abuser. Perhaps Khan was angry that I was no longer his ninth virgin. I wondered if I could hang myself with the rope, but I didn't want someone to find me like that. I curled myself up into a ball and cried, not knowing what would become of me. After a while, I heard footsteps coming towards me. Drug dealers used this park, so I tried to stay as quiet as a mouse, shutting my eyes tight as the footsteps grew louder. Whoever it was, they walked past without troubling me.

After about 15 minutes, I heard a second set of footsteps approaching. I lay motionless, my heart thumping in the still black night. The footsteps stopped and Khan whispered in my ear. 'I'm back.' Sometimes, I feared Khan's whispering more than his shouting. It was controlled, deliberate, and sinister. But now, Khan started talking just like a normal person. He said he loved me, kissed me on the forehead and gave me a cuddle. On reflection, Khan had decided that my abuse as a child wasn't my fault. Then he took me home and raped me, explaining that *that* was true love. The next day, Khan asked me about my childhood abuse in more detail. Not trusting Khan's motives, I clammed up.

Chapter 11

PARTING IS SUCH SWEET SORROW

As the weeks passed and autumn turned to winter, Khan began to trust me more. He granted me a little freedom and I was fed a bit better. No longer locked in the bedroom, I could use the bathroom, but Khan kept the house keys, so I was still locked inside. But I had ways and means of sneaking out through windows while he was out. I would go for short walks during daylight, but only if I knew he was gone for a while. Khan also started to show more kindness on occasion. There were longer cuddles, or he would gaze into my eyes and run his finger gently down my forehead and the spine of my nose. It was now getting colder and there was no central heating in the house. Khan bought me a long, black woollen coat. 'I'm sick of you shivering.' It also seemed that Khan was caring for me a bit more by collecting my prescriptions from the chemist's. In fact, he probably preferred doing that to letting me out. But my expectations were low and getting lower, so I seized on any sign of kindness. The reality was, the beatings continued, and the cuttings, and the rape.

One day in December, a strange thing happened. Khan told me he loved me. He did the same the following day, and the day after. Then he told me his mother was ill and that his family wanted him to marry a sixteen-year-old girl from Pakistan. 'Look, I can't leave you on your own, but I'm allowed three wives and I want you all to live together.' I tried to imagine how someone else could squeeze into this room to be tortured. Then he changed tack. 'My family won't accept you because you're Indian.' I didn't understand. Was I being dumped by my torturer?

'But you've forced meat down my throat and made me dress the way you like, and changed my name. Aren't I already your wife? Shabana Khan?'

'No, you're not fully Muslim. You're not this, you're not that. I could never take you home to meet my mother. You'll never be accepted. I don't know what to do. I genuinely do love you, but I really don't know what to do.'

Perhaps Khan meant what he said. Maybe he was in two minds, but I couldn't imagine him letting me go.

'Will you kill me, then? Are you just going to bury me somewhere?'

Despite Khan's cruelty towards me, I felt rejected. If he did release me, would my parents have me back? I saw no future. Today, I'm a single mother. I control my own life and am aware that I don't have to rely on someone like Khan, or on my parents. But, back then, although 19-years-old, I was really just a child. I used to dream about seeing my parents, giving them hugs. While he was beating me, I would try and take my mind outside of my body and visualise my parents from a bird's eye view. I thought out loud. 'Could you please let me see my parents before I go?' Khan seemed genuinely shocked.

'What do you mean, "before you go"? Nothing's going to happen to you. I won't kill you. And you'd better not kill yourself.'

A few days later, I questioned Khan about his new wife. 'Please, just don't hurt her. She's somebody's daughter.' – the phrase his brother had used about me. 'She might become a mum one day.'

'That's just it,' Khan replied. 'You're barren, damaged goods. I want children. You can never give me that.' I sensed his mood turning violent and cowered by the TV.

'OK, I'll leave. I'll just go,' I whispered.

'You've got nowhere to go. What will you do?'

'Maybe God will take me home. Maybe something will happen. I don't know. I don't understand why things are like this.' I was trying to make sense of my life. 'What you did to me wasn't right, but in my own way, I loved you.'

I remember saying that. Did I love Khan? He was all I had – he'd taken me away from my family and friends. Especially as I wasn't working, Khan was the only person I spoke to for days on end, so he became my only human contact. In between the rapes and beatings, he would tell me he loved me, which made me feel better, for a while. Because of my low self-worth, I sometimes even wondered whether the violence was my own fault, although deep down I knew it wasn't. I felt I was helping Khan get better medically by pouring his methadone. Above all, I believed I was his wife. Now, I'd had enough, but I didn't know what to do. Would he keep me locked up here while he was with his new wife?

On Friday 5th December 1997, I took matters into my own hands and decided to leave Khan to go and see my parents. It wasn't my intention to return 'home'. I had no game plan, no ambitions other than to see my family, perhaps for the last time as I was contemplating suicide again. Khan had forgotten his house keys, which were on the bed, along with the keys to a maroon Mondeo, which he'd hired on a stolen credit card. I felt the keys in my hand. A sense of freedom, but also uncertainty. It was morning. I put on my black coat and made my exit through the door. Weighing about five and a half stone and dressed in shalwaar kameez and hijab,

I departed with no possessions – no 'go bag' this time and no plans for the future. I drove off down the road. Then I turned around, came back, re-entered the house and went upstairs to the bedroom. I felt scared yet somehow free – I no longer belonged to Khan. But my courage had only taken me so far. I rang Woking Police and asked for Gemma in the domestic violence unit, whom I'd spoken to the first time I came back from Khan. I asked Gemma to find out if my parents would see me. I was already on the radar of Surrey Police, having been reported missing.

'I can hear you've had enough now. I'm here to help you,' said Gemma. Tears of hope filled my eyes. The police rang Mum at the card shop but I didn't know the outcome then. I left the house in Aldershot for a second time, and drove off. Driving fast on the bendy roads, I nearly crashed. Reaching the car park in the Peacocks Shopping Centre in Woking where Mum worked, I pulled in to a parking space as a lady pulled out. I had no money to pay for the car park but a stranger gave me her ticket, which had forty minutes remaining on it. *Someone's looking out for me,* I thought.

* * *

On 5th December 2015, I attended my seven-year-old daughter's school carol concert. Words can't express the joy of watching Maya singing happily with her classmates that day. I thought back to the same date seventeen years earlier, and my mother.

* * *

Nervously, I approached the card shop, a waif returning to her mother. Mum was expecting me, the prodigal daughter, now wearing a Muslim headscarf. Her face like thunder, she hissed, 'Get round back.' We went to an office at the rear of the store. I went to hug Mum but she recoiled. 'I don't want you. I *don't want* you!' I was kind of in shock already, after escaping from Khan. My mother's hostility just left me empty. Mum phoned the police, as well as Dad. I'm not sure why she called the police. Maybe they had suggested it, or perhaps she was afraid Khan would turn up. Gemma arrived with a male officer. Having spoken to Dad, Mum announced that they would have me back, but only under certain conditions. I would have to go to India.

'But I don't want that. I only came to see you.' I didn't want to mention suicide. Gemma told me that I needed to decide whether to go back to my parents' house. I agreed – I wanted to see Dad again. Gemma accompanied me back to the house in the hire car, while Mum went in the police car. The police came into the house. Dad was upstairs. Mum shouted to him that I was here, but he didn't come down immediately. I felt awkward, anxious about how Dad would be with me.

Mum phoned her friends with the news. 'Oh, she want to come back now. Ha!' I had said no such thing but didn't really have a route map, so now I got swept along by events like a twig on a stream. When she came off the phone, Mum pulled the hijab off my head. 'That's disgusting! You can't wear those Paki clothes here! And you get rid of that coat.' The police could see the open wounds on my arms and were asking me about them.

Eventually, Dad came downstairs and looked at me with sadness. Sternly, he told me I had to go to India. 'You are never to see Khan again. Never. If you love me, you'll do this for me.' That bit suited me – Khan was getting married, anyway. I didn't want to go to India, but promised Dad I would. Were my parents planning to marry me off? Was that the condition? Perhaps Khan was right about that. I explained that I didn't have my passport. 'Well, you'll have to go and get it,' Dad replied firmly. Fear gripped me. I dared not go back to Morland Road having run away from Khan. *What if he was in?* I was used to his beatings, but these were usually for no reason. But now, I'd left him. I'd plucked up the courage to leave, so there would be a reason. I pleaded.

'Please don't make me go back there. He's due home any moment.'

Dad was having none of it, so the police offered to accompany me to ensure my safety. I couldn't face Khan and feared what he would do to my parents once the police weren't around, but I had no choice. Gemma could see I was frightened and arranged for more back up. With a police car escorting us, I drove the hired Mondeo from Woking back to Aldershot. Gemma sat with me in the car. I had put the hijab back on, not daring to encounter Khan without it. I was a nervous wreck and thought I might crash.

When we reached Aldershot, Gemma called ahead to the local police station to request assistance as we were now in Hampshire, out of Surrey Police's jurisdiction. I accompanied Gemma into the police station. The Aldershot police put on their high visibility yellow jackets and synchronised their radios with the Surrey police contingent. Five hours had passed since I'd left Khan. I was sure he'd be home by now. Gemma kept reassuring me that I'd done the right thing.

As we approached Morland Road, my heart was beating so fast, I wished it would just stop. I tried to park the car exactly as I found it, on the kerb, as if I could conceal what I'd done from Khan. A police car pulled up alongside me. We all got out and doors slammed loudly.

Gemma waited by the car as the other officers escorted

me to the house. 'There'll be an officer in front of you and another behind you. Do not speak to anyone in the house,' one instructed me. My hands were shaking as I turned the key in the front door. We entered the house. The police wondered about the mattresses on the floor. 'Illegals?'

'Possibly,' I replied, more concerned about Khan than illegal immigration. We walked up the stairs and I unlocked the bedroom door nervously. A policeman barged the door open with his shoulder. The police saw the boarded-up windows and the bloodstains. No Khan. Breathing a sigh of relief, I entered the room and surveyed our possessions, such as they were. There was a nice picture of me with Khan, which I didn't take. I placed my black coat and the keys on the bed and took my passport from under the mattress. I didn't collect any clothes, my 'Paki' clothes, which Mum probably would have burnt anyway. Panicking, in case Khan returned, I forgot my medication. I had now left Khan, although, maybe he would have dumped me to get married, anyway. But I still think of this episode as my *escape,* even if I was mentally not yet rid of Khan.

Gemma and another Woking officer drove me back to Woking. It wasn't Dad's plan to have me married off in India, but I didn't know that at the time, so I had a bright idea on the way back to Woking. I explained to the officers that the car was hired on a stolen credit card. 'How much will I get for that? I'll have to go to prison, won't I?' Khan had stolen the card, I just made the booking, but at least I would be free of Khan and, afterwards, no one would want an arranged marriage with me. Doesn't sound like a great plan, does it? But it was the best I could come up with. The police didn't think it was a great plan, either. Perhaps they thought I'd made it up.

'Look, you've obviously been through a lot. We'll pretend

we didn't hear that. You're going to India now.'

Back at the house, Gemma warned Mum, 'When he realises Sunita's gone, he may come looking for her. If he calls, just say you don't know where she is. Act! Just like it's *Eastenders* or something.' Dilip and Billy were now at home, Mum having called them.

Previously, Dilip had assured me, 'We don't care if you're pregnant. We want you back.' Now he changed tune. 'You fucking bitch. We don't want you here. Why don't you just fuck off and die?' I showered and changed into a clean t-shirt and jeans. It seemed strange wearing western clothes after months of dressing the Kashmiri way. That evening, the phone rang. Mum answered.

'Sunita? Who Sunita? I don't have daughter. Is she with you? Have you lost her? You'll never find her now! Ha! Ha! Ha!' She seemed to be enjoying herself.

Several hours later, the doorbell rang. It was the police, but different officers, ones who weren't aware of the background. 'We have a Mr Khan outside.' I started to shake. 'He says you're holding his wife here against her will.'

I was home because I'd escaped from Khan with police assistance, but now he was using the police to try and get me back. Dad, seemingly unaware of the day's events, looked at me.

'Don't you *dare* go with him.'

'Dad, I don't want to go with him.'

The police could see I'd been beaten up recently. 'Are you alright, love? You'll have to decide if you want to go.'

'No, no. My parents didn't do this. Khan did. I don't want to go with him. Please, just get rid of him.'

I didn't want to go up to my bedroom. I thought the staircase was the safest place, away from the windows, so I stayed there for a while. Dilip walked past and kicked me in the kidneys.

'Fucking bitch.'

* * *

When I was five, I wanted a toy that was on top of a wardrobe in my bedroom, but I couldn't reach it. So I asked Dad, who was in the kitchen. He didn't seem to respond, so I decided to take matters into my own hands. I went into Dilip's bedroom and carried a chair into my room. Then I placed a smaller chair on top of it. I climbed carefully onto the first chair, then the second. Balancing precariously, I reached my toy and slowly climbed down with it before returning Dilip's chair to his room. Dad came in to fetch the toy for me.

'Where's the toy?' asked Dad.

'It's OK, I've got it.'

'How did you get it?'

'I flew.' I didn't know people couldn't fly at that age. Superman flew, so why not me? It seemed easier than explaining about the chairs at that age. Dad looked at me oddly, like he almost believed me. He called for Mum, who, being more practical than Dad, checked Dilip's room and noticed that his chair had been moved. Mystery solved.

'Bewakoof,' laughed Dad. The story about me pretending to fly when I was five was repeated frequently over the years.

* * *

After a few hours, just when everyone had settled, the police returned and marched in – different officers again. 'We've had a report of a young girl ringing 999 from this address. She says she's been mistreated.' They eyed Dad accusingly.

Dad looked at me, hurt, betrayed. 'Sunita, you've let me

down again. I knew I couldn't trust you.'

'No, Dad, I didn't call anyone. I never made the call. I promised to go to India and I will.'

'You lied when you were five,' Dad reminded me. 'You said you could fly.' This was true. 'Why should I believe you?' The policeman looked at Dad, astonished.

I wondered whether Mum had made the call. Dilip now intervened. 'Lying bitch. Just give her back to him.'

Mum agreed. 'I have enough of this, just kick her outside.'

I was terrified. What if Khan was outside? I asked the police if they could check where the call had come from. The female sergeant called the police station on her radio.

'Oh, I see … Really?' Apparently, the call had come from a phone box nearby. Khan and his voices – having established I was home, he must have made the call. The police were ever so sorry. None of my family apologised.

Needing emotional support and my family's love, I received Mum's bitterness and Dilip's cruelty, instead. Traumatised by months of abuse, I was, nevertheless, grieving the loss of Khan. I now felt the life drain out of me. I agreed to go to India because I didn't know what else to do. There wasn't time to think.

The next day, from my bedroom window, I saw Khan walking away from the house. He looked forlorn, his head bowed, the old swagger gone. I rushed downstairs to find out what his latest stunt was. He'd placed a shopping bag by the back door. Mum was reading the note and telephoning the police. I tried to read Khan's writing over her shoulder. The note ended, *Take care of her.* Mum screwed it up, so I couldn't see the rest. The bag contained my antibiotics. So, Khan had tenderly ensured I had my pills. A parting gift. The police advised Mum to destroy the medication. They were concerned that Khan had put something in the bottles.

We'll never know.

That afternoon, Dad took me to the sorcerer in Croydon. This time, I had no energy to resist – Dad was the only person in the house who seemed to care about me. The sorcerer asked me if I'd been given meat to eat. On hearing that I had, he explained to Dad that this was how the black magic was done. Supposedly, Khan had bewitched me with meat. The sorcerer gave me another *taweez* to wear. Back home, Dad called Auntie Anita in India and confirmed what had, apparently, been her suspicions. 'You were right, she ate meat.'

I was scheduled to fly to India on Monday 8th December, in the morning, but Dilip had other plans. Having personally arranged my fast track visa to India on the Sunday evening, Dilip rang the police to report me for credit card fraud. This was the first time Dilip had mentioned this, although he must have known about the fraud for some time, before he told me to come home and before he went with Dad to offer to buy me back. Khan first used Dilip's card back in May, using the card details from the receipt for the tracksuit bottoms. Transactions had been traced to Khan's brother's house. Although I hadn't used Dilip's card, and had not benefitted from Khan's deception, Dilip wanted me prosecuted, rather than Khan.

The police interviewed us separately in the living room. They stated that they were duty bound to investigate Dilip's complaint. But, their hearts weren't in it and they suggested to Dad, 'Why don't you keep this in-house? It'll be on insurance, anyway.' Dad pleaded with Dilip too, but he wouldn't budge.

'No, I wanna see her get done for this!'

I didn't want trouble for Dad. 'It's OK, Dad. I'll just deal with it the best I can.'

Dilip turned to the police and insisted, 'Arrest her now!

She's flying to India in the morning.'

Dad explained to the police that I was only going for three months, which was news to me. 'She's going there to recover.'

The police agreed with Dad and tried to reason with Dilip. 'Look, your sister's going to India tomorrow. We can sort it out when she comes back. It would probably only be a caution, anyway.' At this stage the police didn't know about the other credit card numbers I *had* obtained for Khan, albeit under duress.

Early on Monday morning, Dad drove me to Heathrow Airport. No one else came to see me off. Dad had arranged for money to be sent to India, to relatives, to look after me. Mum stuffed a wad of rupees in my pocket to give to her brother, Bantoo Mama. Dad was emotional and we both cried when we parted. I was now alone and scared. Calling Khan from the airport on a payphone, I told him I was going to India, asked him to leave my family alone and wished him happiness.

Khan was driving, and Khan was angry. 'Stay there. I'm coming to get you.'

'No, I'm going to India.' I put the phone down and kept my promise to Dad.

Chapter 12

KNIGHT IN SHINING ARMOUR

The Sikh religion was founded in the early 16th century by Guru Nanak, a Punjabi who preached unity between the religions. Unlike Hindus, Sikhs believed in only one god. Guru Nanak and the later Sikh gurus also preached equality and protection for the poor, opposing caste distinctions. My maternal grandmother was a Sikh.

* * *

When I was 15, we visited Mum's family in Yamuna Nagar in India during the summer holidays without Dad, who was working. Mum argued with her brother and we got kicked out of the family home in the middle of the night. We ended up at Mum's friend's house, where we slept on the roof terrace and stayed for about three weeks. Mum didn't like Dad's relatives, so didn't want to go to Ambala. Mum's friend was a Sikh woman, Jasminder. I used to place my hands on her head to relax her. She believed I had healing powers. Jasminder had two sons – Shami and Rinku – but was very fond of me, I was like a surrogate daughter. One morning, I was walking in the village with the boys and Dilip when a boy on a bicycle made a rude comment. I was wearing jeans – I think Mum liked the idea of us being from England and fashionable when we were in India. This boy charmingly suggested I was a prostitute. Rinku ran up, knocked the boy off his bike and punched him. Shami and Dilip were listening to my Walkman, so hadn't heard. Shami said 'Whoa, what's going on?' Rinku repeated what the boy had said. Shami asked Dilip, 'That's your sister. Aren't you going to do anything?'

'No, not really.' Dilip wasn't bothered, but Rinku made the bicycle boy apologise to me. I liked the fact that someone had stood up for me and gone out of their way to protect me. The respect – I wasn't used to that in my family. We had quite a bit of holiday left, which we spent with Rinku's family. Rinku and I developed feelings for each other. When I woke up in the morning, I couldn't wait to see Rinku and when I did, butterflies would flutter in my stomach. Every now and then, we'd make eye contact and smile. We couldn't kiss or hug, or even hold hands – that wasn't done – and we couldn't really talk much, but there would be this shy awkwardness. Rinku was lovely. Being Sikh, he wore a beard and moustache. He was funny in a quiet way, with a slightly sarcastic sense of humour, but kind and thoughtful, a Cancerian like me – born in July. He liked *bhangra* – modern Punjabi dance music and was also artistic. Mum would sometimes take us to Hindu temples in India, but that summer we went with Rinku's family to *Paonto Sahib*, a famous Sikh temple or *gurdwara* in the far north of India. I remember Rinku looking out for me, treating me like a lady. His mum thought we made a lovely couple.

When I came back to England we wrote and sent little gifts to each other, just trinkets, but they meant a lot to us. Things cooled off a little but, two years later, in 1995, we went to India again. I brought a school friend, Nicole, and she got to see where my family lived. Rinku and I held a joint birthday party with a shared cake and we fell in love. This time I was on the rebound from Moonie. After I returned to England, Rinku and I were writing to each other almost every day, sending each other photos. Later, when I was working at Modo Merchants, Rinku's parents installed a phone so I was able to call him. Just to hear his voice was lovely. His family were keen on a match. But this was all kept secret from my family. We wanted to get married, but Rinku worried, 'I don't think your mum will allow it.'

'But your mum and my mum are best friends. What could be better than that?'

'I'm Sikh, you're Hindu.'

'But I love you and you love me.'

'You know you'll have to change your name to Simran Bedi?'

'Well, I don't like my name anyway. I'll change it for you.'

'It's very basic living here – you've seen it. There's no real toilet, it's just a hole in the ground, no bath, just an empty room with a bucket. Why don't I come and live in England? There are better prospects.'

'Whatever you want to do, I love you. It's not about the house, or the area, or what we own. I really care for you.'

I adored Rinku's parents and his brother was lovely. I was excited at the prospect of being with Rinku. 'Let me earn enough money. If you want, I can come to you,' I suggested. This was the 'done thing' – the wife living with the husband's family.

I told Dilip of my desire to marry Rinku. He declared, 'You can't marry him. He's Sikh. And I think he's gay anyway. He just wants a British passport.' Dilip informed Mum, who agreed with him.

'You can't marry him. He ugly, he got beard and he too poor. I know he Jasminder son, but they got nothing. They got crap house. Dilip think he's gay. He just want British

Passport. Anyway, he Sikh – he not same religion. You never marry him. I won't allow it.'

Sikhs are Punjabis like us, and marriages between Sikhs and Hindu Punjabis were quite common. Mum's own mother was born Sikh but married my Hindu grandfather when she was thirteen.

I started self-harming again. I cut my arms and wrote Rinku a letter, saying, 'I can't take this pain. Mum has refused, because you're Sikh.' I couldn't say the rest of it.

'I'll cut my hair,' replied Rinku. 'I'll become a Hindu. I'll shave my beard off. I love you dearly. We'll just have to pray and put our trust in God.'

'God's put us together. If it's meant to be, it will be,' I replied.

This was when I first had a mobile phone, which I used to call Rinku so I could hear his voice. Mobile phones are universal now, but this was 1995 and he'd never seen one. He wondered if they were connected to a cable of some kind! So, I drew a picture for him. I worked overtime and saved up, hoping to join Rinku in India. I learnt the Sikh prayer and about their way of life.

Big brothers have a large say over their sisters' lives in the Indian community. So, I approached Dilip again and told him I really loved Rinku and wanted to marry him. Dilip softened. Maybe he was pleased to be asked and agreed to support me. He phoned Rinku and his parents and gave us his blessing to wed. But Dilip bends like a reed in the wind and Mum got to him. The two of them turned up at my workplace to demand my passport, which I carried with me to buy cigarettes and alcohol. Why they didn't do this at home, I don't know. Perhaps they didn't want Dad involved or maybe Mum decided to act while she had Dilip onside. She must have feared that I was about to fly off to India.

I was signing for a parcel in the warehouse when the phone rang. A colleague warned me that my Mum and my brother were here to take my passport and were coming over to see me. 'Could you please ask Giuseppe to come over?' Giuseppe was my manager and I thought he might be able to stop Mum and Dilip. Panicking, I took out my passport to hide it.

Parcel Delivery Man asked, 'What's the problem?'

'My mum and brother are coming to take my passport.'

'Give it to me, I'll look after it for you.'

'No, no. It's OK. Thank you.' I thought it was a kind offer, but I didn't know him.

Mum stormed into the warehouse with Dilip behind her. 'Give me your passport and come home now!' she barked. Parcel Delivery Man looked Mum and Dilip up and down.

Giuseppe arrived and intervened. 'We need Sunita here. I'm going to have to ask you to leave.'

As Mum and Dilip sheepishly turned to go, Parcel Delivery Man said, 'Don't worry, I will make *sure* they leave.' Although they were leaving anyway, he strutted along behind them. Parcel Delivery Man – *Khan* – turned and smiled at me as he escorted Mum and Dilip from the building. This was about 18 months before he reintroduced himself at the bandstand in Woking.

Back home in my bedroom, I discovered that all my letters from Rinku were missing, presumably destroyed. Mum fell out with Rinku's mum over her refusal to let us wed. Several years later, they made up when Mum visited India. Her friend showed her how much money she had. They'd bought a bigger house with a proper bathroom suite and flush toilet. It was too late. Khan had got hold of me. He'd ruined me big time.

A couple of years after Khan, Mum told me that Rinku

was pining for me, that he wouldn't marry anyone else. I wrote Rinku a very emotional letter telling him not to wait for me. Rinku has since moved on. He's married with children. Mum once showed me photographs of his children and told me how happy he was. 'Oh, look, he not gay! Such a shame, you two would have been so happy together. He got such lovely wife. He miss you lot.'

Chapter 13

A PASSAGE TO INDIA

I flew into Indira Gandhi International Airport in Delhi on 8th December 1997, broken, exhausted and still carrying open wounds on my back, courtesy of Khan. Three days earlier, I was a captive in Morland Road, but now, I was amongst a throng of people. Strangers. It was overwhelming. Used to being controlled by Khan, I found it difficult to think for myself and find my way around the airport. I stepped out of the airport terminal with my luggage, and into a gust of polluted smog. The near silence of the long flight was replaced by the bustle and noise of Delhi, the Indian capital. My uncle, Bantoo Mama, was picking me up with a driver, but it took a while to find him. Punjabis call their paternal uncles *chacha* and their maternal uncles *mama*. I called Mum to tell her I'd arrived, but couldn't find anyone. Eventually, Bantoo Mama located me. I wanted to call Mum again but Bantoo Mama said it could wait. We drove through the streets of Delhi, her rickshaws, tuk tuks, buffalo and elephants, then out north, overtaking brightly coloured buses as we headed for Yamuna Nagar, Mum's home town. We were delayed by fog and traffic and I think the journey took eight or nine hours, almost as long as the flight from Heathrow. Bantoo was Mum's brother, the one who'd kicked us out in 1993 when she asked for some wedding jewellery back. There was a language barrier – my Punjabi wasn't great and my uncle didn't speak much English. I didn't know how much they knew about me and Khan, and I felt nervous about my reception – the Hindu girl who ran off with a Muslim.

When we arrived at Yamuna Nagar, Bantoo Mama's wife, Sangita Mami, was screaming the place down. 'Why didn't you call your parents? Your cousins are looking for you at the airport! Why are you playing games?'

Bantoo Mama stopped her. 'Don't shout at her. Can't you see the state she's in? She asked me to call home but we needed to get on the road.'

Bantoo Mama and Sangita Mami (auntie) quickly realised I wasn't the same as before. I was undernourished and physically damaged. I couldn't eat properly, so they had to serve my food in baby bites. I had over sixty open wounds when I left England. The bath was a bucket of water, which you would drain away from the bathroom in a channel when used. The children of the house saw blood in the water from my wounds. 'Look, *Didi* (sister) is bleeding!' Indians refer to first cousins as brothers and sisters.

Sangita came into the bathroom once and saw the open wounds and scars on my back. She was a tough woman, but treated me with great kindness. 'Look what he's done to you!' Wrapping me in a towel, Sangita cleaned and bandaged my wounds.

By mid-December, I was beginning to settle into a routine in Yamuna Nagar. I was still in a state of shock, but I was starting to eat normally. One day, Sangita answered a telephone call in English. 'Hello? Who? Surrey Police? OK, OK. Sunita, it's Surrey Police for you.' She looked concerned. I was worried, too, thinking something must have happened to Mum or Dad. Joining Sangita on the sofa, my hand shook as I took the phone.

'It's me.' It was Khan – he had my mobile phone and address book. 'I miss you … I love you.'

I froze. Sangita wasn't fooled. 'Huh? Policeman say he loves you? It's him, isn't it?'

Khan provided confirmation. 'I will *burn* your parents' *fucking house* down.'

As I dropped the receiver, Sangita grabbed it and yelled, '*Harami!* (bastard)' at Khan down the phone. 'God will never forgive you for what you've done to Sunita. Don't call here again!' she added, slamming the phone down.

Later, I heard Sangita on the phone to Mum. 'Look. You've got it wrong. I don't think she's obsessed with him. Have you seen what he's done to her? You should think about what you're doing.'

It was well known amongst Asians in Woking that Khan was a heroin addict. Therefore, it followed that I must be a junkie, too. The reality was, Khan took all my money and wouldn't have needed me as a customer if he was still dealing. And he would no more have bought me drugs than fly me to the moon or take me out for dinner. It didn't fit in with his idea of Asian womanhood. No one bothered to ask me whether I had a habit, but my parents had arranged for me to enter a rehab clinic in India. I was unaware of this when I flew out. Bantoo Mama took me to the clinic and I filled in a questionnaire, on which I answered no to various questions asking whether I was taking any narcotics. Some of these drugs I'd never even heard of. My urine sample and blood test came back all clear and the clinic refused to admit me. By now, Sangita realised the problem wasn't drugs, but the aftermath of physical and mental abuse.

Sangita had an idea. 'You know that Sikh boy, Rinku, a few streets away? You loved him, didn't you? He's not married, yet. Would you like me to speak to your mum? Would you like to marry him?'

The tears fell. 'Look at me, Auntie. Yes, I loved him with all my heart. But who would marry me now? I couldn't do that to him. He deserves so much better. I couldn't look him in the eye.' Sangita understood and smiled sadly.

* * *

Both sides of my family in India were poor. Although, they didn't quite live in cardboard boxes, the toilet was a hole in the ground, cold water was extracted from a well, and children of both sexes shared a bed. When we went to India in the summer holidays, there were poor people begging by the sides of the street. I remember one beggar from when I was a teenager. His skin was dark and wrinkled by the sun and dehydration. He looked at me, his arm outstretched, his expression resigned but patient, like he could wait for death. I took out some coins to offer him, but Mum shouted to stay away from him. Apparently, we didn't associate with people like that. My family are *Khatris,* part of the *Kshatriyas*, the caste of warriors and kings. Historically, many Khatris were in fact merchants, some were silk weavers who made sarees, but they claimed membership of the warrior caste. The reality is that, those boasting upper caste status in India, are numerous and many are poor. Dad's father made bars of soap in his house for a living, whilst my grandfather on Mum's side was a labourer in a paper mill.

* * *

Both sets of my grandparents lived in towns in the north of the state of Ambala, where Hindi- and Punjabi-speaking India merge. Dad wouldn't speak to me at Yamuna Nagar where Mum's family lived, and Mum wouldn't call Ambala where Dad's folks were. So, I was being passed frequently between the two families. In Ambala, there lived my grandfather, Pita Ji, Dad's two brothers, Pappu and Dud Chacha, their sister, Anita, and Pappu's wife and children. Following Partition in 1947, Dad's family moved to Malerkotla, but moved again in shame when Dad's other sister, Ghudi Bhua, married out of caste for love.

Dud Chacha was now made to live apart from the others in a shed with no windows. They were cruel to him, didn't feed him properly and, in the winter, he suffered from the cold. I would try and give him a blanket or a cup of tea. He had such a big heart. I always loved him. I suppose we were fellow outcasts, like Ghudi Bhua. Dud Chacha was now seriously ill. They claimed he would drink white spirit if they let him in the house, or he would steal light bulbs and sell them for money to buy drink or cigarettes. The family didn't like me talking to him, but I couldn't ignore him. As soon as I got the chance, I visited his little shed with its empty door frame. 'Dud Chacha, do you remember when I was a little girl and you used to show me the stars?'

Dud Chacha looked at me with sadness and replied in fluent English.

'I was heartbroken when I heard you were on drugs. They're no good for you. I should know – I used to smuggle them to England.' He wished he'd been there to look out for me. I protested that I wasn't taking drugs – I don't think he believed me. He told me to toughen up and be strong.

The family would give Dud Chacha cold leftovers, shoved on a plate, as though he were a dog in a kennel. I was helping in the kitchen once and took a plate of warm food to Dud Chacha. Anita followed me and took it back off him.

'*He* doesn't eat with the rest of us,' she sneered.

I wasn't having that. 'If he isn't fed properly, I won't eat either.'

'I don't care,' replied Anita sourly. 'Don't eat then.' But my proposed hunger strike put Anita in an awkward position. Dad had provided money for my keep while I was in India, and would be ringing up.

Eventually, Pita Ji, the head of the family, made a ruling – 'Let the child eat. Bewakoof!' – and Dud Chacha ate hot meals, at least while I was there.

* * *

When I arrived in India, I had the shakes. My body would shudder violently. Perhaps this arose from me coming off various prescribed painkillers, or maybe it stemmed from my psychological condition after months of abuse. But my family decided I was possessed and must see a holy man. Mum knew about my medication, but didn't pass on the information. Over the phone from England, Dad said, 'If you love me, you'll do it. Otherwise, I won't call you again. I won't ever speak to you. You'll be nothing to me.' I already felt like nothing – worthless. There was constant pressure to prove my love for my family.

My Auntie Anita took me the first time and it was awful. The holy man was a con artist and a pervert who looked like someone from an *Indiana Jones* film. He pretended to be blind, but I could see his eyes leering at my body. White hair and a long white beard were presumably compulsory for magicians of his order. His heavily scarred face suggested acid had been thrown on it, perhaps by a dissatisfied customer. He wore a black bomber jacket, which looked odd over a shalwaar kameez, and was accompanied by two young helpers and a group of followers – people out for an evening's entertainment with the Witchfinder General.

I sat with my back to the audience, facing The Holy Pervert, who draped a shawl over my back. He then pulled me closer to him and wrapped his legs around my body. No one seemed to think this was inappropriate. Partially concealed by the shawl, he touched my breasts and groin. I tried to back off but was trapped between his thighs. I pleaded with Anita. 'I don't like this.' The Holy Pervert pronounced that I had *jinn* in me – I was possessed by evil spirits. He muttered in my ear and pulled my hand to his groin, trying to make me masturbate him. I shouted, 'He's not blind.' But I'm not very fluent in Punjabi, so I don't think it came out right.

'*Chupkar!*' – shut up – yelled an audience member, as if I were interrupting their favourite show. The Holy Pervert grabbed my mouth, just like Khan used to do. I panicked and struggled. The shawl fell to reveal his erection. Unembarrassed, he pulled my hand close to give him satisfaction and no one batted an eyelid.

'You must do as you're told,' warned Anita. 'Otherwise, he won't like it and he'll curse you.' Then my watch beeped, as it did every hour.

'Where did that noise come from?' asked the Holy Pervert. 'The jinni in this girl is very rebellious. We need to plan an exorcism.'

'It's a watch!' I showed them.

Anita was in awe of the Holy Pervert. 'OK, we're very sorry, Holy One. You must come to our house and we can do it there. Tell me what you need.'

He named his price, thousands of rupees, and gave Anita a list of items she needed to buy in preparation. And the moon had to be aligned with the stars.

'Before you go, I need to antagonise the jinni to show who's boss. I have to stab the jinni.'

'You're not gonna let him stab me!'

He fiddled with my top, attached a magnet and stabbed me four times in the chest and kidneys, which hurt. But it was all trickery; he was using a retractable blade. I shouted, 'It's a magnet!' in English but no one paid any attention to me.

On the way home I asked Anita, 'Did you see what he was doing?' Anita observed that some girls do have sex before marriage. She told me I would have to obey the Holy Pervert.

'You're damaged goods, anyway. And you ate meat.' I think Anita's view was that since I'd already slept with a man – a Muslim man – it didn't really matter if the Holy Pervert groped me. While we were waiting for my parents to arrive in India with the money for the full exorcism, I was forced to see this man a second time with my grandfather who tried to give him a ten rupee note instead of 100.

'No sir, that's not enough.'

'How would you know, you're blind?' asked Pita Ji, not unreasonably.

* * *

Pappu was Dad's youngest brother. He stayed in India when Dad and Dud Chacha came to England. When I was very young and the family visited Ambala, there was a man, a neighbour, who used to come up to me, pull a scary face and shout '*Gudiya,*' which means doll. This occurred again, after I had been sexually abused in England, and I would run and hide. Later, Pappu would invite him into the family house to repeat this performance for Dilip's amusement. When I was a teenager, I remember Pappu going through my bag, taunting me, seeing if I had anything worth selling. He was a resentful man, often scornful of others and jealous of Dad living in England.

Pappu came to me in the courtyard a few days after I'd seen the holy man. He'd been drinking and we were alone. 'You're damaged goods. No one will marry you now.' This was the kind of motivational talk I would normally expect from Khan or Mum. Pappu started rambling. 'All those bodies overboard. All those people who drowned for your dad. They've cursed you.'

'What do you mean, Uncle?' We spoke a mixture of Hindi, Punjabi and English.

'Damaged goods. Girls like you don't get very far. Anyone can have you now.'

'Uncle, why are you saying this? You wouldn't like it if someone said this to your daughters.'

At the mention of his daughters, Pappu looked down at the floor. But then he persisted. 'Your dad smuggled immigrants to England and some of them drowned. They don't curse the boys, they curse the girls.' The television blared from the main living room, where the rest of the family were. Pappu grabbed my wrists, like Khan used to, and pulled me into a side room. Then he let go, poured himself a whisky and a glass for me – *Johnny Walker's Black Label*.

'No, I don't drink,' I lied. He produced some packets of condoms from his pocket with pictures of naked white women.

'They give you pictures in case your wife doesn't do it for you!' he smirked.

'Did you know your dad slept with his girl cousin when she was 14? She had to have an abortion. Damaged goods, just like you.' He staggered to a cupboard, rummaged through some photos and selected one. 'Look at her on her wedding day, all dressed in red. She was lucky to get married. Now your dad's karma is coming back on you.'

'Dad wouldn't do that. Why are you saying this?' But I wondered. Dad's karma. The souls of those drowned people. Was I bearing their pain?

Pappu drunkenly grabbed my arms. I was about to scream so he put one hand over my mouth. Then he let go, looked away from me and laughed bitterly. I left the room wondering what kind of family I had.

The next morning, I was struggling to carry a bucket of water to the bathroom. Pappu appeared and helped me with it. In the bathroom, he tried to rub up against me and grabbed my clothes. I made as if to scream and he backed off. Later, he asked me to get Dilip to bring him some pornographic magazines. I protested to Pappu that I didn't have that kind of relationship with my brother. I couldn't ask him that! I didn't add that Dilip was having me prosecuted for credit card fraud. In the end, I did ask Dilip for the porn mags, which, no doubt, provided satisfaction for Pappu.

A frosty atmosphere now descended on the house. I avoided Pappu as much as possible, although he continued to follow me around. Guilt was written on his face while his wife, Mansi Chachi, wore a worried frown. I wanted to call Dad but there was a padlock on the phone. 'I need to call Dad.'

'No, there's a time difference,' stammered Pappu. In fact, it was early evening in England.

'I want to call my father!'

Pita Ji heard the commotion and asked what the matter was. 'What's it to you if she wants to call him? Let the child use the telephone.'

'No!' shouted Pappu, almost pleading, his face coated in nervous sweat.

'What is it you've done to her? What are you scared of?' Pita Ji seemed to know something.

A couple of days later, Dad called, but I couldn't tell him what had happened. I just suggested it would break things up a bit if I went to Bantoo Mama in Yamuna Nagar. Once again, Dad preferred emotional blackmail to reason.

'If you love me, you'll stay in Ambala. If you go to Mum's family, I won't speak to you.'

Mum arrived in Ambala in late January '98. She was here to arrange Dilip's wedding. I told Mum about Uncle Pappu's advances. Mum didn't usually take my side, but she loathed Dad's family. 'Fucking, bloody bastard!' She confronted Pappu, who then disappeared from the house, just before Dilip, Billy and Dad were due to arrive. He missed the pre-matrimonial festivities, so Mum blamed me for casting a shadow over the wedding. Pappu slunk back to the house after a week, to his wife and two young children.

Chapter 14

THE EXORCIST

When I was born, I was in intensive care for three weeks, fed through a tube. Mum found this inconvenient and left after two. Afterwards, she would refer to me as 'damaged goods'. Dad prayed to the goddess, Maa Vaishno Devi, vowing to make a pilgrimage barefoot to her shrine if I lived. I survived and Dad kept his promise. He flew with me, aged one, to India, travelled to the Trikuta Mountains in Jinnu and trekked to the shrine of the 'Mother Who Fulfills Whatever Her Children Wish For' with me on his shoulders. Maybe Maa Vaishno Devi still looks over me.

* * *

While Dad had his black magic, Mum had her own ideas on how to 'cure' me. She and her sister-in-law, Sangita, took me to the holy city of Hardiwar on the River Ganges. The Ganges is the sacred river of India where Hindus bathe, pay homage to their ancestors, have their ashes scattered or wash away their sins. Guess why I was brought there.

In Hardiwar, for reasons best left to the imagination, the Ganges is brown and murky. Various objects floated down river as I waded into the cold river. The current was strong so everyone was holding on to a metal chain to avoid getting swept away. Despite my fear of water, I decided to go along with whatever was planned and get it over with. Many people wade in up to the waist, cup their hands and take a little water to wash in, but I was destined for the deluxe service, the full submersion. Mum was next to me but on the steps at the river bank with Sangita. Mum grabbed the back of my head and dipped it into the river. I was immersed in the brown liquid. As I was allowed up, I coughed, a putrid taste on my tongue. My eyes were blurred, my hair dripping with the Ganges. I welcomed the hot sun. Mum cackled. 'This for God to forgive all your sins, all you done.'

* * *

In the early 1970s, Dad set up in business with some Dutch sailors smuggling illegal immigrants from India. After a spell in prison, Dad went to India to find a wife, quickly married Mum and settled in Woking. Afterwards, he trained as an electronic engineer and learnt how to fix computer hardware. In England, Dad discovered slot machines and strong lager. Indian men of his generation tended to drink whisky. But Dad drank Stella Artois as well. Sometimes, he would come back from the pub and sing along to Bollywood songs on a cassette recorder. He also gambled on horses and played the fruit machines. Players win cash prizes if they get three matching fruits, lemons say. After the initial spin, players can hold or nudge the three buttons to increase their chances of hitting the jackpot on the next spin. *Hold, hold, nudge. Play!*

'If you love me, you'll do this. If you don't, I'll never talk to you again.'

When I was little, Dad used to take us to the Woking Liberal Club. This was basically a pub rather than a political establishment. Dad believed I would bring him luck on the fruit machines. He likened me to Lakshmi, the Hindu goddess of prosperity. 'Hit that button!' Dilip and Billy played Space Invaders while I helped Dad on the fruits. Dad's lucky mascot, named after an old girlfriend, Sunita. But Dad wouldn't quit while he was ahead and any winnings would usually end up back in the machine.

* * *

Dad phoned me from England. 'If you love me, you'll do this.' The time had come for my exorcism. Unsurprisingly, the Holy Pervert had confirmed the family's suspicion that I was possessed. The jinni – evil spirit – needed to be chased from my body for good. Why were his previous attempts to do this not exorcisms? Presumably, because they cost less. An exorcism was his top of the range product, so couldn't happen until Mum arrived from England with sufficient rupees.

A rickshaw pulled up at the house, with two boys aged about eight and eleven, hanging off the sides. The Holy Pervert emerged carrying a kind of rosary, but no white stick. He managed not to bump into anything as he made his way into the house. The boys carried a chest – his box of magic tricks. The elder one was draped in the Holy Pervert's shawl. Floor space was cleared in Pita Ji's room and the family children were dispatched to a safe place with Mansi Chachi. It was a starlit evening and we waited for the planets to align. The Moon also needed to be at a certain angle.

I had to sit cross-legged with my back to my persecutor, facing Mum, Pita Ji, Pappu and Anita, who all looked suitably fearful. This was before I told Mum about Pappu. Banished from the house, Dud Chacha wasn't present. For the family, Anita seemed to be in charge. A great believer in black magic and, reputedly, no mean sorceress herself, Anita was also a schoolteacher. I wanted to hold someone's hand but this wasn't permitted. A terracotta pot was placed in front of me, in which various herbs and seeds were boiled up. The Holy Pervert sat behind me, the two of us encircled by the rosary beads. Towards the end with Khan, when I no longer feared him as much, I liked to face him when he assaulted me, to show defiance, to shame him. But with my back to the Holy Pervert, I couldn't see what he was up to. He wrapped his legs around my body and squeezed up against me, his groin pressing against me. I tried to move forward but he kept pulling me back. Then he pushed his fingers into my spine. My body shuddered – further proof I was possessed. The Holy Pervert began chanting and rocking me backwards and forwards, his penis pressed against my body all the while.

'Mum, this is a load of crap!' I shouted.

'Be quiet!' snapped Anita. The chanting continued. I coughed to wind up the Holy Pervert. Or perhaps it was my jinni. Anita looked furious. Pita Ji had advised me to repeat the Prayer to Lord Shiva a sacred 108 times. I recited the mantra under my breath, just moving my lips a little. The Holy Pervert released me from his grip, but my ordeal had only just begun.

'We've got to beat this jinni out of her.' Then he hit me on the back where my scars were still tender. This hurt like hell but I was also angry, although powerless. I had become accustomed to a certain level of violence with Khan, but even he would usually get bored after a while. The Holy Pervert's assault on me lasted more than an hour, using various wooden and metal implements while he continued to chant. He clearly enjoyed his work. The adults looked on in terror. I screamed out, 'Mum, please help me!' She turned her back on me and looked away. When the beating was over, the contents of the terracotta pot were emptied into the bucket. The Holy Pervert claimed this was the jinni. The younger boy took the 'jinni' down to the river, accompanied by Pappu. The rest of the family left the room without acknowledging me as I sat on the floor, beaten and humiliated. The Holy Pervert remained with the eleven-year-old boy and then started to masturbate.

Mum came back in with the money and saw him. 'Eurghh, that's disgusting!' she spluttered, handing the helper a wad of rupee notes with distaste. Later, by way of explanation for my ordeal, Mum said, 'Well, Dad said need doing'. None of the family enquired as to my well-being or said 'Well done'. Perhaps they thought I should have been grateful.

Chapter 15

TISSUE OF LIES

Mum had come to India bearing gold jewellery for the bride's family. Dilip had chosen his own wife back in September – Shikta from Delhi. Financially, my brother would have been considered a catch – an Oxford graduate working in IT. Mum and Dad rented a flat in Delhi, around the corner from Shikta's family.

When I met Shikta, she made little effort to conceal her dislike for me. Whether Dilip had briefed her against me, told her about Khan, or whether it was competitive jealousy, I don't know. I said I was glad Dilip had found someone to make him happy and suggested we could be like sisters as we both only had brothers. Shikta responded with a strained smile. I bought Shikta some gold earrings for her 21st birthday at the end of January. Having been cleaned out financially by Khan, I had to borrow some money from Mum, which I later paid back. A few days later, I discovered she'd given the earrings away. Dilip was still in England at this time, but being nice to me on the telephone. He needed me to help with the wedding arrangements and told me not to worry about the credit card fraud, explaining cheerfully, 'I didn't lose a penny!'

Dilip flew to India in February with Dad and Billy, just a few days before the wedding. Mum and I went with

Shikta and her family to the airport to meet them. We were supposed to be grown-ups, but Shikta would stand in my way or push into me. I still had painful scars, tender areas. She was very immature, like a playground bully. I don't know what Shikta thought about marrying Dilip. She wasn't one to open up. We went back to her parents' place, where Dad was asking after my health – he was pleased to see me. Whether people knew the full story, I don't know, but they knew I hadn't been well. Shikta sulked because she wasn't receiving enough attention.

As the wedding approached, more of our distant relatives began arriving in Delhi from Punjab and Haryana provinces. They wore their best, brightly coloured clothes to celebrate Dilip's forthcoming wedding. Mum's eldest brother, Dev, also came with his family. He was a retired Indian Air Force wing commander. We didn't get to see him very often. The outside of the flat was decorated with bright lights and garlands of marigolds as we welcomed our guests at the gate with plates of food lit with candles. Dad was on the *Kingfisher* lager and playfully picked up a heavy Sangita, his sister-in-law.

The engagement party, the *shagan,* was scheduled for the day before the wedding because Dilip was on a flying visit to India and would take Shikta home to live in England. The day before that, Mum had arranged a morning appointment with a beautician for Shikta and me. Shikta's brother drove me, but Shikta was already there, having had henna – *mehndi* – applied to her hands. Shikta looked at me but spoke to the beautician, announcing firmly, 'I need to practise putting make-up on for the wedding.' The beautician obliged and attended to Shikta's face for some time while I watched. Shikta now decided she needed to have her hair arranged and smirked in my direction. This performance carried on for two hours. Mum had pre-paid for the appointment and our time was now up as Shikta's brother arrived to collect us. Traditionally, the groom's sister plays an important role at Indian weddings, but I now left the beautician without henna. Shikta knew exactly what she was doing. I didn't challenge her or make a fuss, although Mum did ask why I had no henna, so I explained what had happened.

The following day, the shagan took place in the afternoon at a nearby wedding hall. Billy was standing on his own – he didn't really speak much Punjabi or Hindi. I approached him nervously. Billy had stopped talking to me during the Khan era but now said he had missed me. I told him I missed him too and we hugged. Some distant relatives came over and asked after my health. Perhaps they'd heard I was 'unwell', but they seemed kind and concerned. From the corner of my eye, I saw Shikta scowling at me. I didn't respond. Shikta's parents were making a present of cash to Mum – notes on a plate under a handkerchief – but Dilip intercepted the plate and refused the money on Mum's behalf. Mum was stunned – she was paying for most of the wedding. Shikta entered later. Mum had bought her 21 outfits, of Shikta's own choice, including special ones for the shagan. Shunning Mum's presents, Shikta wore an everyday shalwaar kameez trouser suit. Mum was saddened by this. She worked in a card shop and had saved hard to make Dilip's wedding special.

That evening, the night before the wedding, my family held a reception for our relatives in the small flat we were staying in. Shikta's family weren't in attendance so there were about 30 guests. I was serving nibbles and chatting to various aunties and uncles. They said it was nice that I could make it to India for my brother's wedding and complimented me on my outfit. I replied that it was lovely to see them. Suddenly, out of the blue, Dilip lobbed a grenade in my direction.

'Do you remember, you were abused as a child? And I saw

it. There was no one there for you. I witnessed you get raped as a child. Do you remember? You'll never be happy, you'll never be loved. You'll never get married. You're damaged goods, you are.' Those nearest to us were shocked but not everyone heard, so the silence spread through the room slowly, in ripples. Stunned by Dilip's bile, I put the plates down and made towards the door.

'I'll just go. I'll go off somewhere!' I cried. Dad grabbed my wrists. Khan used to grab my wrists.

'No, please, *beta*. Please, please, Sunita, please don't. He doesn't know what he's talking about, he's being stupid. He's being foolish. I don't know why he's done it today.'

Dilip continued to rant. 'She'll never be loved. She doesn't deserve to be loved.'

'Dad, I've tried so hard. I'll just go now and carry on walking till I drop dead.'

'No, you won't,' said Dad, giving me a big hug. I collapsed sobbing into his arms, as he comforted me, saying, 'Just ignore him.' I had wanted to hug Dad for so long, but now I just felt miserable.

'Why is God punishing me? When will God stop punishing me? What is it that I've done so wrong, dad?'

'Maybe God's punishing you for what I've done,' whispered Dad. Dilip heard and now turned on Dad.

'Yeah, what have you done? Come on, you might as well say it in front of all these people. What *have* you done?' The room was now silent. I let go of Dad and looked at my brother. Out of helplessness, I now took control.

'Not here, not in front of everyone. Let's go outside.' I wiped my eyes and left the flat, accompanied by a confused looking Dilip.

Delhi was alive. Horns blared, cats and dogs hurried about their business and a lorry tried to squeeze through tuk-tuks, and what seemed like a thousand scooters. A majestic elephant seemed to preside over all. 'Why would you do that?' I asked Dilip. 'How could you do that to me? How could you do that to dad? What if Shikta's relatives had been there? I hope you're a dad one day and your kid throws up your past.'

'Is it true, then?' asked Dilip. 'All those things mum said about dad? Are they true?' A feature of my parents' marriage was that Mum would bring up Dad's indiscretions from time to time, including his time in prison.

'It doesn't matter. This is your life. My life is my life and dad's life is dad's life.'

'I don't know if I'm doing the right thing. Should I get married, or should I not get married?'

'Do you love her? Do you know her enough?'

'Well, I don't really know. That's what arranged marriages are all about, aren't they? You get to know the person, you grow to love them, I suppose.'

'What's the rush?' I asked.

'Well, if Mum dies due to the stress you've caused her by going with that Paki Khan, I'll be single for the rest of my life.'

Dilip's bitterness shone through. I reminded him about Mubina. 'What about *your* Muslim girlfriend?'

'She couldn't have children, so I forced Mum to start the arrangements. Anyway, a wife is cheaper than prostitutes.'

I wanted to punch Dilip in the face. Instead, we spoke a while longer, but normally this time, without rancour. Then we hugged.

After about half an hour, we returned to the party, where our relatives tried not to stare at us. Dilip asked me again about Dad and the drowned migrants. I shrugged. 'Karma, I guess. It gets us all in the end.'

I looked over at Dad who was standing nearby. His face

dropped. 'I know. Pappu told me,' I said, by way of explanation.

* * *

On the morning of the wedding, Dilip was like a bear with a sore head, although he doesn't drink alcohol. He was irritable, snapping the heads off all who crossed his path. Our aunties applied turmeric to his arms and legs. In Hinduism, turmeric signifies fertility and prosperity. As early evening approached, Mum and the aunties placed a *sehra* – a headdress with hanging garlands – on Dilip's head. Then we made our way to the wedding venue, where Dilip mounted a white mare. As his sister, I now tied sacred threads to the horse's reins and our girl cousins followed suit. Dilip slowly rode his horse to the banqueting hall, with Billy and me marching proudly on either side as a brass band played.

Shikta's male relatives greeted us at the entrance to the hall. Then Shikta appeared with her mother for the *jai mala,* where she and Dilip placed garlands of flowers around each other's necks.

Mum surveyed Shikta's outfit and looked at me with concern. 'Why she wearing same as you? She with us when we buy yours.' Usually, Indian brides wear red, but Shikta wore a long, cream skirt with a maroon border, part of a two-piece *lengha*, identical to the one she'd seen bought for me. So, I was attending my brother's wedding without the traditional henna and dressed the same as his bride. Did Shikta plan this to discredit me? I'll probably never know. Inside the hall, Dilip and Shikta sat on the top table. I joined briefly for family photos but stayed in the back row, trying to hide my clashing clothes.

Time came for the tying of scarves ceremony, where the bride and groom tie the knot, literally, with pink cotton scarves placed around their necks and tied together. Mum sent me forward to perform this ceremony, but Dilip put up his hand. 'No, not her!' Dilip's mood swings and U-turns are hard to predict or fathom. So, I don't know whether I was rejected for the clashing outfit, the credit card fraud, or for being sexually abused as a child in front of him.

During the ceremonies, there was some confusion over gold. Mum had already given presents of gold to Shikta and her family, but the priest and Shikta's parents now declared she must make a further gift at the ceremony. Mum took off her gold necklace and put it around Shikta's neck but stressed it was a loan, whispering, not very quietly, 'You can borrow this.'

After the wedding, an Indian bride leaves with her new family for further festivities and games before spending the night with her new husband. Dad was staying elsewhere in New Delhi with his relatives and didn't come back to the flat with us. So Dilip and Shikta were joined by me, Billy, Mum and Mum's relatives, who were staying with us for the next stage of the celebrations. Dilip and Shikta disappeared, rather than sit with the family. Eventually, Sangita stood up with a plate of food – *thali* – and announced that we were ready to greet the newly-weds. Mum's eldest brother, Dev, was waiting to make gifts of jewellery to Shikta in the main room. Mum was suffering with a migraine and went to lie down in the back room for a short while. Sangita wondered if Dilip and Shikta were outside, or maybe on the roof terrace, and asked Billy to go and fetch them while she and I took a glass of water and some aspirin to Mum. As we entered the back room, Dilip stormed past us in a fury, straight out the door without speaking to anyone, a grinning Shikta following in his wake. Mum was lying in a heap on the floor in a state of shock.

'Couldn't they have waited?' she whispered. 'Look! They never even clean up the tissues.' Dilip and Shikta had consummated their marriage and left without saying goodbye to Mum or her relatives. Mum was distraught. Sangita and I made excuses for Dilip and Shikta to the other relatives, explaining it was late and they had an early flight in the morning. The happy couple spent the rest of their wedding night in their five-star hotel, before jetting off to Seville for their honeymoon the next day, breaking Mum's heart in the process.

In the morning, Mum was in a daze. She looked broken and kept repeating, 'That family liars and now they take my son from me.' Apparently, Shikta's family had exaggerated their financial status. I tried to console Mum but she didn't want me, she wanted her golden boy.

* * *

Hijras are transgender people in the Indian subcontinent. Facing discrimination and danger, they band together for comfort and security. The word hijra has been translated as eunuch. In reality, those identifying as hijras are more diverse. Whilst a number are born with irregular genitalia, others are men who have adopted feminine identity and dress, although some undergo castration on initiation into the hijra community. Employment opportunities are few, so many hijras resort to prostitution or begging. Despite their low status in Indian society, many people believe they bring luck. So, some make a living by turning up, uninvited, at weddings and birth celebrations, trading on the good fortune they supposedly bring. But, if the parties are unwilling to pay, the hijras don't always leave quietly.

That morning, we got a phone call from Shikta's parents,

warning that a band of hijras were on the way to the flat. They had presumably been told we were richer pickings, but, I suppose, at least Shikta's folks had the decency to warn us. 'Some eunuchs are coming! I not pay them!' said Mum defiantly, before retiring to the back room. The hijras arrived, rang the doorbell and then banged on the gate. Billy and I looked at each other, not knowing what to do. I opened the inner door and saw about eight or ten hijras gathered outside in the street, women at first glance, but with deep voices when they spoke. My Hindi is even worse than my Punjabi, but the demand for money translated well enough. I held my hand up to indicate 'five minutes', to buy time. I consulted Mum, who washed her hands of the problem. 'No! I spend enough on wedding. *You* get rid of them.'

After several minutes, there was a commotion as our visitors started shaking the gate and shouting angrily. I opened the door again. A couple were starting to undress – this was how they extorted money. The leader pointed at me, her face etched with pain, but also a kind of pride. She uttered a curse. *Too late,* I thought. I went back inside and locked the door of the flat, but the demonstration continued. Eventually, after about twenty minutes, the hijras gave up and left. Their indignant moans and curses grew quieter as they trudged away, disappointed.

Chapter 16

BACK TO BLIGHTY

A week after Dilip's wedding, I flew back to England with Dad and Billy, a few days before Mum, who stayed behind in India to collect Dilip's wedding albums. My passage to India had not been uneventful, but at least I hadn't been married off – yet. Physically, I was in marginally better shape, but I was mentally scarred and dangerously low. Much remained unresolved in my life. Possible criminal prosecution loomed on the horizon, as did the spectre of an arranged marriage. And, of course, there was Khan. I didn't know where he was. Would he leave me alone, or would he come after me back in England? In Woking, Dilip and Shikta were already back home, following their honeymoon in Spain. The house needed cleaning, with several days of dirty dishes and Dilip and Shikta's dirty underwear on the floor, so I set to work. Shikta stayed mainly upstairs in a black dressing gown, although she would come down to give Dad shopping lists like the lady of the manor. Dad wasn't working at the time, but was expected to pay for their food. Dad asked Dilip and Shikta if they wanted to come and meet Mum at the airport. Shikta replied on their behalf. 'No, there's no need.'

I accompanied Dad to Heathrow Airport. On the way back, Mum asked how Dilip was. There was no reply. 'Billy's looking forward to seeing you,' I said after a while, changing the subject. When we got back to the house, I went to hug Mum but she sidestepped me and put her arms around Billy. Dilip and Shikta were still upstairs. Mum had gifts for her sons – cricket pads and gloves for Billy, and two beautifully bound wedding photo albums and a video for the newly-weds. She called for Dilip a couple of times, telling him she had the photos. Eventually, Dilip and Shikta emerged, sullenly. Mum seemed nervous, her son cold and distant.

'Oh, you change your hair,' remarked Mum innocently. Dilip had a centre parting.

'I made him change it,' explained Shikta, who now took centre stage on the sofa to view the wedding photos. There was a nice picture of me hugging Billy. Mum turned to me.

'Oh, you beautiful in picture, Sunita.'

Shikta exploded. 'Dilip, how dare your mother not say I'm beautiful.'

Mum was visibly shocked by Shikta's rudeness but tried composing herself, spluttering, 'But Shikta, I never mean upset you. Of course, you beautiful. You are bride. I never meant to say Sunita beautiful. I made mistake.'

Ironically, Mum had managed for nearly twenty years not to pay me a compliment and frequently called me ugly, so this was an avoidable error. Dilip took Shikta upstairs to look at the albums in private. I made Mum a cup of tea but she shooed me away, saying, 'It's all your fault.'

The following morning, Dilip snapped at Mum, 'Are you going to do the arrival ceremonies or what?' For once, Mum stood up to her golden boy.

'It's too late. You already sleep with her and you gone early on wedding night.' Shikta stormed back upstairs.

Later, Shikta asked me to show her Woking, so I took her shopping. I was trying my best, despite her animosity towards me. Back home, she complained to Dilip loudly.

'Sunita wore me out.'

'That's 'cos she's stupid,' snorted Dilip, loyally.

Shikta didn't get the hang of the dishwasher and broke it. Fair enough, but she blamed me.

'Sunita did that.'

'That's 'cos she's stupid!' chirped Dilip. My parents knew it was Shikta, but said nothing. They didn't want to upset Dilip. Shikta would make meals for herself and Dilip only, which they ate apart from the family, leaving Mum and me to cook for everyone else. Mum was disgusted – this wasn't the Indian way.

One evening, the house phone rang. I answered – it was Shikta on her mobile. She was walking home from Woking town centre and claimed Khan was following her, but then she laughed, apparently unconcerned. I told her to stay on the phone as I called for help. As soon as Shikta heard help was on the way, she hung up. Following previous incidents, provisions had been made, so Dad, Dilip and Billy now mobilised against Khan for the first time. Taking a cricket bat, hockey stick and Dilip's baseball bat, they set off to rescue Dilip's beloved. I couldn't help wondering that my family's response to Khan was very different now. I was happy for Khan to be dealt with and waited anxiously by the front door. Dad and my brothers returned within a couple of minutes, with Shikta safe and sound. Apparently, Khan had disappeared. The princess had been rescued from the dragon.

Dilip shoved me as he came in. 'It's all your fault, you fucking bitch.' Dad heard and turned a blind eye, while Shikta seemed delighted. Mum was puzzled. 'But Shikta, how you know what Khan look like?' Mum had a point. Shikta had only lived in England a couple of weeks and, as far as we knew, had never met Khan. Shikta didn't answer and smiled, seemingly unembarrassed by the question, before trotting upstairs, followed by the still fuming Dilip. Mum and I both knew that if she'd encountered Khan, she wouldn't be smiling. The atmosphere in the house was now toxic, making it difficult for me to fit back in. There was a viper in the nest, who seemed to be doing her best to turn Dilip against Mum and Dad.

Mum was unhappy and took it out on me. One day in mid-February, she brought two black bin bags in from the garden shed, a special surprise she'd been saving up.

'Look what your Paki man left here!' When I was in India, Khan had returned my clothes, some deliberately stained with semen. 'They disgusting.' Khan had also thrown the hire car keys into the garden and called the police. 'We went through so much because of you,' Mum complained. Not all the garments were soiled and Mum asked if I wanted to keep any. No, I did not – they carried too many painful memories. Mum heard Dad coming towards the kitchen and hurriedly began putting the clothes back in the bags.

Dad was astonished that Mum had kept the clothes.

'Why are you showing her? I don't want them in the house. Burn them.' Mum disposed of the clothing, apart from a blue cardigan, which she still wears.

Unchallenged by Mum and Dad, who were frightened of angering Dilip, Shikta's spite towards me became more blatant.

'She's too dark. She's ugly. Who would marry her?'

There was also the credit card fraud, mentioned frequently. 'Perhaps we'll have her arrested,' always accompanied by her nauseating smirk and a joyless fake laugh from Dilip.

One evening, Mum, Dilip and Shikta were in Dilip's bedroom looking at the computer as I walked past. Shikta asked, 'How tall is she? Shall we say she's fun?' They all laughed. Mum seemed happy being with Dilip and called me in to ask my height. They were putting me on Hindu wedding sites to get me married off. 'We've got you on five sites,' announced Shikta, gleefully.

'Surely, somebody'll take her!' added Dilip, much to Shikta's amusement.

Not wanting them to see I was upset, I walked over to the bedroom window. Down below in the back garden, something was moving. A gas lighter flickered in the twilight and its owner looked up at me. Khan was back.

I shuddered and left the room quickly. 'She's so ungrateful,' whined Shikta sarcastically, assuming my departure resulted from her bullying. 'The sooner we get rid of her, the better.' I saw Billy in his room with his headphones on. I thought of telling him Khan was here, but didn't. Around 11 p.m., I was in my room at the front of the house when the neighbour's security light came on and a small stone hit my window. I didn't look, but hid in the darkness. Then another stone, a bit larger – Khan's calling card. Mum was in the bathroom, heard the noise and came into my room.

'He outside is he?'

'Leave it, Mum. Leave it – he'll go away.' Instead of ignoring Khan, Mum chose to antagonise him. Opening the window, she shouted, 'Go away or I call police!' I kept my head down so Khan wouldn't see me and I wouldn't see him.

'I just want to see her!' he shouted. Khan began throwing more stones at the window, but big ones this time. I pulled Mum down to protect her but she just looked at me, stood up and shouted at Khan.

'Just you see what we do with her!' Mum was hinting at an arranged marriage. Dad came to see what the commotion was just as our neighbours' house lights switched on. Khan disappeared into the night.

At around 2 a.m., there was a loud knock on the door and the bell rang. Mum and Dad both went downstairs to answer – I followed. It was the police.

'Do you have a Sunita Khan here?' asked a policewoman. 'Her husband's outside, says you're holding her against her will.'

I thought he was supposed to be getting married, but he still wouldn't let me go.

'No, I'm not being held,' I explained.

'Well, will you go outside and talk to him?'

'No!' I protested. 'I don't want to see him!'

We were joined by Dilip and a bleary-eyed Shikta, who glared at the policeman.

'You've disturbed my sleep.' The policeman's mouth opened but he couldn't find the words to respond to Shikta's arrogance.

Dilip turned on me. 'She must have called him. Kick her out.' Dad looked at me sadly.

'No, Dad, I didn't call him.'

Dilip believed, or claimed to believe, that I'd called Khan in response to the arranged marriage plans. Perhaps I should have pointed out that I no longer had a mobile phone. Khan had taken it. Oddly, some months later, it transpired that Dilip was still paying the account. Dilip had arranged the contract for me when I was under 18 and I used to pay him cash for the bill. When I disappeared with Khan, and then when I left Khan and was sent to India, Dilip carried on paying for it by direct debit. After this incident, I was moved into the spare room at the back.

After a couple of days, Khan rang the house and left a message on the answerphone. If my parents didn't let him see me, he would throw acid in Mum's face. He called, repeating the threat several times and we had this on tape. The police were informed and took away the answerphone, which included the phone itself. Mum blamed me for the loss of the phone, although it was returned a few days later. Dilip and Shikta had already installed a separate landline in their room, but wouldn't let anyone else use it in the meantime.

When I left Khan, I'd done everything asked of me by my parents. I'd gone to India, endured a bizarre 'exorcism' from a pervert and been dunked in the Ganges. I'd also helped Dilip with his wedding arrangements when he asked, while he was still in England. He'd said, 'Don't worry about the credit cards. It's all on insurance. I didn't lose any money.' I even tried to welcome Shikta into the family. But all this wasn't enough. Everyone believed I was somehow responsible for the return of Khan, who was now threatening my family. There was no vigilante party to protect me from Khan. Dad was hardly talking to me, Mum was promising an arranged marriage, Billy was distant and didn't say much and Shikta and Dilip were constantly hostile, spiteful, threatening to have me arrested. I wasn't allowed out on my own. Khan and Mum, between them, had cut me off from my friends. My suffering at Khan's hands was something I had to live with. I still do – he appears in my nightmares. I was feeling desperate and isolated with no one to really talk to. A couple of times, when no one was around, I rang the Samaritans on the house phone.

With Khan's credit card fraud being dangled over me by Dilip and Shikta, I decided to take the initiative. I went to Woking Police Station and told the officer on the front desk that I'd come to make a confession and explained about the cards. He looked confused, probably thinking it was a wind up. 'Come again, love?' I repeated the reason for my visit. I guess this doesn't happen very often, so maybe there was no procedure. The officer went away and came back with a police sergeant, who formally arrested me. I had come out without a bag, so they took what few possessions I had in my pockets and checked for a belt so I couldn't hang myself. It now hit home that this was for real. I was now a criminal suspect, having owned up to theft, but I didn't feel like a criminal – these were Khan's crimes. The sergeant led me down to the cells and locked me in.

The cell was cream coloured, the walls scratched where people had tried to carve their names or patterns, presumably with their fingernails. I was left there for some time. The silence was amazing and, after a little while, I began to feel peaceful. I was safe from Khan. There was no Shikta and no Dilip mocking me, threatening me. No Mum making me feel worthless. I burst into tears, but these were tears of release, of pain flowing out – peace and quiet. An officer checked up on me and I asked for a pen and paper, on which I wrote a mantra, which my grandfather, Pita Ji, had taught me to recite, Om Namah Shivaya – In the name of Shiva. I just kept writing it, again and again – Om Namah Shivaya – and I felt calm. A policeman came into the cell and told me Dad was upstairs and was very upset because he couldn't see me. I'd left a note at home to say I was going to the police station to discuss the credit card fraud. I didn't want Mum and Dad to think I'd run away. I asked if I could please see Dad as I didn't know if I was going to be released. I was told that wouldn't be possible.

'Well, there wasn't much point telling me he's here then, was there?'

Two police officers came in to question me about my crimes – a man and a woman. I had decided to own up to all offences associated with Khan, even if they were nothing to do with me. I thought I would go to prison, but I would have to be strong and go through with it. The prize was that

I would be rid of Khan and no one would want an arranged marriage with me afterwards. And after that? Well, I didn't really have a game plan. I told the officers what Khan had done to me – the abuse. I gave them details of the crimes – the use of Dilip's cards which had already been reported, the credit card details I obtained for Khan under duress when I was working at Galleon and the cars Khan was hiring. My role had been to book the cars on the telephone – Khan collected them for his own use and paid by credit card. I wanted to make sure I went to prison. The policeman went outside to consult a senior officer. When he came back, they asked me whether I would like to own up to a further 14 offences. These are called 'TICs' – taken into consideration. The 14 later piled up to 30 as the police cleared their paperwork. I knew nothing about these crimes and I don't even know if they were anything to do with Khan, but I put my hands up to them to be helpful. I was allowed one phone call and called a duty solicitor, who arrived and warned me that what I'd owned up to was serious.

'It's not just petty theft, you know – it's, "obtaining services by deception".' I asked what the maximum sentence was. 'Five years.' To my surprise, I was bailed to return on 30th May. I had no 'previous' and it was credit card fraud, but I didn't know about these things, so I seriously believed I might be remanded in custody. It was late evening and Dad was waiting for me. He'd been crying and drove me back to the house. Dilip was delighted and, for Shikta's amusement, asked me what it was like in the cells.

Chapter 17

FRED

Gemma from Woking Police Station arranged counselling for me at a place called The Crescent. With difficulty, I started to open up about Khan, about V, and all the abuse. I talked about my low self-esteem and my relationship with my family. But, after two sessions, my treatment was stopped abruptly because, according to hospital notes, Khan had threatened staff there.

Khan resumed making threats to my family – perhaps he'd only stopped briefly because the phone had been taken away. I was now sleeping in a room at the back, but Khan watched the house constantly and had worked this out. One night, at about 2 a.m., he came into our back garden, like Romeo below Juliet's balcony. He threw small pebbles at my window. I tried ignoring him but he carried on, so I opened the window and asked him to go away. Unlike Romeo, Khan warned in a menacing hiss that he would throw acid on Mum's face if I called the police and that I must come to the window whenever he called. He also threatened to set fire to the house. My room was between Dilip's and Billy's, but no one heard him.

Khan now changed tone. He wanted to chat and whispered that he'd won his court case against the parcel company that used to employ him. He'd been sacked for concealing his criminal record but his lawyer argued successfully that Khan had answered 'not applicable' so hadn't actually lied. I said I was pleased for him, although I didn't really care – it wasn't my problem.

Khan asked, 'Who's that girl in the house? Is she your brother's wife? She's not much of a looker!' Then he ordered me to write him a letter saying I loved him and wanted him back. I thought it a bizarre request but didn't want to antagonise him. So, I took a pen and paper and quickly scribbled the note as instructed. I was accustomed to obeying Khan, terrified of the consequences of not doing so.

The next morning, the police came around, furious. They'd received a complaint from Khan, stating that I'd harassed him by throwing a love letter at him. No one thought to ask what he was doing in our back garden, trespassing, in the first place. Despite the tape recordings of Khan's threats to my family, and the rescue from Aldershot three months previously, the police decided to file this as a 'no crime' on both sides – six of one, half a dozen of the other. They had better things to worry about. The atmosphere in the house became unbearable. My name was mud and even Dad was barely talking to me. Khan had put a stop to my counselling and now I feared the police wouldn't believe me. Khan was a very persuasive liar – after all, he had me practically brainwashed.

When I was living with Khan, he used to attend counselling sessions with the Windmill Team, the drug and alcohol unit based in St Peter's Hospital in Chertsey. Sometimes, he took me inside with him, or he would leave me in the car park. I now needed someone to talk to. I wanted to tell someone about Khan and what he'd done to me. So I rang the Windmill Team. I don't know who I spoke to – a psychiatric nurse possibly, who took notes. I told her about the rape and the torture, the cigarette burns and the cutting. I spoke of being locked in the room in Aldershot for days on end. And I told her about Khan raping a twelve-year-old when he was at school.

* * *

I decided to leave home so Khan wouldn't know where I was, and maybe he would stop bothering my family. But, I was also running away. Running from the threat of a forced arranged marriage and from Dilip's and Shikta's bullying. The trouble is, I wasn't yet working so I had no money to rent anywhere. I made contact with a homeless shelter – Woking Association for Single Homeless – the WASH. It was a start, but I couldn't really see beyond that. I wrote a letter to my younger brother, Billy, saying I was sorry but I had to leave. Only Shikta was in the house when I left. I told her I was going.

'I don't care,' she sneered.

Leaving with just a few possessions – my 'go bag' – I wandered for an hour until I didn't recognise the streets any more. I didn't know where I was or where I was going immediately, or in life. Lost and alone, I broke down – despair had taken over. Finding a phone box, I rang the WASH asking for help as I didn't know how to get there. They telephoned the police, who came to collect me. I'm sure they were sick of me in those days, but, as always, they responded to the call. I was taken to Gemma at Woking Police Station, who spoke to the WASH, arranged for me to be admitted and drove me there. Gemma returned later with some clothes and my teddy bear from home, and gave me a hug. It was decided that I should use a false name, so I was introduced to the other residents as 'Fred'. No one was to know of my whereabouts, not Khan or my family. There were about 12 young people staying in the WASH, male and female, aged between 16 and 25, all white except for me. The first few nights were scary. Nervous of Khan finding me, the noises made by the other residents cast shadows on my mind. Fellow lost souls, some of my housemates seemed hostile, others withdrawn. Several were cocaine users, smoked dope or were alcoholics; although drugs were obviously not allowed in the hostel. A few had been in prison or young offenders' institutions. A couple seemed 'respectable' and went to work every day, but most were on the dole. One man offered me sex and marijuana, in that order. I declined. We each had our own room, so had some privacy, but the bathroom and shower was shared. At first, I kept largely to myself and only ever really spoke to a few of the others. The staff in the hostel told me to sign on for benefits, which didn't go far, although the Salvation Army provided some tins of food to the residents. Initially, fearing Khan, I went out mainly at night for some fresh air. My feet were cold because I didn't have any socks. But, as I needed to buy my own food, as well as socks, and was looking for work, I started to venture out more during the day as well. I would hide in car parks, away from the road, to avoid Khan. With my giro (benefit cheque), I bought a painting by numbers kit and a little plant in a plastic pot. I came to think of my plant as a companion and even thought of naming it, but decided I had no right. I didn't want to *own* the plant the way Khan had owned me.

Tending to my plant and painting my masterpiece – a scene with boats in a harbour, which I still have – I began to find some tranquillity. Life was far from 'normal' – I was jobless and living in a homeless hostel, but I had food, shelter and some kind of routine. Credit card fraud was on the backburner for now, arranged marriage not on the table and I was away from my family, although I missed them. I also seemed to have shaken off Khan for the time being, although, he still haunted my nightmares. I got to know a girl called Julie, who had the room opposite mine. One Friday evening, we went for a walk into Woking town centre. On the way, we saw a group of Asian guys. I knew a couple of them, Jamal and Khaliq. They invited us to go clubbing in Guildford. Not feeling in the mood for partying, I wasn't keen, but I didn't want to disappoint Julie, so I went along. We drove to Guildford in two cars. At the club, I was uncomfortable, probably a party pooper, but I didn't particularly want to be around boys, or to drink. I was kind of broken and would rather have just had peace and quiet alone with my plant and painting. Julie got off with some guy and said she would spend the night with him. There was a curfew at the hostel so I went outside the club, wondering how I would get back. Jamal joined me and we chatted for a while. A little drunk, Jamal clumsily moved around and kissed the back of my neck. I stepped away quickly – I hadn't expected that. Jamal seemed embarrassed but we carried on talking. Eventually, the whole group, minus Julie, drove back to Woking, long after curfew time. The gang went to a bedsit a few doors up from the hostel, where a Muslim girl named Mumtaz lived alone. Upstairs lived a white girl, who was in a casual relationship with Jamal. In Mumtaz's room, a crowd were drinking and sharing a joint, including a couple of girls from my class at Winston, as my old school is known. They were on holiday from uni – I could have died of embarrassment, living in a homeless shelter. I went to leave, thinking I would just hang around in car parks until the morning. But Jamal begged Mumtaz to let me stay, so I slept on the floor. Mumtaz slept in her bed, whilst Moonie's boy cousin was on the sofa. We spoke of Moonie during the night.

* * *

Khan found me during the day, sitting on the kerb near the shelter. It was cold and I had no jacket with me, but I needed some fresh air. Woking's a small town. Maybe someone spotted me and rang Khan on his mobile – my mobile. Or perhaps he knew I was there and was driving past regularly. It was the bad Khan, not the nice Khan saying he loved me, but the Khan of seemingly limitless anger and bloodshot eyes. 'Fucking bitch.' Using both hands, he grabbed my hair and neck, hauled me to the car and slung me into the passenger seat. Then he slam-dunked my head on the dashboard – twice. I nearly blacked out but regained my senses as Khan ran around to the driver's seat. He'd locked the passenger door, so I had to unlock it but wasn't quick enough. Khan sped off with me in his Capri and drove to a secluded area of a business park, which was empty at weekends. Khan asked me about India. I told him about Pappu.

'What did your family do about that?' asked Khan. I looked down. 'See? They don't care about you,' he crowed.

With sadness in his voice, Khan now said, 'When I realised I forgot the keys, I had a feeling you would go. It hurt me when you left.' There was a brief, menacing silence. Khan didn't ask why I left him – perhaps he'd worked that one out for himself. Nor did he mention the credit card fraud, although I found out in 2014 that he'd been arrested for it and, presumably, bailed.

Then Khan raped me. Again. He walked around to the passenger side of the car and escorted me out. Suddenly, he put his hand over my mouth and bundled me into the back seat where he attacked. He was struggling to pull my jeans and pants down in the back of his Capri, so he was too pre-occupied to punch or bite me this time. When I lived with

Khan, I wore *shalwaar kameez*, which are easy to remove – you just pull a cord to untie the knot. This was the first time for months, but relatively tame by Khan's standards, because we were in a car. When he was done, I asked, 'Is that it?' Although I felt humiliated and violated, the sad truth was, I missed the cuddles afterwards.

When I lived with Khan, he raped me regularly, violently. After the first time, I was never offered the chance of consenting to sex, even if I would only be 'consenting' to avoid rape. Sex for Khan *was* rape, nasty and brutish. Rape was a form of control, degradation with aggravated features. The punch in the face. Villa lost again? Bad day at work, dear? Run out of methadone? The screamed abuse. 'You fucking bitch.' But worse, torture. Cutting with glass. The head held under water. Biting, sinking his teeth in or tearing at my skin like a rabid dog. Cigarette burns. Whipping with his leather belt – fifty shades of black, blue and red. It never got easier because each rape was different, sadistic, calculated to inspire fear. But afterwards, mostly but not always, there were cuddles, with my head nestling in Khan's chest. It would all be over. After the terror, Khan showed some affection and my feelings of rejection subsided for a while.

Khan left me in the car for a couple of minutes while he made a phone call, which he didn't want me to hear, before driving me back to the WASH. In the car, he explained, 'I just wanted to fuck you one last time.' He warned that he'd reported me for harassment. He claimed the police and my parents would be waiting for me back at the hostel and that I would be kicked out. Violated once again by Khan, I now felt scared, as well as ashamed. No one would believe me. When we reached the hostel a police car pulled up behind us. An officer knocked on the window and asked Khan if he was OK. He replied that he was and the police went away.

Pathetically, I nodded my thanks to Khan for not following up his complaint. Back in my room at the hostel I cried. My fragile peace was shattered.

The following day, I hatched a cunning plan. I would record Khan talking to me, expose his behaviour and prove that *he* was harassing *me*, not me him. With my dwindling dole money, I bought a Dictaphone in town. I knew Khan would come for me again. He called on the hostel payphone and told me to come outside. I knew that if he came into the hostel, I could be kicked out, so I obeyed. But I first switched on the Dictaphone, which I hid in my blouse. When I got in the passenger seat, Khan saw the bulky Dictaphone almost immediately and snatched it, roughly. My plan was in ruins – my heart sank. Khan drove to town. 'I'll show you what a Dictaphone's for,' he promised smugly. As he parked up, Mum's boss from the card shop walked past and saw us together. This was not turning into one of my better days. Khan went into *The Planets*, an amusement arcade, while I stayed in the car. If I escaped, he would only turn up at the hostel.

The Planets was named after HG Wells' novel, *War of The Worlds*, in which the Earth is conquered by Martians whose invasion kicks off at Horsell Common in Woking. *The Planets* housed the usual fruit machines, pinball tables and other games, as well as a bar. The crowd was young, supposedly over 18, white and Asian – some kids bunking off college, older men up to no good. It was particularly popular with Asians because you couldn't see in from the outside, unlike the *Wetherspoon's* pub and the sports bar opposite, so they wouldn't be spotted drinking and smoking by disapproving parents. Drugs were dealt in *The Planets*, too. I used to go there occasionally with Moonie. Recently, I'd been a couple of times with Julie. Ironically, I felt safe there because of the cameras – I didn't know Khan also went there. Khan was in *The Planets* for about half an hour. When he returned, he didn't seem quite so pleased with himself and threw the Dictaphone back at me. 'See what people are saying about you?' he said in mock disgust. The day got a little better – Khan didn't rape me, but kindly dropped me off near my parents' house, about two miles away from the hostel. Back at the hostel, I listened to the tape – nothing.

Many months afterwards, I listened to the other side and there it was – Khan's recording. Khan had flipped the cassette. Oddly, the recording is fifteen minutes into the tape. But now I have it on MP3, with copies – Khan's voice from 1998. The first speaker is a young woman. Khan follows.

'What's the idea, then?'

'Was anyone looking for me? In the last couple of days?'

'Yeah, Kaalia, Shaf, Khaliq, Jamal.'

'No, any Asian girl? You live in the WASH don't you?'

'No. Sunita?'

'Who's Sunita?' asks Khan.

'Your ex. Indian girl. Asian girl?'

'I don't know her.'

'You DO know her. Kaalia was telling me you had a relationship with her and you were nearly married. And she's changed her name.'

'Where's she living?'

'Near the WASH. Her friend Julie lives in the WASH.'

'I – I don't know a girl with that name. Someone called at my workplace.'

'This girl, Sunita, she's small, small Indian girl, very pretty, very short.'

Khan gets straight to the point. 'Have you spoken to her?'

'No, I've seen her though. But Kaalia was saying you, er, you had a relationship with her.'

'Does she go with anyone then?'

'Kaalia was saying she loved someone, but he won't tell me who.'

'*(Inaudible)* ... went out with who?'

'Sunita is in love with somebody, but I don't know who. *(Inaudible)* ... not going out with anyone.'

'This ... Sunita,' Khan pauses. The girl laughs. Khan continues. 'I don't know her. I'm not even from round here. Is she from round here?'

'I think so ... *(Inaudible)*. Jamal knows her.'

'Does he? Alright, you do me a favour, yeah? You tell Jamal, right, to keep away from her.'

What's the idea then? It may be that Khan is using the Dictaphone openly, so the girl wonders why. I think she's a certain white girl who knew Jamal and his crowd. – Chantal? Charmaine? Champagne? According to Julie, Champagne was threatening to knock me out because Jamal's crowd took me to Guildford. She was jealous of me being on her turf, although I wasn't looking for a boyfriend. She obviously knows Khan, even taking messages for him like a secretary. Oddly, Khan's accent in the recording is Asian, in contrast to the English accent he used with me. Champagne also seems to know a lot about me, although we'd never spoken. She says I'm in love with someone. I had made up a secret love interest to ward off a couple of guys at Mumtaz's place. What was Khan up to with the recording? I don't think he really had time to plan anything as he'd only just discovered the Dictaphone. He seems to be digging for dirt on me, but the recording seems to backfire. Khan alternates between asking questions about me and denying any knowledge of me. But Champagne knew about me and Khan and enjoyed teasing him. *You DO know her.* At one point, she seems to be laughing, maybe at the Dictaphone, maybe at Khan's lies. Khan would have hated this – he liked to be in control. At the end of the recording, all pretence evaporates as Khan issues a clear warning intended for Jamal's ears.

'You tell Jamal, right, to keep away from her.'

I hadn't told Khan anything about Jamal and his clumsy pass at me – not that there was much to tell. The recording is two minutes long, but Khan was in *The Planets* for about half an hour. I suspect he'd heard something about me and Jamal before the recording took place, perhaps before he entered *The Planets*. Maybe Jamal had expressed an interest in me and this got reported. I don't think Khan was happy with the recording. Maybe I wasn't supposed to hear it – he just threw the Dictaphone as a gesture. Did he try and delete the recording, but accidentally missed this extract? But then why flip the tape? Whatever his thinking, the tape demonstrates that Khan was prying into my personal life and making a thinly veiled threat to another man to stay away from me.

The following day, Khan turned up at the WASH in his Capri and called me on the payphone from my mobile. I was terrified he would get me kicked out, so I quickly ran outside. Khan's visits aside, I had some peace of mind at the WASH – I wouldn't have known where to go if I couldn't live there. He was parked right next to the hostel and had Jamal in the back of the car. Khan ordered me into the front passenger seat while he sat in the driver's seat. Turning to Jamal, Khan grabbed the top of his Kappa tracksuit with his left hand. With the palm of his right, he slapped Jamal's face hard, repeatedly.

'SHE'S … MY … WIFE … FUCKING … STAY … AWAY … FROM … HER!'

Jamal offered no resistance – Khan's reputation for violence preceded him. Then he grabbed my foot and lifted it up, twisting my whole body in the process. He screamed at

Jamal. 'Kiss her foot!' Jamal's lips caressed my trainer.

I was scared as well as sorry for the humiliated Jamal, who now stammered, 'I'm – I'm sorry. I only kissed her like a sister.' Khan couldn't have known about the kiss, such as it was. Jamal's needless confession earned him several more hard slaps across his already bright red face, before he was dismissed.

Khan shouted at me at first, but then smirked before boasting, 'Look at the respect I command!' He then drove me to St Peter's Hospital and told me to stay in the car while he went in to see the Windmill Team for his counselling session. After about half an hour, he came out and ordered me to get out of the car. He looked towards the window of the Windmill Team and smiled at me, put his arm around me and kissed me, as if putting on a show for someone in the building. Khan wasn't one for kissing – rape, torture and cuddles, yes, but not kissing. 'I love you,' he said. Then, quietly, Khan asked me, 'How could you? How could you tell them about the twelve-year-old?' before adding, chillingly, '*No one* will believe you. I will *make sure* no one ever believes you.'

Chapter 18

ONE FLEW OVER THE CUCKOO'S NEST

The next morning, I went into Woking to cash my fortnightly giro and do my shopping. When I returned to the WASH, I was called into the office and informed that, regrettably, I would have to leave because Khan had found me. My place in the WASH was conditional on him not doing so. Only in 2015, from hospital notes, did I discover that Khan had threatened to petrol bomb the hostel. I felt a lump in my stomach. I'd come to the WASH partly to escape Khan and now he'd ruined that. I rang my friend Lindsay on the payphone. She kindly offered to put me up. I went upstairs to pack my things – clothes, plant, painting material. The rest of the day is a blur. While in my first-floor room packing, I heard two voices downstairs. Khan and Mum arguing, baiting each other. I'd had three weeks without family contact. I ran downstairs and could see Khan through the opaque glass window of the door. Mum taunted him. 'I'll marry her off in India now!' I didn't know what to do. I called Lindsay again.

'Just get a taxi. We'll pay,' offered Lindsay. Then Mum came into the hostel. I told her I was leaving and to stay away from me. Mum was fired up from her confrontation with Khan and now turned her fire on me.

'Ha! You got nowhere to go. What you gonna do?'

'I'll stay with friends.'

'You don't have any friends,' scoffed Mum. 'Time to marry you off.'

Although Lindsay had offered me a lifeline, I suddenly saw no way forward. Khan would never leave me alone. There was no one to protect me from him and my family's solution appeared to be marriage to a stranger in India. The fragile peace I'd acquired before Khan returned was built on shallow foundations and I now broke down, shouting at Mum, 'Stay away or I'll kill myself.' Mum just mocked me.

'Ha! You can't even do that properly. No one want you anyway.'

Mum's taunts raced around my head as I ran upstairs. Locking myself inside my room, I decided to end my life. It wasn't planned, but I meant it. I say it wasn't planned, but I already had the pills. I'd made provisions to commit suicide, just in case – suicide was always on the cards. The last year had been hell with Khan, the abuse and the hatred from Mum and Dilip. Now something snapped – I'd had enough. I took a cocktail and quantity of pills, which would normally be guaranteed to do the job. I'd been saving diazepam, prescribed for anxiety attacks, in twos and threes and I had thirty coproxamol, a painkiller no longer prescribed in the UK because of its frequent use in suicide bids. To begin with, I took the pills one by one over the sink with bottled water, so as not to be sick on the floor. Then I heard Mum's voice and the hostel manager's as they came up the stairs. I barricaded the door with a bedside table and began taking handfuls of the pills, chewing them. I remember the sour, chalky taste as I tried to eat the pills as quickly as I could. I broke some disposable razors to cut my wrists and speed up the process further. I wrote Khan's name on my arm – a gesture, I suppose. *Happy now?* I wondered whether my organs would fail and thought there might be internal bleeding. As I started to lose consciousness, my eyes felt heavy like lead.

I've tried to explain what made me try to kill myself, but I don't want to justify attempting suicide. I didn't know life could get better, but eventually it did. Suicide was something Mum had often threatened. 'Oh, I'll kill myself.' So suicide seemed to be a possibility, an option, something mentioned fairly often, so not an unfamiliar phenomenon. But suicide is not glamorous, it's painful and it hurts others, especially those who care about you. When I look at my daughter now, when I hear her laugh and see her smile, I'm happy to be alive; glad I failed that day. To anyone feeling suicidal, I would beg them to seek help. You may feel alone, but many others have been there. Life is precious, and human life unique. I didn't see any way forward then, but the future is a mystery and things *can* get better.

The next few hours are hazy. I lay on the bed and looked around the room. I whispered, *sorry*, to the plant. In my head, I asked God to take me back. I remember Mum being in the room a bit later, packing my things and cursing me – 'Stupid girl.' I fell on the floor and had to be helped downstairs, where I heard Dad's voice. This was around 10 a.m. My eyes were shut – I remember motion and voices. I was taken to the doctor, who advised Mum to take me to hospital straight away. Instead, I was driven home. I remember being left alone in the car outside for a while – I didn't go inside the house. Billy and Shikta came out with Mum – Dilip must have been at work. Shikta said to Mum, 'Mummy, why does she look all funny?' I guess I was flopping about, kind of dying.

'Just let her die. I had enough now,' suggested Mum. Perhaps she didn't mean it.

'No, take her to hospital,' insisted Billy. 'You must take

her.' Then I remember Dad coming back out. He and Mum drove me to St Peter's Hospital in Chertsey. I was taken to A&E and admitted at 7 p.m., nine hours after the overdose. The hospital notes, which I now have, confirm, '*Mother admitted she wanted her dead.*'

* * *

I don't remember much about my treatment, so I must have been unconscious during it. I do recall Mum complaining that she was hungry. Later, Mum told me there were tubes sticking out of me. Next morning, I woke up in a strange bed. When I realised I wasn't dead, I was disappointed. Powerless, I couldn't even control my death, let alone my life. I hadn't thought of my suicide bid *not* working. I wondered if I was paralysed from organ damage and started to move my hands and toes. I was alive, but dead on the inside. My clothes felt funny, like they weren't on properly. I was wearing a tracksuit and felt in my pockets – I had no money. A woman stood at the end of my bed, swaying. She was about 40 with short brown hair and a piercing stare. She made imaginary scissors with her fingers. 'I'm going to cut your pretty hair off!' Her finger scissors cut the air as she swayed.

I didn't know where I was, so I went to the window. We were on the first floor and I could see rabbits in a field. I tried opening the window. 'Don't open it. They'll tell you off,' warned Mrs Scissor Hands. The window wouldn't open fully, anyway. Some staff came in and explained that I was in the Abraham Cowley Unit, the psychiatric wing of St Peter's Hospital in Chertsey. I'd been here before with Khan when he was attending one-to-one counselling for drug addiction. They returned my shoes, which, apparently, they had prevented Mum from taking. Hospital notes confirm this, and also confirmed that Mum had confiscated my money.

I shared a room with Mrs Scissor Hands. Outside our room, the ward was mixed. I walked past a man with his boxer shorts around his ankles doing a chicken dance. 'Bug, bug, bug, baargh!' In the recreation room, the other patients asked what I was in for.

'There's nothing wrong with me.'

'That's what we *all* say.'

One young man had tried to kill himself in front of a train. I'd read about him in the *Woking News & Mail*. He'd also tried to steal an ambulance with a screwdriver in a bid to escape. He said, 'If you make it out, that'll give us all hope.'

On my second day, a nurse told me that Surrey Police were on the phone. In fact, it was Khan. I wonder who'd told him I was there. 'Come outside. Oh, no you can't, can you? Look what your family have done to you.' Later, I was informed that Surrey Police had called again. They'd received a complaint from Khan that I was harassing him and told me I must stop ringing him. Yet, the hospital notes confirm I had no money to use the payphone. They also state that Khan had threatened to fire bomb the hostel. The notes also mention that Khan was known to the hospital's Windmill Team – the alcohol and drug dependency unit on the ground floor, below my ward. Records state that Khan was known for harassing young girls and had convictions for ABH (actual bodily harm) and GBH (grievous bodily harm). Perhaps I should have pointed out that Khan's phone was the one he'd stolen off me in the first place!

I've always assumed that the second call was the real Surrey Police, but it might have been Khan, too. Surrey Police called yet again. This time it definitely was Khan. He handed the phone to a male friend who told me stop harassing Khan, who then told me he had a child. 'Her mother's white!' he boasted. I could hear a child crying in the background. Khan hated white people. Come to think of it, he disliked black people, Indians and Bangladeshis, but this woman's skin colour was, apparently, a source of pride to Khan. Early in our relationship, Khan said that 'some white bitch' he slept with after a work function had claimed she was pregnant. He handed the phone to his white woman, Donna, who gleefully joined in the fun, accusing me of harassment. Khan then took the receiver and taunted me. 'She's got my kid. You'll never be a mum. I never loved you! No one will ever love you. You're nothing!' Then he said, '*Talaq. Talaq. Talaq.*' – I divorce you, three times.

From what I've read, my unwitnessed 'wedding' to Khan did not comply with Islamic Law. However, at the time I did think of him as my husband and he frequently referred to me as his wife. Although, he no doubt went through this divorce charade solely to humiliate me. It kind of worked for me. I felt I was no longer Khan's wife – a tie had been broken.

Mum and Dad came to visit with Dilip and Shikta, who brought me a Get Well Soon card with a kitten on it. Remembering that I used to like playing pool at college, Dilip asked if there was a pool table. 'Oh no. I s'pose not. You'd probably only bash each other over the head with the cues!' He'd obviously been saving this one, which seemed to be the funniest joke Shikta had ever heard. I was released after five days. Only recently did I discover that I hadn't been 'sectioned', which means I was a voluntary patient and could have left at any time, but I didn't know this then. According to Mum, the doctor who'd treated me in Accident and Emergency, advised Mum against putting me in the psychiatric unit, but she did it anyway. Mum drove me back from hospital. When we reached the front door, I went to hug her. I should have known better. Mum adapted an old

Indian fable to let me know where I stood in her estimation.

'If my Dilip or my Billy give me poison to drink, I drink it with smile on my face. Even if they cut out my heart, then they fell over, I ask if they OK, if they hurt. That's how much I love my boys. But you! You! I don't want you anywhere near me. I never hug you. Never. You better off dead.'

Chapter 19

LOOKING FOR MR. RIGHT

According to legend, in the days of the Mughal Empire, a daughter was born to a potter named Tulla in the Punjabi town of Gujrat. The girl, Sohni, grew into a beautiful young woman. Sohni would help her father by decorating his pots with pretty patterns and selling them. Gujrat was on the trade route from Central Asia to India and, one day, a wealthy Uzbek merchant called Izzat Baig, arrived in town with his caravan. When Izzat Baig saw Sohni, he was captivated by her beauty and fell head over heels in love with her. Izzat Baig decided to stay in town just to be near Sohni, and he sent his entourage on their way. He would make excuses to visit Sohni's store so he could see her and talk to her, constantly buying mugs and jugs. No longer a merchant, Izzat Baig became a buffalo herder and was known by the townsfolk as Mahiwal. Pretty soon, Sohni fell for Mahiwal and they began meeting secretly in the dead of night. But news of their secret trysts spread, causing a scandal in Sohni's community. She was supposed to wed one of her own kind, not an outsider, so her father arranged for her to marry her cousin, also a potter, who lived some miles away. Mahiwal was heartbroken and wandered far and wide looking for Sohni.

Eventually, Mahiwal found Sohni living with a husband, whom she despised, next to a lake. The reunited lovers were

overjoyed and Mahiwal took a hut on the opposite bank.
Sohni's husband was frequently absent and she would cross
the lake to visit Mahiwal at night, using a large clay water
carrier, a ewer, as a float.

One day, Sohni's sister-in-law spied her making her way to
meet Mahiwal. Instead of telling her brother, Sohni's husband,
the sister-in-law told her mother and the two hatched a scheme
to take Sohni's life. They replaced the ewer with another one
freshly made by the potter. That night, Sohni crept down to the
lake as usual and launched into the water with her vessel. The
clay hadn't yet dried properly and half way across the lake,
the ewer began to fall apart and sink, pulling Sohni under
the water. She let go off the ewer and lunged back up to the
surface. But Sohni couldn't swim. Mahiwal could see her from
the opposite bank as her arms flapped desperately in the water.
Mahiwal dived in to save his beloved, swimming with all his
might towards her. Sohni surfaced one more time and her eyes
met Mahiwal's. Then Sohni disappeared below the water for
the last time. When Mahiwal realised Sohni had drowned,
consumed with grief, he let the lake take him. So, perhaps the
star-crossed lovers were reunited after all.

* * *

Traditionally in India, marriages were arranged between
spouses chosen from the same religion and caste. People
rarely married for love. Now, many pick their own partner,
or at least have a greater say in arranged marriages,
especially in the UK. But, there are still many forced or
coerced marriages.

Once I was back home after my suicide attempt, Mum
and Dilip picked up where they'd left off in planning my
arranged marriage. I'd caused enough trouble. I was a

burden. Mum hired a photographer to take pictures of me in Indian clothes, and in English clothes. Traditional and modern. All bases covered, Mum and Dilip put these on the websites and posted copies to people. I was taken to see a holy woman in Southall, Reena Didi Mata, who danced and shook like a demon as her followers vied to touch her feet. Mum pushed my head down just above this lady's lap. Then we saw a *pandit* – a Hindu wise man – who instructed me to wear a yellow gemstone, which would ensure marriage within a year. The pandit predicted that if I cut my hair off, my marriage would fail. Mum thought this was an odd thing to say – I'd never worn my hair short before. We went to a temple in Southall where there were separate registers for boys and girls, which listed the caste, age, weight and height; a bit like racehorses, I suppose. A lady there, Bhattiya, said to Mum, 'Your daughter's very beautiful. I've got a daughter in Liverpool. I'll see if she knows any single men.' They exchanged phone numbers.

The home phone started to buzz with the mothers of prospective husbands. Mum was in charge. The Hindu marriage sites look a lot more consensual now, but, back then, Mum was vetting everyone. I heard her giving out my details – eye colour, date of birth, academic qualifications, bra size even. One mother declared, 'We don't like her name. We don't like names beginning with S.'

Another said, 'Oh no, she looks so nice. But she's born on Tuesday. She's *manglik*.' The definition in Indian astrology is more complex than just 'Tuesday', but, to some people, mangliks are considered unlucky and unsuitable for marriage, except to each other. Apparently, I'm double manglik. Well, I would be, wouldn't I? Oh, and I also have the *kaal sarp yog*, which means the planets formed the shape of a dragon when I was born, so bad luck times ten.

Twice, when my parents tried to arrange a birth chart for me on trips to India, the astrologer suffered a heart attack. This became a standing joke in my family. On a third occasion, a chart materialised, but it was invalid because the wise man had forgotten about British Summer Time, so it was an hour out.

Other families thought I wasn't educated enough because I hadn't been to university. But some were interested and most weekends, for several months, we were receiving visits from boys with their parents. Mum and Dad would give them tea in the front room while I sat on my own in the back room. The young men and I would be allowed five or ten minutes alone together. Some were nice, some shy, others seemed strange. One boy put his hand down his trousers and fiddled with himself. The cricket was on telly – I pretended to watch it. Mum visited the parents of another possible match, who apparently took great delight in showing off their furniture. Mum seemed a little put out but countered with our five-bedroom house when they visited with their son. The four parents drank tea in the front room, while the boy was sent to talk to me alone in the back. He said nothing but stared at me intently, while rocking backwards and forwards. I broke the ice. 'So, is this what you want? An arranged marriage?'

'Can you look after my children?' he replied.

'You've got children?'

'Not yet.' He carried on staring and rocking. We sat in silence for about five minutes, before Mum came and called us into the other room. In the kitchen, Mum asked me what I thought of him.

'He's a fucking weirdo!' I don't think I'd ever sworn in front of my parents before, but desperate times called for desperate measures. Fortunately, Mum saw him rocking straight afterwards. His parents were keen and pushy, calling the following day to say they were happy for the engagement to go ahead. They seemed desperate to get him fixed up. Mum refused.

'Stupid rocking boy and fancy furniture. You never marry him.'

Sometimes Mum and Dad would go to meet the boys first. There was one who Mum teased me about. 'He got Ferrari and motorbike. He really nice guy. He has lovely mum and sister. But he too nice. You'd really like him but he too kind. I'm going to say no. You not even meet him.' Perhaps there was some other reason, or they turned me down, but Mum decided to rub it in.

There was a guy from Southall called Jag whom I liked and came close to marrying. His family first visited in May, just before Dilip and Shikta moved out. Mum offered them some biscuits. Jag's father warned, 'Don't give them to my wife. She eats like an animal!' Dilip and Shikta burst out laughing while Jag looked embarrassed. His father announced that they were Khatris, the same caste as us, and proudly told us his family name.

'Ooh, ooh, same as me!' squealed Shikta. Mum's tea spurted from her mouth, while Dad slapped his forehead. As Dilip glared at them, Mum tried to retrieve the situation.

'Oh, same as our daughter-in-law. Jolly good!'

Jag's father asked Shikta where she was from. 'I'm from *Dilli*, but Mummy and Daddy are from Lahore.' Jag's father appeared to suffer from foot in mouth disease.

'Ah! Lahore. Pakistan. We don't like Pakistanis.' For once, Shikta was lost for words. Her family were Hindus who had fled Pakistan at Partition, like Dad's. Dad and I smiled at the irony.

Jag's brother had come along, too, and chatted with Dilip about their respective universities. A bit later, in the kitchen,

Shikta sneered childishly, 'You're *only* getting to marry that boy because of *my* husband's Oxford degree.'

Mum intervened, but not on my behalf.

'Huh! He *my* son first.'

Jag was allowed to date me for several months. He seemed nice and kind. But his parents did an astrological chart and discovered I was manglik, so they told Jag he couldn't marry me. Jag turned up at the house one day and said he didn't care about all that. He didn't believe in astrology and he wanted to marry me. But Mum told him that he couldn't go against his parents' wishes. Afterwards, Dad thought it just as well. 'Southall's too close. His parents are a bit funny. They might find out about you.' By which he meant Khan and the credit cards.

In September, we got a call from Bhattiya in Southall. Her daughter knew a family in Liverpool, the Tojals, who owned a business – clothes shops. Their eldest son was Ajay, aged 25. The family drove down from Liverpool one Sunday in October 1998. Ajay joined me in the back room while our parents drank tea. He seemed shy, childlike almost. We hardly spoke but he told me he liked Everton Football Club. After just three minutes, his mother interrupted. 'Come along, Ajay, we've got to go now.'

Events now moved quickly. Our families agreed we would wed. My parents liked the fact that the Tojals lived in a different part of England. So, although they were Punjabis from the same religion and caste, they didn't know anyone we knew and were unlikely to learn of my past. I would be away from Woking and a long way from Khan, should he ever return. Whether we were personally compatible was not considered a priority. I asked if I could date Ajay a few times like I did with Jag, but this time Mum refused. She didn't want any more time wasted. The *rokhna* took place in

Liverpool in November 1998. This confirms the betrothal and is a formal announcement that the prospective bride will no longer receive suitors. My parents brought gifts for the Tojals. Again, I didn't spend much time alone with Ajay. It was almost as if we were being kept apart. Eventually, we walked outside and sat in his Dad's car. I asked Ajay if there was anything he wanted to ask about me. 'No, the past is the past,' he replied. On the positive side, he didn't seem the controlling type, but I was apprehensive.

Chapter 20

EMPLOYEE OF THE MONTH

I discovered alcohol as a teenager at school. I used it to block out life – memories and fears. Alcohol became my crutch again. V, Khan, the abuse, my impending arranged marriage – booze helped them go away, but only for a while.

* * *

Just a week after I was discharged from hospital following my overdose, Shikta and I both got temporary data entry jobs with CCI, a credit control company. After a few days, they decided to let Shikta go – I don't think she had much office experience. I explained to our manager, Steve, that she was my brother's wife and this would cause problems for me at home. I asked if they could fire me, instead. I figured I would find another job and there would be one less reason for Dilip and Shikta to hate me. But Steve said Shikta was too slow, he couldn't use her. He agreed to let me go first, before Shikta. Then the company re-hired me a few days later as a receptionist, without Shikta knowing where I was. At CCI, I made some friends – we would go to the pub at lunchtime. I also had a supply of drinks in water bottles at work – vodka and tequila. Too much was unresolved, so I was blotting things out with alcohol – Khan, the situation at home with Dilip and Shikta, and my parents' plans for an arranged marriage.

After a couple of weeks, I decided to get a tattoo on my shoulder – *Om Namah Shivaya* (In the name of Shiva) – the Hindu mantra Pita Ji had taught me. It was partly an act of defiance. I was defying Khan – *Look I'm Indian.* If he came back, what could he do? Cut off my arm? I was also defying my parents. *I'm 19, I can do what I like, can't I?* Although, I didn't really feel that I could and wasn't going to show them the tattoo. But it was also a continuation of my self-harming – a release of pain, although it hurt like hell and I had a fear of needles. So, I had mixed emotions and motives. Next day at work, the tattoo was covered with cling-film and tape. I went to check out the tattoo in the toilets. A woman came in.

'Oh, is that a tattoo? Your parents won't like that, will they? Being Asian?'

Lots of British Asian girls have tattoos now, but this was 1998.

'I won't show them. No one will see it until I'm married off, and then it will be too late.'

'But your husband will see it?'

'No, he'll probably do it with the lights off.' My assumption was based on what Khan did. Then another girl joined us and they compared their tattoos.

Moonie got in touch around this time – I had a new mobile. He was married now, but we were always close. Moonie's baby son was very ill in Great Ormond Street Hospital in London. Then Moonie stopped calling and wasn't answering his phone. One morning, Mum shrieked excitedly, 'Come downstairs! Look what I got to show you! Your friend Moonie in paper. He been sent to prison!' Mum looked like the cat that got the cream. Moonie was in the *Woking News & Mail.* He'd been driving up to London to visit his baby son in hospital, but without a license, insurance, tax or MOT. He'd already been banned but had carried on – he needed to visit his son and the train was expensive. I was upset and couldn't help comparing Moonie's offence to Khan's crimes. Moonie wrote to me from prison. I replied, giving him my work address so Mum couldn't read his letters. A few weeks later, Moonie turned up at work. I'll never forget the sight. He had his possessions in a bag from the prison and I hugged him.

At home, Dilip and Shikta carried on much as before, taunting me about my looks or the credit card fraud. Once, when they were out, Mum had something else to show me. She'd gone in to Dilip and Shikta's room to reclaim the gold necklace she'd lent Shikta at their wedding in New Delhi and found a letter to Shikta from India, which she felt compelled to read. Parts of the letter were in Hindi and parts in English. Mum can read English in printed form – perhaps she'll read this – but she was having trouble with the joined up writing so she needed my help. I refused at first, but Mum got me fired up, telling me that Shikta had read my diary. According to Mum, Shikta had laughed about Pappu's advances, and had also complained that I didn't treat her with any respect in my diary! So, I read Mum the letter, which was of an intimate nature.

One evening, Dilip suggested a wager. 'I bet you ten grand she won't get married – no one'll have her!' Shikta was in fits. Finally, Dad stuck up for me. 'If you can't be nice to your sister, you'll have to move out.' Shikta chose the second option and they found a place to rent in Woking a few months later.

On Friday 19th February 1999, I stood trial at Guildford Crown Court for credit card fraud. Previously, I'd attended three hearings at Woking Magistrates' Court where, ultimately, it was decided the case was serious enough for the Crown Court. The next stage had been the preliminary hearing at Guildford, where I entered not guilty pleas to five specimen charges. We'd been through several solicitors and eventually ended up with a Sikh solicitor from Hounslow, whom I called, 'Uncle'. Privately, I opened up to him about the things Khan had done to me, things I couldn't discuss in front of Dad – the rape, the cigarette burns, the torture. The solicitor asked me to obtain a medical report from Mum's doctor, which detailed the scars on my back and elsewhere, mementoes of Khan. He also arranged for a psychiatric report, which described my low self-esteem and where I discussed V and my sexual abuse as a child. When Dilip and Shikta moved out, Shikta redirected her post, but we shared an initial and a surname, so my letters, including correspondence from my solicitors and the court, went to their address, much to Dilip's delight. On the morning of the trial, he popped around with a solicitor's letter, which he'd sat on for some time.

The week before the trial, my supervisor had refused me time off as unpaid leave – I'd used up my holiday allocation for earlier court appearances and seeing solicitors. With CCI being a credit reference agency, I felt it unwise to ask for leave on the grounds that I was being prosecuted for credit card fraud. So, for the trial I made up an excuse, but it came out all wrong. 'Can I have Friday afternoon off, please? It's my funeral.' My supervisor, who didn't like me very much, just looked at me as I tried to retrieve the situation. 'I mean … a close friend's funeral.'

She didn't look very convinced. It did feel like my funeral, though. The whole credit card business had been hanging over me since December 1997, when Dilip called in the police. But now, it was nearing crunch time. There was an almost permanent lump in my throat. I really believed I would be sent to prison, although I had mixed feelings on that, since I wasn't really looking forward to the rest of my life on the outside. In the morning, my fiancée, Ajay, had rung the house. This was unusual as he normally rang in the evening. Dad smelled a rat. 'Sunita, Ajay is on the phone. He normally rings at night. Have you told him something?'

'No, Dad. I promise you, I've not said anything.' I put the phone on loudspeaker so Dad could hear. He tried to remain silent but breathed heavily. Ajay explained he was going out that evening, so he wouldn't be able to call – mystery solved.

At work, my supervisor was on fine form. Dragging a heavy mail bag across the floor, she sighed, '*Ooff*, it's so heavy. Like dragging a dead body. Oh, sorry, I forgot, you're going to a funeral!'

At lunchtime, I prepared to leave work and tidied my desk. Perhaps for the last time, I thought. Opening my water bottle, I downed the remaining neat vodka. I picked up the phone to call Moonie and began dialling, but had second thoughts. There was no point upsetting Moonie – this was my mess. Thinking of his time in prison, I was convinced that I, too, would be jailed. Dad was picking me up so I used a body spray to hide the smell of alcohol and cigarettes – vodka is not completely odourless. Dad looked sad and didn't say much on the drive to Guildford. I thought about Khan, the mastermind of our petty crime wave. What if he turned up in court? As Dad was pulling into the car park, I noticed the special van used for transporting prisoners. The possibility of prison loomed larger. Dad saw the prison van, too. He looked gutted – he knew I hadn't committed the crimes. I wondered which seat would be mine.

Inside the court building, a colleague spotted me, Reggie. I didn't know him well, but he and his girlfriend had helped me on a work arranged booze cruise to France, where I drank too many neat Jack Daniels. Dad had allowed me to go on the trip so that I could buy him a crate of duty free Stella lagers. 'Dad, he works with me. I need to ask him not to say anything at work, in case I don't get sent to prison.' Dad and Reggie shook hands. I tried to make a joke.

'Fancy seeing you here.' It turned out that Reggie was standing trial following a pub brawl. We agreed to keep each other's secrets – Reggie is not his real name.

Eventually, my barrister arrived and took me and Dad into an office. He asked what holy book I would prefer to swear on. It turned out the court didn't have the Hindu holy book, *Bhagavad Gita*, so it was agreed I would use a bible. The barrister thought I had a good chance of getting off because of extenuating circumstances. I wasn't so sure. We were still here after all those hearings, so it seemed to me that the prosecution were winning so far. Three days were pencilled in for my case if I pleaded not guilty. I couldn't face the trial and didn't want Dad to hear about the details of my abuse – the rape, the cigarette burns and the beatings. They were all in the paperwork, but Dad hadn't wanted to read any of the details. Weighing up the prospect of prison against a further drawn out process, I wasn't sufficiently in love with my life on the outside at the time to fight for my freedom. I just thought I'd get it over and done with and decided to plead guilty. On the pros side, prison would put paid to an arranged marriage. No one would want me after that. I didn't let Dad or my barrister in on my change of plan.

A court official called out my name. I looked at Dad. The barrister explained that I had to use a separate door, while he and Dad used the main door. I crept nervously into the court room, where I was shepherded towards the dock, raised up from the body of the court. This was it – I was on trial. *The accused.* The atmosphere was eerie, out of this world. The barristers wore wigs made of horses' hair. The only sound was the court stenographer typing. I looked around for Dilip and Shikta, the 'victim' of crime and his beloved. Dilip and the infamous tracksuit bottoms. They weren't in court. I even imagined Khan might be in the public seats, turning up to see if I incriminated him, or maybe just there for a laugh. But he wasn't there, either.

'All rise,' intoned the court clerk, and I rose to greet the judge, who arrived in a long wig. The clerk asked me to confirm my name and date of birth. My voice shook as I whispered, 'Sunita W–, 4th July 1978.' We sat. Then, Judge John Michael Bull QC addressed me from his bench at the opposite end of the court room. He explained kindly that the charges against me would be read out and I needed only to answer guilty or not guilty to each charge. The judge asked me if I understood. 'Yes, Your Honour.' I dug my fingernails into my hands, trying to remain composed. Then the court clerk began.

'In the matter of count one, obtaining services by deception, how do you plead?'

I paused. A tear ran down my cheek as I replied, 'Guilty.'

Then came a voice from down below. Dad wasn't having it. 'No! No! She didn't do this. It's not her fault. Please listen.' The judge looked at Dad and asked for quiet in court before the clerk continued to list my alleged crimes.

'In the matter of count two, obtaining services by deception, how do you plead?'

'Guilty.'

I was prosecuted for a sample of five crimes that had occurred between September to November 1997, out of a total of thirty-five charges on file, some of which were from 1998, after I'd left Khan.

Dad sobbed as I pleaded guilty to all five charges. The court clerk told me to be seated. Dad's crying became more audible. The judge told Dad to be quiet again. I couldn't stand it – I wanted it over and done with. There were gasps in court as I stood up and said my piece.

'Please, Your Honour, don't make my dad cry anymore. He's gone through enough. Please, just put me in jail.' The court clerk warned me not to speak in court.

Judge John Bull spoke. 'No, I'm not going to send you to jail. It's clear you didn't commit these crimes on your own. I have read the evidence.' Addressing the police prosecutor, he asked, 'Why is Miss W here? She shouldn't be here? Where is Mr Khan?'

'We don't know, Your Honour. He left the country.' Throughout the build-up to the trial, the various meetings with solicitors and the earlier hearings, I didn't know whether Khan would be prosecuted, nor where he was. I hadn't seen or heard from him since my overdose attempt and our telephone 'divorce' ten months earlier. The newspaper report of my trial states that he was in Pakistan. He could equally have been in Birmingham. Either way, he lay low for a while and avoided prosecution.

In the witness stand, Dad placed his hands together in supplication and, through tears, appealed to Judge John Bull. 'She didn't do this, Your Honour. He is a very bad man. He did bad things to her.' Dad explained how I didn't eat when I was with Khan and outlined my plans for an Indian wedding in May. He also told the Judge of my 'Employee of the Month' award at work.

Judge John Bull summed up the case. 'Quite clearly, you have been carrying the can for Mr Khan.' Glancing at the police prosecutor meaningfully, he added, 'It shouldn't be *you* here. However, as you have pleaded guilty to all five counts, I have to sentence you.' Adding a cautionary note, His Honour continued, 'There comes a time when you have to say, "No".' I was given a twelve-month conditional discharge, fined and ordered to pay costs. Far from being delighted, I just saw the arranged marriage looming closer.

We bumped into Reggie again after the trial. 'I escaped jail by a whisker!' he told me cheerfully.

Back home, about twenty minutes later, Dad took all the paperwork from the court case and burnt it in the back garden in a large oil drum, page by page, ashes to ashes, declaring, 'It's all in the past now.'

Mum returned from work and walked past me, remarking, 'Oh, she still here.'

I made the front page of the *Woking News & Mail* 'A WAIF-LIKE 20-year-old Asian girl from Woking, who succumbed to the pressures of a man twice her age to carry out various crimes of deception, appeared before Guildford Crown Court on Friday.' At least the article was sympathetic and quoted my barrister at length stating that I was, '… a vulnerable young lady, whose actions were completely out of character. She had got nothing out of it; her bank account had been drained of money. During her time with Mr Khan, she had been living in conditions of squalor. It was an impossible situation and the scars would take a long time to heal.'

The morning after the paper came out, I went to work. I was a receptionist so everyone saw me. Apart from Reggie, who exchanged a knowing nod, no one approached, but I felt their eyes on me. Waif-like Asian girl. Convicted fraudster. Removing my water bottle from my handbag, I opened it and took a swig of vodka. Employee of the Month.

Chapter 21
KNIGHT ON A WHITE CHARGER

Indians prize gold above all other commodities. Gold has long since served as an unofficial reserve currency, seen as a safe investment, a nest egg. The yellow metal is entwined in Indian culture, too. Gold is believed to bring good luck and is offered to the gods in Hindu temples. Gold jewellery takes centre stage at Indian weddings, too, both as a gift and as something to be worn as a display of prosperity. For many British Indians, the place to buy gold is Southall in West London, the heart of Britain's Punjabi community – Sikhs live there, predominantly, but also Hindus and Muslims. Coming from largely-white Surrey, a trip to Southall was always something exotic, an adventure often combined with a trip to Dad's relatives in neighbouring Hounslow. Dilip would play count the white man. Southall Broadway is alive with the colour, sounds and smells of the Punjab. Shops selling saris or jewellery nestle amongst the usual British high street stores and banks. Bhanghra and Bollywood music blare from passing cars, whilst the smells of tasty spices sizzling in the Indian restaurants and cafés conjure up visions of Lahore and Amritsar. When I started work, Mum encouraged me to invest in gold jewellery, something for a rainy day. Aged seventeen, I bought a gold set – necklace and earrings – which I wore at my eighteenth birthday party. I also bought a gold chain with three pendants, representing Hinduism, Islam and Sikhism. The shopkeeper was puzzled. 'Are you sure you want all three together?'

'Yes please,' I replied. 'I don't understand why we shouldn't all be together. We're all human, aren't we?'

'She stupid. She got Muslim friends,' explained Mum. There was also Rinku, a Sikh. But Mum saw the practical side, too, adding, 'Never mind, gold is gold.' Later, Khan kept the chain and the Allah symbol.

For my forthcoming wedding, there were further trips to Southall to buy more gold jewellery. Dad bought gold bangles, a wedding necklace and earrings from his *bhua's* (aunty's) shop, whilst I bought the *naath* – nose ring, *tikka* – head piece, as well as bracelets and more earrings. Mum bought various Indian outfits and insisted that I had my legs waxed, which hurt like hell.

In February 1999, Ajay came to Woking for a brief visit. We got a phone call from his family. He was at Euston Station, where the trains from Liverpool arrive. They wanted Dad to drive into the centre of London to pick him up. Dad was less than impressed. Why couldn't Ajay get the tube across London to Waterloo, then a train to Woking? But Ajay could no more have done that than climb Mount Everest. And it wasn't his fault. The family had put him on a train at Liverpool and he'd got off at the other end. Job done.

Ajay and I took a short walk to the newsagents to buy a soft drink. It was the week after the credit card trial and there was a pile of newspapers on the floor – *The Woking News & Mail* – with the headline 'Girl Influenced by Older Man.' Although I felt ashamed, part of me wanted Ajay to read the article, although, with hindsight, I know he would have struggled with that. After about two hours, Ajay's auntie, who lived in Hampton in Middlesex, came to pick him up.

Our engagement party – the *shagan* – took place at the Park Royal International Hotel in Warrington, near Liverpool, on 5th April 1999, just six weeks after the trial. This is a higher profile occasion than the rokhna and the Tojals put on a show. There were seven or eight hundred guests, all catered for with a free bar and disco. Presiding over the ceremony was a Hindu priest, who spoke Sanskrit, an old Indian language, rather than Punjabi, which would be used in a Sikh wedding. Our side of the family travelled by coach from Hounslow in West London, a centre of the Punjabi community. We brought five *thalis* – plates of food – together with gifts of gold jewellery for the Tojals. Dad washed Ajay's feet symbolically and placed a *tilak* on his forehead – a vertical smear of red paste applied on auspicious occasions. My older brother, Dilip, presented Ajay with a diamond ring, which my parents had bought from India. As bride-to-be, I wasn't present for this part of the ceremony. I appeared later, wearing a mustard coloured sari, which I'd chosen especially with sleeves to cover my Shiva tattoo. The Tojals gave me a lovely, pink *lengha,* a suit weighing ten kilos and comprising a long skirt and top. They also presented me with gold bangles, a necklace and earrings. Then followed the *chunni* ceremony, where Ajay's aunts made further gifts of gold, signifying my impending entry into the Tojal family. Then I was joined by Ajay, who placed the engagement ring on my finger, awkwardly. Then he looked away, enchanted by the pretty pink and blue balloons emblazoned with *Congratulations Sunita and Ajay.*

After the shagan, Ajay started to ring me at home every day. He sounded different. The same Liverpool accent, but more animated and chatty – more intelligent. I put this down to shyness when meeting me in person, and I started to feel a little bit better about marrying a stranger. Ajay told me he loved me and called me his princess. We were married at Weybridge Registry Office in Surrey, on 14th April 1999, about three weeks before the Hindu wedding, a year to the day since the overdose and two years to the day after Khan and I exchanged vows. The date of the ceremony was shrouded in secrecy until a few days before. Well, it was for me, because my parents feared I might run away. Or perhaps they thought Khan would gate-crash proceedings. Mum announced, 'You'll have to take Wednesday off work. You getting married.'

On the morning of my 'English' wedding, a hair and make-up artist arrived late, turned my hair into a beehive and also helped me put my orange and gold sari on. Mum complained, 'She done sari all wrong. Too late to change it. La, la, la!' The lady was from Gujrat, a different part of India, so my sari was Gujrati-style, with a drape hanging over my right shoulder rather than the left, so I stood out from all the other Indian women at the wedding. I wondered whether Ajay would kiss me in front of everyone. Mum frowned. 'Oh no. Your dad not like that. Not in public. Not before Indian wedding.' When the Tojals arrived, I wanted to talk to Ajay outside.

'Hi Ajay, what you said to me on the phone last night ...' but he ignored me and walked straight past. This seemed very odd. I'd been getting cards, supposedly from Ajay, saying, *I love you*, and now he wouldn't speak to me.

During the ceremony, Ajay started to drool. Only slightly, but it was a little off-putting. The registrar asked whether there was any reason we shouldn't be married. A couple of young children started to scream and everyone laughed. Maybe the children knew something. Then my wedding ring was too small. The engagement ring had been too big. Now he was forcing the ring onto my finger. Pushing and drooling. We exchanged vows, with some difficulty on

Ajay's part. Finally, the registrar announced, 'You may kiss the bride!' Ajay lunged towards me, grabbed me and kissed my lips with his already wet mouth. A few people cheered. My heart sank. I looked for Dad to show him I'd kept my promise, but couldn't see him.

Afterwards, my parents hosted a reception at the Scout and Guide Headquarters in Woking. This is where I used to go to Brownies, and where I had my 18th birthday party. After their Bollywood-style extravaganza the previous week, the Tojals seemed underwhelmed by the choice of venue, and our plastic plates and cutlery. We had sixty or seventy guests and my cassette player, although, to be fair, we still had the main Hindu wedding to come. Everyone was congratulating us, apart from Dilip and Shikta, who were smirking. Ajay sat playing with a napkin with a childlike smile on his face. Some people were now starting to see something wasn't right. One of Mum's friends said to her, 'What you've done to Sunny is wrong. Look at him!' Dad heard and came over.

'What's the matter with him? Why is he doing that?'

'Why don't you ask him?' I replied.

Dad approached Ajay and asked if he was OK. 'Yeah, I'm just waiting for me mam, like, so I can go to the toilet.'

Dad looked perplexed and came back to where I was standing. 'I don't understand it. I think he's waiting to go to the toilet. There must be a queue.' Apart from anything else, Dad had a problem understanding Ajay's Liverpool accent. Presently, Ajay's mother, Behnji, appeared and escorted her son to the bathroom. Behnji means big sister – that's what everyone called her.

People were waiting for food and nothing was happening, so I went to help in the kitchen. Shikta had offered to sort the food out but apparently changed her mind. Someone said, 'Sunny, you shouldn't be doing this. Where's your brother's wife. Why isn't she helping?' I accidentally burnt my hand. Dilip came in. 'I thought Shikta was here? Oh … Sun's burnt her hand.' He seemed genuinely concerned. Later, cooking duties over, I left the kitchen and re-joined the party. Dad looked relieved. 'Oh, I thought you'd run away.'

I tried to talk to Ajay outside, but he ignored me, again. I was beginning to suspect that the person telling me he loved me on the phone was not Ajay, but possibly one of his cousins or uncles. Looking back, it seems probable Ajay was told not to speak at any of the ceremonies. His mental incapacity was to be covered up as far as possible until we were married. Eventually, the Tojals and their guests boarded their coach back to Liverpool. I wouldn't be joining them until after the Hindu wedding, so tonight was not our wedding night. It was time to say goodbye for now. All eyes were on us and, just as Ajay was preparing to kiss me on the lips, I dodged in and kissed his cheek, saying, 'Bye.'

'I'll see you on our wedding day,' replied Ajay.

'OK,' I said.

'I'll see you on our wedding day,' he repeated, as if it were a prepared speech. I went back inside the hall and began tidying up.

The next day, I went back to work legally married. Colleagues asked why I wasn't on honeymoon. Taking a swig of vodka from my water bottle, I explained I still had the Hindu wedding to go.

On 1st May 1999, the day before my Indian wedding, Dilip and Shikta arrived at the house early, adding to the already tense atmosphere. I wanted to go out and buy some cosmetic tweezers, but Mum said I wasn't allowed. Dilip said, 'I bet she doesn't go through with it. She'll do a runner and let you down again.' Shikta chuckled joylessly. Dilip added, 'Mind you, he is a retard, so I wouldn't blame her!'

I had no intention of running off. Dad told Dilip to be quiet. 'You're not helping.'

The *mehndi* lady arrived to apply henna to my hands and feet. This is an ancient tradition – the henna symbolises the inner sun and the outer sun. Its colour is supposed to deepen over the following hours, which is why it is put on the day before the wedding. Shikta sulked. 'Why can't I have henna?' Me, me, me.

'Because not your wedding!' replied Mum sharply.

'Let her have some,' I said. It made no difference to me. When Shikta left, she turned to me, smiled and wiped her henna off.

As with Khan, marriage would entail a wedding night and sex. At this time, my experience of sex consisted of being sexually abused as a child by V and raped regularly as an adult by Khan. I asked Mum if I could have counselling, but she refused. This wasn't something Indians did. Now, of course, I wouldn't think I needed anyone's permission, but, then, I was living under my parents' roof, a kind of broken refugee from Khan. I no longer had the confidence to go and seek help alone. My fear of the wedding night grew as the big day approached. There was no one in the family I could talk to.

About fifty women arrived at the house to commence festivities with the *chura* ceremony. Chura are red and cream ivory bangles, which are washed in milk, placed on the bride's arms and worn at the wedding. Although, nowadays, thankfully, plastic is used. Female guests touch the chura, wish the bride luck, perhaps give words of advice, and tie little gold-plated or silver ornaments to the bangles. Traditionally, the bride's *Mama-Ji* – her mother's brother – provides the chura, so my uncle Bantoo Mama, who was visiting England at the time, performed this role.

We played CDs of Punjabi folk songs, to which the crowd sang along. By tradition, I wasn't allowed to try the bangles on beforehand. I have very skinny arms – 'waif-like', as the local newspaper might put it – but relatively broad wrists. The bangles the guests slid on to my arms were becoming progressively narrower. So, whilst the first few destined for near my elbow fitted perfectly, the smaller ones wouldn't go around my fist. I was squeezing my hand in tightly over my thumb, but the bangles started to cut me. I didn't want to let everyone down so I carried on. Blood was now dripping into the milk. The singing continued. I started to panic. Everything was coming to a head. I was marrying a virtual stranger tomorrow. I wanted to do this for Dad, but now I felt despair. The lovely music contrasted with the pain on my hands and the trickling blood. I'd completed my right arm and was now doing my left arm. Dad could see something was wrong. 'Leave it! The bangles don't matter. You've got most of them on.' The milk was streaked with blood. I felt everyone staring. I stood up and left the room with a handful of bangles to finish the job in privacy. Dad followed me into the hallway and put his arm around me. 'Leave the bangles.'

'I'm doing this this for you, Dad.'

I composed myself and we returned to the throng. Someone commented, 'She's only got half the bangles on one side.' I'd managed the regulation twenty-one bangles on my right arm but only nine on the left.

'Oh, she *Daddy's* girl,' Mum explained sarcastically. 'He say she doesn't have to. I don't know *what* Tojals will think.'

My wedding took place on the same date my parents got married. I used to buy wedding anniversary cards from my parents to each other. This time around, I couldn't because I wasn't allowed out. On the morning of the wedding, Mum was unhappy that she hadn't received a card from Dad. She didn't buy him one, either, despite working in a card shop, but maybe that wasn't the point. So, the atmosphere was already frosty when we received a call from Liverpool to say that Ajay's father had been taken to hospital. He needed an emergency operation on his nose and wouldn't be able to attend the wedding. 'Drink probably,' sniffed Mum. Dad felt sorry for Mr Tojal. It was unheard of for a man to miss his son's wedding and Ajay was the eldest boy.

'Will the wedding still go ahead?' I wondered aloud to Dad, secretly hoping it wouldn't.

'Yes, it's all booked now. Their coach will be leaving soon.'

Mum phoned various people to float her theory. 'He probably been drinking too much. La! La! La!' Dad kept telling her to be quiet. I asked her why she was making up rumours. 'Well, what else could it be?' Mum didn't need any evidence.

Dad exploded. 'Shut up, you stupid woman! Leave the man alone. How many more times? You don't know what's wrong with him. BEWAKOOF!'

* * *

Our Indian wedding was held at The Four Pillars Hotel in Osterley, West London, on 2nd May 1999. Two coachloads of Ajay's family and friends drove down to London from Liverpool. Others travelled under their own steam from there and elsewhere, including India and Canada. Like Dilip in New Delhi the previous year, Ajay rode in from nearby on a white mare, Punjabi style. The bride isn't supposed to watch the groom's arrival procession, the *baraat*, so I was confined in a hotel room. But I can describe events from the wedding video. It was a sunny, spring day as the party kicked off with the *dhol* man, playing a two-headed Indian drum. The young men from the north, in their smart dark suits, danced joyously to his rhythms in the streets and car park outside the hotel. Two young cousins acting as bridesmaids left me alone to go and watch the fun. The dhol's two heads produce a bass sound from one end, and a higher, tinny sound from the other; almost a melody. The drummer's song penetrated the hotel walls, as if seeking me out, speaking to me. I felt a knot in my stomach. Outside, Ajay wore a traditional Indian costume, including a *sehra* – a headdress with hanging beads and flowers. Normally, the strings of beads are spaced out, but Ajay's face was entirely covered so he couldn't see. He had to be guided towards the horse and lifted onto her. To his front sat a young boy, a relative who acted as his groom, dressed in an identical outfit – Ajay's 'Mini Me'. Ajay's female relatives then tied sacred threads to the reins of the horse, his mother Behnji presiding proudly, before he made the short journey to the wedding venue. Ajay's father was absent with his mysterious nose problem.

The drumming and dancing continued until the *milni*, when my male relatives came out of the hotel to greet Ajay's family with a garland of flowers, and a Hindu priest joined proceedings. Neither of my two grandfathers, nor Dad's brothers, my *chachas*, travelled from India, but Dad had more distant male relatives in attendance from nearby Hounslow. My brothers, Dilip and Billy, Mum's brother, Bantoo Mama, and some other London-based relatives of hers completed the family contingent. As the bride's father, Dad wore a pink turban, while Ajay's close male relatives wore bright red headdresses. Men from each family took turns to bear hug a counterpart from the other side, one attempting to lift the other from the floor in a good-humoured test of strength.

I now made my appearance for the *jai mala* ceremony, which took place outside the hotel. As I walked nervously down the hotel steps, I was a little disconcerted to see Ajay's face completely hidden behind the beads. I tried speaking to him, but he remained silent behind his mask. Under instruction from the priest and our mothers, we placed garlands of flowers around each other's necks. This signified my acceptance of Ajay as my husband. We then went inside the hotel for further rituals. Auntie Anita in India had foretold that marrying on the same date as my parents would bring bad luck, and, for the superstitiously minded, our wedding was beset with such ill omens. According to tradition, richly-coloured henna on the bride's hands means she will be welcomed warmly into her new family. The henna on my hands was barely visible. 'Ooh, look how pale her henna is,' chirped one guest, disapprovingly, as she viewed the anaemic efforts of my mehndi lady. Our priest was a last-minute replacement for the first choice, who had been taken ill. Hindu priests – *pandits* – come from the Brahmin caste and can earn a good living handling the religious aspect of weddings and funerals, and conducting havans (blessings on special occasions). The substitute priest may or may not have known the correct Sanskrit – who would have known? – but he kept getting our names wrong, much to Dad's annoyance. We were instructed to put certain items in a sacred fire. Ajay found this very confusing and kept making mistakes. Then the fire went out, unexpectedly. Several guests gasped as black smoke belched from the pot, causing me to cough.

The producer of the video super-imposes a still shot of me at regular intervals throughout the film. In this, I bear the traditional nose ring of an Indian bride – the *naath*. I look sad and helpless, as if carried along by events, which makes it a pretty accurate portrayal. Perhaps the cameraman thought I looked 'dreamy'. I had approached the wedding with apprehension. This was not a consensual arranged marriage – I had no input. I felt I was an embarrassment, a burden being passed on to a stranger. Anxious about moving to a different part of the country, the prospect of sex with Ajay frightened me, too. So far in my life, 'love-making' had not been a pleasurable experience, but I was resigned to my fate. Suicide hadn't worked, I hadn't been imprisoned for fraud, and I had now promised Dad I would go through with the wedding. I saw no other option. No one briefed me on protocol, the order of events, where and when to stand or sit, so I didn't know what to expect. I was accompanied by two female second cousins around my age. But I barely knew them and really had no one to confide in. In the film, Mum can be seen constantly yapping in my ear, telling me to go this way or that. I smile briefly when I joke to my cousins about escaping through the fire exit. Mum and others pull me and prod me in various directions. I am passive, resigned to my fate.

The video triggers further memories of the day. In the *kanyadaan* ritual, Dad literally gave my hand in marriage to Ajay. We also 'tied the knot', again literally, with two long, pink, cotton scarves around our necks, bound together. More ceremony. In the *saat phere*, Ajay and I walked seven times around the fire with four guests acting as 'pillars' to support us, including Dilip, Billy and a friend of his. The fourth pillar was the Indian doctor who attended my suicide attempt and later suggested a marriage of convenience between me and his brother to enable him to live in the UK. We also had to tread barefoot on a path of rice. This brought back memories of walking on broken glass for Khan's amusement. As I hesitated, Mum snapped at me to tread harder and press forward. Then, I swapped places with Ajay to sit on his left, a symbolic statement that I was now his wife. Behnji presented me with a magnificent gold necklace. I belonged to the Tojals.

Ajay's headdress was removed and his face emerged, blinking into the lights. I looked him in the eye and spoke, trying to make a connection. I was now his wife, for better or worse. I felt very alone, so was trying to build a rapport with my new husband, making friends. Someone purporting to be Ajay had recently told me on the phone that he would treat me like a princess. But again, Ajay wouldn't speak to me face-to-face. He looked to the left, then to the right, like a beast in a zoo, but not at me. I don't know what Ajay felt at this moment. Perhaps he was as frightened and confused as I was. Tufts of hair were sticking up, which the pandit tried to pat down. Dad came over with a comb and attempted to tame Ajay's plumage. Ajay accepted this as perfectly natural – he was used to his mother, Behnji, doing this for him. The film highlights the change in my parents' demeanour, almost from the moment Ajay's mask is removed. Their concern was obvious. Their faces seem to ask, 'What have we done?' It's not as if they hadn't met him before, but I think the occasion and the sticking out hair left little room for doubt about Ajay's helplessness.

Eventually, Behnji marched Ajay away to change into Western clothes for the evening celebrations. He returned presently in a suit and tie, order restored to his hair. On the top table at an Indian wedding, the bride and groom, their parents and sometimes select older relatives, sit on one side only, facing the guests. Dilip and Shikta weren't scheduled to be there, but Shikta kicked up a fuss. Why wasn't she on the 'A List'? Although neither she nor Dilip spoke to me throughout the day, she wanted to be the centre of attention at my wedding and vied to appear in as many photos and video clips as possible. Mum didn't want to upset Dilip, so space was found for them at the top table. The video captures the sad spectacle of Dad perched on the end of the table, facing longways, looking like a gate-crasher at his own daughter's wedding. He had dispensed with his pink turban early on and appeared mainly with a pint of lager in hand. I don't blame him! Dilip sips fruit juice and chats with Shikta, while Mum looks uncomfortable next to her pushy daughter-in-law.

The call came for the first dance. The guests applauded as Ajay and I walked on to the empty dance floor, more as two separate lost souls than as a couple. I wore a *goonghat*, a headscarf which can be used as a veil, which is supposed to remain in place until the wedding night. When the music began, a shiver ran down my spine and I felt the eyes of the room on me. This was *our* tune, one Khan used to sing to me when he was being nice – '*Pyar Kiya Toh Nibhana*', which translates roughly as, 'You have loved, now keep the promise'. The track features in a 1998 Bollywood film – '*Major Sahib*' – but songs are released in advance of the films, so the recording came out in 1997. It wasn't all happy memories – a cassette of this was also playing the time he smashed my head against the dashboard. So, Khan made his appearance after all. Perhaps he was there all along – the ghost at the banquet.

The song is about promises between lovers. The first two lines, translated from Hindi, are …

Becoming crazy, my heart tells you time after time
Even for a moment, darling, don't go far from me

A lump leapt to my throat. It was now my turn to wear a mask. Pulling my veil down to hide my tears, I buried my head in Ajay's shoulder.

Ajay promptly ripped my veil off, roughly, earning a stern telling off from his mother. This was considered dishonourable, but he didn't know any better – maybe he thought it was romantic.

We were then joined by the other guests and the dancing continued with Bollywood hits, *bhangra* (modern Punjabi dance music) and Western pop songs. Some of the young female guests tried their hand at solo Bollywood-style dance performances. Then guests formed a circle and danced the hokey cokey to Kool &The Gang's '*Celebration*':

Cel-e-brate good times – COME ON!

* * *

Dowry is the payment in money or kind by the parents of a bride to her new husband's family. The practice is deeply rooted in many cultures worldwide, but has been illegal in India since 1962, although there is no statute law banning dowry in the UK. The final act in a Punjabi wedding ceremony is the *doli*, where the bride says farewell to her family and leaves to start a life with her new husband. But, before that, Behnji had a question – a real show stopper. 'What about the dowry?' The moment when she asks Mum, who then consults Dad, is captured exquisitely by the wedding photographer. My parents spent £35,000 on the wedding and had made the traditional offerings of jewellery, but there was no dowry. In the photos and video, Mum looks concerned, Dad embarrassed. He even opens his wallet, as if hoping for a miracle. Behnji is clearly not impressed. At our betrothal – the *rokhna*, my parents had asked the Tojals what else they wanted, to which they'd replied, 'Nothing'. But now, Behnji had changed her mind. Or perhaps they never really meant 'nothing' but said what was necessary to secure a bride for Ajay. We rose from the table and walked outside for the final goodbye.

In an unusual display of maternal concern, Mum warned, 'They want dowry. There's no more money. I don't know what they do to you.' This bombshell was the last thing I needed, but I couldn't back out now. I couldn't dishonour Mum and Dad.

In the video, Dad cries as he escorts me to the Tojals' car. His face is etched with pain as I throw rice over my shoulder from a plate held by the grinning Shikta. Even Mum manages to shed a couple of tears. It had been a long day. Dad was tired and emotional. He never really 'got' the Khan scenario, believing I was either drugged up or bewitched by magic, rather than listening to me. But Dad loved me, stood by me in court at the credit card trial, and stood up for me against Dilip and Shikta. Like all of us, to some extent, my father is a product of his upbringing, and thought an arranged marriage was the best solution under the circumstances. Now, he was losing his daughter – his *Lakshmi* – and possibly having second thoughts about the choice of husband. I cry as I approach the car, telling Dad, 'I kept my promise.' The video shows Billy gently touching me, as if offering encouragement. We hugged. Dilip joined us, the three embracing for the last time before I joined my new family. I felt happy and sad at the same time. I would like to think Dilip was genuinely moved and not play-acting for appearances. Dad hugged me and we cried.

I joined Ajay in the back of his uncle's Jaguar and held my face to his body. We were driven around the corner and dropped off to join the coach party destined for Liverpool and my new life.

Chapter 22

A BOX OF CHOCOLATES

Two coachloads headed back to Liverpool in the early hours. Ajay and I sat with the womenfolk, whilst the rest of the men went in the other coach. Behnji sat behind us, periodically poking her head through the gap to whisper to her son. I asked Ajay how his father was. He didn't reply, which wasn't out of rudeness, he just didn't know what to say. Behnji answered for him, explaining about her husband's nose operation. Sitting by the window, I watched the night go by and wondered what lay ahead. I thought about Mum and Dad, Dilip and Billy, Woking, the only home I'd known, apart from Khan, and felt sadness at leaving. It had been a long day and I was emotionally drained. Khan's face appeared in my half-slumber. Sensing his anger, I shuddered and woke with a jolt. One of my wedding shoes turned up a couple of rows back – I'd slipped them off earlier. Someone found it and made a joke about Cinderella and Prince Charming. I considered Ajay, the giant man-child sitting next to me. I knew I had to make the best of things. As we neared Liverpool, at about 3 or 4 a.m., Behnji handed me a pocket mirror, snapping sourly, 'Sort yer face out, the cameras are ready.'

As the star attraction, Ajay and I were billed to leave the coach last, and were greeted by the blare of flashing cameras. Ajay looked left and right again, overwhelmed by the attention. Once inside the Tojal family home, there were further ceremonies and we played traditional Indian wedding night games. The women gathered around to watch while the men mostly drifted off for a drink or a smoke in the garden. First, I had to try and scoop some 50p coins from a small pouch. I suggested tipping them all out.

'No, you can't do that!'

'Didn't her mother teach her anything?'

I'd never seen the games before, and didn't really know what to do. Dilip and Shikta had more urgent priorities on their wedding night. The second game involved both Ajay and I trying to find a 50 pence piece in a large tray of milk. The loser tries to prise open the hand of the winner to take the coin. Some people play this with the wedding rings. It is sometimes claimed that the partner who triumphs at this game will have the upper hand in the marriage, but it's also a chance for the bride and groom to touch hands, supposedly for the first time. We had three goes. My heart wasn't really in it and Ajay found the first two coins. As I tried to retrieve the coin from him the first time, the guests sighed – *Woooh!* And *Ahh!* – as our hands met and Ajay opened his hand. I found the third coin. As Ajay tried to open my hand, I decided to resist. My grip is quite strong, so Ajay used brute force to pull my fingers back. 'Careful, Ajay!' gasped one guest.

One of the men shouted, 'Come on, love, lerrim 'ave it. I wanna go 'ome!' so I surrendered the coin. The final game involved breadsticks and jewellery. I was having trouble understanding the rules, which provoked much comment from the women.

'Ah! She's so simple!' cooed one of Ajay's aunties.

'I wonder what Ajay will be like with 'er tonight!' cackled another.

First up was Behnji. I had to pass breadsticks from my palms to hers. Then, she presented me with a box of jewellery. This process was repeated with Ajay's younger brothers, followed by other close relatives. All the while, one of the older women chanted a ritual commentary in Punjabi. In all, I received 15 boxes of jewellery – rings, earrings, necklaces and bangles. Behnji's eyes bulged at the treasure trove.

Ajay and I were to live in this house, along with his parents and two younger brothers. I went to use the downstairs toilet briefly. As I was washing my hands, Behnji came in, knocking on the door. 'Get out. We need to go upstairs.' There seemed to be some urgency, something she wanted to say or do, perhaps out of earshot of the guests. I followed her upstairs and into what turned out to be Ajay's bedroom. Like me, Ajay had a mini-temple to Lord Ganesh, pictures and statuettes, which Behnji instructed me to bow to. I knelt and bowed. Scowling, Behnji growled, 'I'm 'avin' that.' She grabbed my nose ring, the *naath*, and yanked it off. As I stood up, she went for my gold bangles. 'Them 'n'all.' Mum and Dad had bought the gold bangles, which are separate from the ivory, chura bangles. I tried to take them off myself to make it easier, but Behnji wouldn't let me. She pulled the bangles off forcibly, causing my hands to bleed again. This was all so unnecessary. I could have given her the jewellery, but Behnji needed to show who was boss.

Behnji shoved me. 'Now, go downstairs. You're gonna be taken to a hotel now.' The wedding night. No escape. Behnji called for Ajay and ordered her younger brother, Robbie, to drive us to the hotel. Family members and guests followed us out to say their goodbyes. Behnji provided us each with a back pack. I didn't know what was in mine, but it seemed Behnji was planning her son's wedding night with military precision.

On the way to the hotel, which was in Warrington, neither Ajay nor I spoke. I was still in shock from Behnji's assault. To break the silence, Uncle Robbie tried to make us laugh with his repertoire of accents – Brummy, Geordie and so on. Then, in his own Scouse, 'Come on, princess, give us a smile! It *may* never 'appen!' At the hotel, Robbie checked us in, as if Ajay were incapable of handling such a complicated transaction. It was getting light, about 5:30 a.m., but check-out was at 10 a.m. It seemed we were there for one purpose, in and out, no fripperies, and too late for a candlelit dinner. When we entered the room, Ajay took one look at the double bed, jumped in the air and dive bombed face first onto it. I went to use the bathroom to compose myself, and to also put off the dreaded moment, but Ajay barged past me. When it was my turn to use the bathroom, I opened the backpack Behnji had given me. Inside I found a purple negligée and thong – Behnji's idea of sexy. I'd never had 'sexy' underwear – Khan didn't bother with such finery. I felt distinctly uncomfortable, like a lamb being dressed for the slaughter, but there was nothing else to wear.

Eventually, I re-joined Ajay in the bedroom. He was lying on the bed, motionless, facing away from me. I dimmed the lights, not keen on him seeing my revealing costume, or my scars. I called his name but he didn't answer, so I hoped he was asleep as it was getting on for 6 a.m. I decided to sleep on the floor. I crept onto the bed and took a pillow. But Ajay wasn't asleep. 'What you doin', like?'

'I thought you were asleep. I didn't want to disturb you.'

'Don't be silly, get into bed.' As I got under the sheets, Ajay suddenly pulled me towards him, lifted my nightie and climbed on top of me. He was big, almost a foot taller than me, and strong, so I couldn't move.

'Look, can we talk about this first?' I didn't want sex with

Ajay, but I especially didn't want it with no discussion.

'No, we've gotta do it. We've gotta do it. We've gorra get it over and done with.' Ajay seemed to be working to a script and now had my arms pinned – I was helpless. Just as I resigned to my fate, he got up abruptly.

Literally breathing a sigh of relief, I thought that, perhaps, I might be safe after all. But Ajay wasn't finished yet. He produced a red condom from his bag. I watched in horror as I beheld my husband stripping off his clothes and putting the condom on. Believe it or not, I'd never seen a fully naked man or a condom. Mum had excused me from sex education at school, and as for Khan, he didn't use contraception, or ever let me see him completely naked. He would be half dressed with me underneath him, or it would be dark. Ajay sat on the bed and played with himself for a couple of minutes. I looked away. Then he came for me, climbed on top again and raped me. It was all over in a few minutes.

Rape is rape, but Ajay's rape was much quicker than Khan's and was not accompanied by the same level of gratuitous violence, although he did drool over my face throughout the ordeal.

Afterwards, as I lay on the bed, sore, Ajay went to the bathroom. When he returned, he was flicking water off the condom, which he seemed to have washed, and he put it back in his bag. Being naïve, I didn't realise people washed and re-used condoms. Now I'm no longer naïve, I *know* they don't. Ajay sat on the end of the bed, ignored me and called his mother on his mobile phone.

'Mam, I've done it.' I heard Behnji ask Ajay to check for blood. She wanted to see if I was a virgin. Ajay inspected the sheets inch by inch, like a cartoon detective and found no blood on them, but some on the pillow cases. This came from my wrists where Behnji had yanked off the bangles. Ajay knew no better and reported blood to Behnji, probably not knowing why, before asking, 'Can I come 'ome now, Mam?'

'Yeah, I'll send your Uncle Robbie.'

'Can I have the chocolates now, Mam?'

'Yes, you can.'

'Do I 'ave to share 'em?'

'No.' Ajay retrieved a box of *After Eights* from his backpack, opened it and devoured the lot, his reward for a job done.

When he'd finished his *After Eights,* almost as an afterthought, Ajay fetched a necklace, gold with black beads, from his back pack. This was the *mangalsutra,* a sacred necklace worn by Hindu brides. The presentation of the mangalsutra is itself an important part of the wedding ceremony, traditionally symbolising the consummation of the marriage. ''Ere you go,' chirped Ajay, plonking the necklace into my hands. Who said romance is dead?

I showered and changed into *shalwar kameez.* Ajay and I sat apart in the hotel lobby, husband and wife, awkwardly silent for about an hour, until Robbie returned with one of Ajay's brothers to drive us back to the house. We skipped the hotel breakfast. In and out. Job done.

* * *

Back at the Tojals' house, there were still about ten guests. One woman had stayed at the hotel before and asked if we'd used the jacuzzi. I didn't respond. Behnji squirmed uncomfortably. Someone asked about our honeymoon. We were scheduled to fly to Bali, but I said I didn't think it was right to go whilst Ajay's father was in hospital. I wanted to visit him, so our honeymoon was postponed. Behnji told me I'd gained a lot of respect within the family by putting my father-in-law first. I think this was the last positive thing she said to me.

After a while, Behnji called me into a side room, away from the other guests. She had decided to lay down the law. 'Right. When you see me, you come over and you touch my feet. If you see me ten times in a day, you do that ten times. Every time you see me. Do you understand?'

Aarshivaad is the Indian custom of touching another's feet with the hands. People might touch the feet of a pandit or a guru, who in return touches the head to grant a blessing. It's a mark of respect, but it's also a two-way process, not meant to be demeaning. Younger family members touch the feet of elders, parents or grandparents, again in return for blessing. In families, this would normally be done as a greeting or on departure, not every time you walk into a room, ten times a day. Not everyone observes the custom these days, especially in England. Mum and Dad didn't practise foot touching at home. Ajay's parents were, in many respects, more westernised than mine – I think they'd been in the UK longer and Behnji spoke with a Liverpool accent – but Behnji was one of many control freaks to enter my life, and an extreme interpretation of the foot touching tradition suited her agenda and ego. She also dispensed with the blessing part, breaking her part of the bargain. So much for tradition.

As part of my induction into the Tojal household, Behnji informed me how she took her coffee – black no sugar. Sour. The reason for Behnji's hostility soon became apparent. 'Your parents should have given me dowry. I want dowry. I wanna washing machine.' Behnji already had a washing machine, but she wanted a new one from Mum and Dad. Since they hadn't provided one, I would have to wash all the clothes for the family by hand. But the washing machine was just one item on Behnji's wish list. 'I wanna dishwasher, ten grand in cash, and I wanna Mercedes with personalised number plates.'

Behnji proceeded to outline my other responsibilities. I was to do all the cleaning in the house and help prepare meals. My hands were still very sore and I wasn't expecting this. Indian brides are not supposed to lift a finger while their wedding henna is still visible, but Behnji only bought into those Indian traditions that suited her, like dowry. So, without any sleep since the night before my wedding, I was put to work as soon as the remaining guests had gone home. I felt as if this was my punishment – karma – for being with Khan, and that I had to accept it. I spent much of the first day of married life, indeed much of my time in Liverpool, on my hands and knees, cleaning skirting boards or over the sink, hand washing dirty underwear. But, it wasn't all housework and foot touching. During the course of the day, Behnji would make me change outfits. 'Go and put the blue one on.' A couple of hours later … 'Sunita, go upstairs and put the red one on.' To begin with, in the aftermath of the wedding, it was Indian clothes, *shalwar kameez*. Later, I wore western clothes, also of Behnji's choice. Through her son's marriage, it seems Behnji had gained not only a skivvy, but a doll, too. But what she really wanted was her dowry.

In the afternoon, Behnji ordered a coffee. Behnji put the cup down. ''Ere let me have a look at yer 'ands.' My hands were cut from the *chura* ceremony on Saturday and, again, from where Behnji had pulled the gold bangles off. There was now puss in the wounds. Behnji squeezed my hands spitefully. 'There's something wrong with you.'

In the evening, there were five for dinner, including Ajay's two teenage brothers. I helped Behnji prepare the meal, which she served at the table. For some reason, Behnji ordered me to sit apart from Ajay. Whilst Behnji was in the kitchen, Ajay regurgitated his food and spat it back onto his plate. His brothers shrieked, 'Eurggh,' and 'That's disgusting.' They'd probably seen this trick before, but were embarrassed in front of me. Ajay smiled sheepishly.

At half past seven, Behnji said, 'Come on, Ajay, it's your bedtime now. Up to bed.' I was astonished – he was 25 and being treated like a young child. I was still doing housework. Life is full of choices. Carry on with chores, or sleep with Ajay? At eight o'clock, Behnji chose for me, telling me to go to bed. I showered, cleaned my teeth, changed into pyjamas and, accompanied by a large dose of wishful thinking, slipped nervously into bed next to Ajay. He'd consummated our marriage the previous night, so I hoped that maybe he wouldn't be interested tonight. I was wary, but Ajay seemed to be resting. The bedroom door was open and the bedroom and landing lights were off, so it was dark.

At around nine o'clock, I heard creaking floorboards and flinched. Because of Khan, I'm sensitive to sounds. 'What's that?' I asked Ajay.

'It's me mam.'

I looked around and saw Behnji silhouetted in the doorway, just standing there, silently. 'What's your mum doing there? Does she want something from the bedroom?'

'No, she's watching us.'

'Why?' This was creepy.

'She wants me to do it with you,' replied Ajay, almost apologetically.

I was disgusted. 'Are you serious? While she's watching!?'

Ajay struggled to put forward an argument. 'Please, let me do it with you … because me mam's watching.'

'No way!'

'You've got to. She wants me to make you pregnant.'

'No, Ajay, no! Not like this. Not with your mum watching.'

Behnji spoke. 'If she says no, just 'it 'er, Ajay. Just punch her. Take her clothes off and just do it, Ajay.'

I whispered in Ajay's ear, trying to reason with him. 'Please don't do this. If you hit me, I'll hit you back.' But Ajay was conditioned to doing what his mother told him to. Ajay started to undo my pyjama buttons. I suppose being with Khan had toughened me up, so I fought back. We wrestled, fell out of bed and I banged my head on a cupboard. Behnji turned on the light and urged Ajay to hit me. My husband stood up and kicked me in the side, the kidneys, again and again. I screamed at him to stop. Ajay's younger brother, who was doing his homework in his bedroom came running in, followed by the middle brother from downstairs. They saw Ajay now stomping on me, while Behnji looked on. Ajay's brothers pulled him off me.

The middle brother shouted, 'What are you doing? You don't do this to *bhabi* (sister-in-law). You just don't do that.' At last, someone had come to the rescue. Behnji stormed off, her plan thwarted, but she wasn't done yet.

On the Tuesday, everyone went to work or school and I was left in the house alone, but without a key. Behnji gave me a list of chores to do: washing, cleaning the floors and vacuuming the carpets. Mum had snatched my mobile phone the night before the wedding, telling me I wouldn't be needing it. Behnji ordered me not to use the landline, although I could answer the phone and take messages. During the day, Behnji phoned to monitor my progress. I'd finished washing all the clothes by hand. 'Good. Now clean the floors. I'll be checking when I get back. And if your parents ring, say you're busy. Get rid of them.' Behnji called several more times for further reports, adding further jobs to keep me busy.

I called Dad at home and told him about my pussy hands. Behnji had refused to let me see a doctor. Dad knew an Indian lady doctor in Liverpool, perhaps a family friend. He called the doctor, who rang the house later after Behnji had returned home. Behnji answered and glared at me as she handed me the phone. I took the phone into the kitchen, away from prying ears. The doctor asked if I could talk freely – I hesitated. She seemed to have a pretty good idea what was going on. I think she knew the Tojal family.

'Just reply yes or no.'

'Yes.'

'Is someone there?'

'Yes.'

'Are you OK?'

'No.'

'Can you explain what's happened?'

'Not now, sorry, Auntie.'

'Are your hands pussy?'

'Yes, Auntie.'

Auntie promised to get me some antibiotics. She asked if I was on the pill and prescribed some more for me.

That evening, Ajay and I were sent to bed about 7:30. Behnji came in the night again and stood in the doorway. 'Go on hit her. Rape her.' The boys were downstairs. This time, Ajay was too strong. He got his way and forced himself on me. Afterwards, I just lay there, sore, violated, despondent. When Khan raped me, there were cuddles afterwards. My reward. Ajay didn't cuddle me and the sad truth is, I missed Khan's cuddles. Talk about low expectations.

Oddly, when Ajay raped me on our wedding night, he wore a condom, which he washed out afterwards. It may be that he had been taught sex that way. But, with Behnji looking on, he didn't wear a condom. It later transpired that Behnji wanted me pregnant, so the condom wasn't her doing. But I was on the pill. A female relative of Ajay's had telephoned me in Woking. She advised me to use contraception if I didn't want to get pregnant. She felt Ajay and I should get to know each other first. It was strange – I didn't know this woman. I think she wanted to make sure she had a baby before me, but the advice suited me. I was in no rush to have a child with Ajay.

Later that night, I woke up and went downstairs for a glass of water. Ajay wasn't in bed. Downstairs, I could hear noises, which sounded like a man and a woman making love. They were different from the sounds Khan and I used to make, but I knew the sounds from videos he made me watch. I wondered whether it was Ajay's middle brother with a girl. As I tiptoed past, I realised the noise was coming from the television. Peeking in, I glimpsed the bizarre spectacle of Ajay watching a pornographic video with his mother. Behnji wanted to make sure Ajay knew exactly what he was doing. They didn't see me, but they'd probably heard the tap running in the kitchen. I crept back upstairs where Ajay joined me a little later.

* * *

The city of Liverpool is divided into the red half and the blue half, Liverpool Football Club and Everton Football Club, although Liverpool FC's fiercest rivalry is with Manchester United.

On Wednesday evening, we visited Pavan in hospital. My new father-in-law was in bed and seemed pleased to see me. I went to touch his feet, assuming that was expected, but he was embarrassed, particularly being in public with other patients and visitors. 'Ooh, no, no, no. Don't bother with all that. You've always got my blessing.' Pavan smiled at me proudly, 'Today, I haven't gained a daughter-in-law, I've gained a daughter.'

'And today, I've gained a dad,' I replied. Pavan told me to call him 'Dad'. I felt happy. My expectations were low to start with, but despite what had happened so far, Pavan made me feel I could maybe fit in with my new family after all. I asked after his health.

'Well, I'm missing the match. I support Man United. We're playing Liverpool tonight.' I went to see if I could find a radio so he could listen to it. Luckily, there was a transistor radio in a recreation room. I asked the nurses if I could borrow it so Pavan could listen to the game. Behnji fumed silently. She didn't like me doing something voluntarily without being ordered around by her. Pavan was delighted and chatted about football. It was nearing the end of the football season and Manchester United were neck and neck with Arsenal in the race for the Premier League title. Pavan explained that Manchester United had beaten Aston Villa the previous Saturday, the day before my wedding. This reminded me of Khan, who would turn hooligan on me when Villa lost. I looked down.

'You don't support Villa do you?' Pavan joked. He must have seen something in my face. Pavan went on to explain that his youngest son supported Liverpool, whilst Ajay and the middle boy supported Everton. 'Have you ever been to a game? I'll get Ajay to take you to Everton.' Ajay was thrilled. Manchester United and Liverpool drew 2-2 that evening, but over the next few weeks Pavan's team, United, went on to win the league, along with the European Champions' League and the FA Cup. As I began to bond with Pavan, Behnji scowled at me from the other side of his bed.

Chapter 23

TOY SOLDIERS

Hindu brides are believed to bring good fortune, literally the goddess Lakshmi, to their new families. Shortly before I married Ajay, Pavan rang Dad with some news. The Tojals had suffered a fire at their clothes' warehouse. Fortunately, no one was hurt but they had come into a £70k windfall from the insurance claim. Pavan was delighted. 'It's your daughter! Our Lakshmi!'

* * *

Traditionally, Punjabi newly-weds visit the bride's parents shortly after the wedding night. This is the final formal ceremony, called *phera dalna*, so we travelled back down to Woking on Thursday 8th May.

'Bang, bang! You're dead!' The hulking frame of Ajay, my new husband, lay on the floor of my parents' living room in his Everton football top. He was playing with the plastic toy soldiers he'd brought along for company. Dad came in, stepped over Ajay awkwardly, and joined Mum on the sofa. Dad glanced at me briefly, then looked away. Ajay's face lit up. He'd spotted a bowl of chocolates on the coffee table. He hauled himself up, strode over to the chocolates and grabbed a handful with his great ham fist, before putting them in his pocket. Mum eyed Ajay with contempt, as only Mum can. Dad just looked stunned.

'Would you like a chocolate, Ajay? Would you like a bowl?' I asked. 'They'll melt in your pocket.' Ajay wasn't listening. His face contorted with childish desire. He unwrapped one of the sweets and began scoffing greedily. Mum and Dad watched in horror as Ajay took out another chocolate and then began drooling as he chewed. He did nothing about it because he didn't know any better. But it wasn't his fault. I took out a tissue to wipe his face.

'Can't he do that himself?' snapped Mum.

'No, he'll get his top wet.'

'Who?' asked Ajay, only vaguely aware that we might be discussing him.

'Have you finished with your soldiers, Ajay? Shall we put them away?' I asked.

Mum and Dad tried talking to Ajay in English, but he didn't respond, so Mum tried Punjabi. Still, Ajay ignored her. It wasn't as if he couldn't speak – he just didn't do adult conversation. Questions were too challenging. At last he spoke up to ask for a drink, in the unmistakable tones of Liverpool. 'Can I 'ave a R*iiibeee*na, like?' But Mum and Dad didn't understand his Scouse accent.

'What language is he speaking?' asked Dad.

A little while later, Ajay left the room. I assumed he was going to use the downstairs toilet. Mum came in shortly afterwards. 'He just standing there outside toilet? Why he just standing there?'

I realised what the problem was. 'Ah! At home, he won't go to the toilet without Behnji's permission. Or take a bath. He's waiting for permission to go.'

'So, he take chocolates without asking? But he won't go

toilet or bathroom unless someone say? That why he stink?'
Mum was trying to make sense of Ajay's behaviour, and
also his aroma, which was becoming overpowering. I went
and explained to Ajay that he *was* allowed to use the toilet
without asking and an accident was averted.

The approach to my arranged marriage had been like a
game of poker between the two families. Mine had a big
house in the Home Counties, but I was 'damaged goods'.
I'd run off with a Muslim, was not a virgin and was being
prosecuted for obtaining services by deception. Ajay's family
ran a business in Liverpool and Manchester, but he had the
mind of a child, couldn't tie his shoe laces and wouldn't take
a bath unless his Mum told him to, although they claimed
he'd been on a two-year computer course. So, posh house in
Surrey versus family business in the North. Secrets and lies.
Damaged goods together.

Later, we were sitting in Dad's room watching television.
Mum and Dad had their own rooms downstairs, but Dad
was kind of hovering in and out of his room. He seemed
uncomfortable around Ajay, embarrassed, and also unable
to look me in the eye. While Dad was getting a beer, Ajay
punched me on the shoulder and giggled. He wasn't being
malicious, just play-fighting, but it hurt and I was bruising.

'Don't do that!'

Once again, Ajay didn't seem to be listening. He grabbed
my top and wrestled me to the floor, I tried to push him off,
but he rolled on top of me, and then off me, as if to give me
a chance.

Dad came back in and asked Ajay, 'What are you doing?'

'Dad, tell him to stop!' I yelled.

'Stop it!' shouted Dad. Ajay didn't respond. He was too
busy enjoying himself. Dad shouted in Punjabi, '*Bas, bas,*'
– stop.

Mum heard the shouting and came in. 'What's going on? What's he doing now? Stop it!' Finally, Ajay obeyed and got off me.

Like many Hindus, my family are vegetarian, which comes from Dad's side. Vegetarianism stems from Hindu principles of non-violence and karma. But many Punjabi Hindus do eat meat – Mum and Shikta both grew up in meat-eating households, as did Ajay. Mum prepared six dishes of vegetarian food to welcome her new son-in-law. 'But I don't like it. There's no meat.' Ajay wasn't being deliberately rude – he was just used to eating meat. This went down like a lead balloon, but at least Mum and Dad were spared the revolting sight of Ajay eating. After the meal, which Ajay hardly touched, I took him out to get some takeaway food so he wouldn't go hungry. He left a half-eaten chicken burger in the fridge next to Dad's beers. Later, Mum tackled me in the kitchen. 'Dad not happy. Move burger quick.'

'So why did you marry me into a meat-eating family, then?' I asked.

'Hmmph!' Mum didn't have an answer.

As evening drew on, Dad announced he was going to bed early. He'd lost his job the day after my wedding, but said he would be getting up early to do his prayers. Hindus pray to a number of gods. Dad is a devotee of Hanuman, the monkey god. Mum asked me what time Ajay and I would be going up.

'Ajay's mum normally sends him to bed at 7:30.'

'What?' Mum was astonished. Dad held his head in his hands.

Mum had made the spare bedroom up especially, with clean towels laid out for us like a hotel. The stench of Ajay's body odour was overwhelming as we entered the room. After the wedding night rape and the Behnji-inspired rape, I decided not to spend the night with Ajay, at least while I was in my parents' home. I also had sleep to catch up on. I hadn't really resolved how I would handle the matter of sex with Ajay long-term.

'Ajay, there's your bed. Do you want to take a bath first?'

'No. Aren't you sleeping with me then?'

'No, I'm sorry, I can't, Ajay. Not here. And you really do need a bath.'

I went to sleep in Billy's room – he was away at university. A few hours later, I heard someone clomping along the landing and Ajay came into the room. I got up abruptly and walked to the door, wary after the previous four nights. Then Mum appeared.

'What's going on? Why all doors slamming?'

'Mum, I'm sleeping in Billy's room tonight.'

Mum was exasperated. 'You have to sleep with him. He your husband.'

'*You* sleep with him.' Mum's jaw dropped – I'd never spoken to her like that before. Then Mum sniffed and looked at Ajay. 'Ajay. Do you want bath? Or shower? Bath or shower?' Ajay blinked, but didn't answer. Despairing of the pair of us, the reluctant bride and the reluctant bather, Mum went back to bed. I spent the night on the sofa downstairs. Dad came down in the early hours for his prayers, saw me, but said nothing.

The next morning, Mum complained, 'Sunita, he stink. Can't you get him have bath?'

'No, I've told you. He won't have a bath unless his mum tells him to. You made me marry him. You tell him.'

Late on the Friday afternoon, Mum and Dad were taking me and Ajay to Reena Mata's in Southall, Middlesex. The newly-weds were to be shown off. This was where Mum brought me when she was looking for husbands for me, where we received the blessing and advice of Reena

Mata. It was also a place to meet other Indians. By now, I suspect Mum had misgivings about parading Ajay around the Punjabi community, but this outing had already been arranged. Ajay was wearing a t-shirt. 'Haven't you brought shirt?' enquired Mum. Ajay had not. He also hadn't yet washed. Mum asked Ajay if he would like to borrow Dad's aftershave but Ajay didn't see the need.

In the car on the way, Mum sat in the passenger seat and could see me and Ajay in the rear-view mirror, sitting in awkward silence. Mum tried to make conversation, asking Ajay which gods he prayed to. 'Huh?' Either Ajay didn't understand the question, or he didn't pray to any gods.

Dad preferred praying at home rather than in temples. He was driving and, on the cassette, playing the *Hanuman Chalisa*, a Hindu hymn in praise of the monkey deity, associated with wisdom and intelligence. This hymn is widely popular in India and details Hanuman's heroic exploits and qualities. Dad joined in the theological discussion to ask Ajay if he knew the hymn.

'Eh?' Apparently, Ajay did not. Ajay started to drool, so I took out a tissue and wiped his chin. Mum saw me in the mirror and tutted.

'Stop doing that! Let him do himself.' As requested, I stopped wiping saliva from Ajay's face. As if to drown out everyone's embarrassment, Dad turned the music up. When we reached our destination and got out of the car, Mum took one look at Ajay, turned to me and snapped, 'Get tissue and wipe his chin!'

Inside the venue, various members of the congregation were introduced to Ajay and tried, with limited success, to make polite conversation. Mum seemed distinctly uncomfortable. When Ajay began drooling again, I took out another tissue to perform my wifely wiping duties. In desperation, Mum stood in front of me, as if she could somehow prevent anyone from noticing. After only about half an hour, Mum explained to everyone that Ajay and I were driving back to Liverpool early on Saturday, so needed to get back to Woking. In fact, we weren't due to go back until Sunday, but Mum had decided to cut her losses. On the way back, I thanked Mum for leaving early so Ajay wouldn't miss his bedtime. Mum didn't see the funny side. 'Shut up, bewakoof!'

* * *

When I was living in Aldershot with Khan, he came home once with four cans of lager and a takeaway vegetarian pizza. He seemed normal, happy and smiled at me. I was hyper-sensitive to Khan's moods, always looking for signs of normality, seizing from them the hope that things would be different today – he wouldn't rape me or hit me. Frequently, my hopes were dashed. I smiled back at Khan. His team, Aston Villa, were playing and he let me sit on the bed with him to watch the match and share his pizza – there were no chairs in our room. Khan opened one of the cans. *Tissshh.* The fizzing sound made me flinch, which in turn lit Khan's fuse. His expression darkened and the Bad Khan grabbed me and pulled me towards him. Then he forced me onto the ground, put his foot on my head and ordered me to pray for Aston Villa. Further degradation followed as Khan pulled my shalwar kameez down and raped me from behind. Beer in his left hand, pizza in his right, watching his beloved Villa, Khan claimed this was every man's dream. When he'd finished with me, he put his foot on my face and told me to stop crying as I was ruining the match. Fortunately, Villa won that night so I was spared further violence for a while. Later, Khan cuddled me – the Good Khan.

* * *

On the Saturday, Ajay asked, 'Can I watch the footie, like?'

Dad looked perplexed again. 'What's he saying?'

'Dad, he's speaking English. He's asking if he can watch the football. He supports Everton and they're playing on TV.'

Mum put her foot down. 'He can't touch my telly. He never wash his hands.' Mum had noticed that the tap didn't run when Ajay used the downstairs toilet, so we were banished to Dad's room for the football. Again, Dad was wandering in and out, out of sorts. Everton were playing West Ham United and scored first. Ajay leapt up and landed on his feet with a thud. Then he jumped again and again, punching the air and screaming.

'Yeeeah! Yesssss! Yeah!'

Dad came running in. 'What's happened? What's the matter now?'

Mum followed. 'What *tamasha* (commotion) is this?'

'Everton have just scored. It's one-nil,' I explained.

Dad followed cricket and neither of my brothers were into football, so Mum and Dad weren't used to football fans celebrating. I knew more about the game from Khan. The date was Saturday 8th May 1999 and Everton beat West Ham 6-0, so Ajay had a lot to celebrate. Mum and Dad knew enough to know that 6-0 was a big score and Mum turned football pundit to sum up Everton's success for Dad's benefit. 'Ha! You lost your Lakshmi, you lost your job. He got her, he win 6-0.'

Chapter 24

DUD CHACHA

We drove back to Liverpool on Sunday and, on Tuesday, Pavan was discharged from hospital. Although he was still unwell, he lifted the atmosphere in the house immediately. Cheerful and chatty, he would make jokes or talk about his beloved Manchester United. When he first sat down, I went to touch his feet, but he said I didn't need to do that. I was effectively Pavan's carer for a while. I had to apply a special cream up his nose, as well as massage his legs and wait outside the toilet in case he fainted, because he was still weak. Behnji still supervised my daily chores and would expect me to touch her feet, although not in front of Pavan. The Tojals put me on the car insurance so I could collect Pavan's newspaper and run Ajay's youngest brother to school. For a while, Pavan's return seemed to bring some semblance of normality into my life. Whilst I was helping him, we seemed to bond a little. But most importantly, with her husband back home, Behnji stopped inciting Ajay to rape me.

* * *

When I went to India aged 17, the time my feelings for Rinku blossomed, we also visited Dad's family in Ambala. One day, I was with Dad's family in the main room. Dad was in England working and Mum was elsewhere in the house. I'm not sure where Dilip and Billy were, but Mum wanted as little to do with Dad's family as possible. Banished from the house to his shed outside, Dud Chacha's health continued to decline. His clothes were now rags and he wore broken flip-flops without socks, even in winter. Sometimes, he would leave his shed for a smoke. On this occasion, I could hear Dud Chacha's footsteps on the stone floor at the back of the house. *Flip … flop … flip … flop.* Then the smell of cigarette smoke wafted into the house and my grandmother, Mata Ji's, eyes lit up – her son was still alive! She looked into my face, trying to communicate, but the words wouldn't come out. Mata Ji had suffered a stroke about ten years previously, and was now immobile with impaired speech. I would try to bring her some comfort, comb her hair or hold her hand, much to Auntie Anita's annoyance. Mata Ji was pining for Dud Chacha, separated by a brick wall, but struggled to say his name. She desperately wanted to see him but this was forbidden. 'Dud … Dud … Dud …'

In a high-pitched voice, Pita Ji mimicked his wife contemptuously. 'Dud … Dud … Dud …'

Auntie Anita joined in the fun. 'Dud … Dud … Dud …' This brought tears to my eyes. I didn't see Mata Ji often, but I felt we had a special connection.

Pita Ji used to tell Mata Ji that he wished he'd married her sister. Mata Ji was a quiet, kind, gentle woman who had endured a hard life, one of toil and subservience, and marriage to a man who seemed to despise her. Made a refugee at Partition, Mata Ji's children were her world, although not all repaid her kindness. She was especially close to Dad, who was the eldest, and Dud Chacha. She must have missed them terribly when they were sent to England. Dud Chacha was now back in India, but locked out of her life. Mata Ji could no longer do the cooking and cleaning, and Pita Ji and Anita didn't really see the point of her. Anita would tell her she'd be better off dead – she was a burden. Mata Ji slept on a hard, wooden bed in the main room where Pita Ji would turn up the volume on the TV if she fell asleep. He would also slap her, or kick her legs, and mocked her constantly. This would bring tears to Dad's eyes when he witnessed it, but he didn't say anything. He was unable to defy his father. Dad sent money to India for Mata Ji's treatment and care, but there was no hired help, no improvements for her benefit. Pita Ji had built four shops, which were leased out. While Pita Ji and Anita continued to taunt Mata Ji, I went outside to see Dud Chacha. I called for him, but he didn't answer. Peering into his shed, I saw my uncle passed out, a *beedi* – Indian roll-up – smouldering beside him on the floor. I heard Anita follow me out with a water bucket, as if to use the hand pump, although I didn't hear the usual clanking sound. I put a sheet over Dud Chacha. Anita glared at me, but didn't say anything to Pita Ji. His favourite game show had just started on TV, so she knew better than to interrupt. I held Mata Ji's hands and smiled to indicate that Dud Chacha was alive.

Mata Ji passed away in 1997 when I was with Khan in Aldershot.

* * *

In Liverpool, one of the many chores on my 'to do list' was to make chapatis – Indian flat breads made with flour and water. Behnji decreed I must prepare sixteen chapatis every evening for the family, of which I was allowed just one. I think Behnji was surprised that I could make perfectly round chapatis. I'd been helping Mum in the kitchen since I was nine-years-old. But Mum wasn't very good at making chapatis. They weren't round and they didn't rise up whilst cooking, as they were supposed to. Dad would tease her. '*I'm a better cook than you.*' Ironically, it was Khan who taught me how to make round chapatis using a rolling pin, often by candlelight. You learn fast when the penalty for failure is a lit cigarette on the back of your hand.

One evening, as I was completing the sixteenth chapati, the phone rang. Behnji answered. Soon after, I heard Pavan's voice. 'You *must* tell her.' As I left the kitchen, Pavan approached me awkwardly. 'Your Dad's on the phone. It's bad news, I'm afraid.' Behnji smiled maliciously. I shook as I picked up the phone. Dad was in tears at the other end.

'What's happened, Dad? What's happened?' But Dad couldn't say the words. My first thought was Mum – Mum's dead. But then I heard Mum shouting at Dad.

'*Bewakoof*! Speak! Stop crying. *Tsoh, I'll* speak to her.' Mum took the phone, opting for directness over tact. 'Dud Chacha dead. He found dead in his shed.' Then, already embroidering the story to tell her friends, Mum added, 'Perhaps your auntie poison him.' Mum hated Anita.

I was stunned. My brain wanted to stop to take in the news, but at the other end of the telephone, Mum was ranting at Dad, who was clearly grief-stricken. 'What you crying for? You all want him dead. You never help him. Now he gone, you crying!' Without pausing for breath, Mum now addressed me. 'Anyway, we know you were close, so we let you know.'

Behnji squeezed my sore hands spitefully as she took the receiver from me. 'Yeah, I've had a word with me 'usband. We can't all come down. I'll bring 'er down tonight, as it's custom. You can't keep 'er. Just for a few hours, OK?' She didn't add that chapatis don't make themselves, you know. Mum had absolutely no intention of keeping me.

'No, it doesn't matter, it's a long drive.'

Pavan intervened, telling Behnji, 'Please take her. She was close to him.'

Later, my chores completed, I cried in the toilet. I cried for my tragic, kind uncle, Dud Chacha. Now, even more alone in the world, I cried for myself, too. I wished I'd told Dud Chacha what really happened.

Behnji rapped on the door – she'd found some more jobs for me to do. I prayed silently for Dud Chacha and hoped his suffering was over. Behnji drove me down to Woking in the early hours. I think the drive was about four hours. It wasn't in Behnji's nature to put herself out for others, especially me, but Indians set great store by tradition. It would have looked odd if I hadn't been allowed to visit Dad on his brother's passing and Pavan was in favour, too. Behnji also hoped she might not leave Woking empty-handed.

'Let's see what they give you.' On the drive down, Behnji subjected me to one long, repetitive monologue about the lack of dowry so far. Washing machine, Mercedes, *blah, blah, blah*. Behnji had arranged to stay with a relation in Middlesex. She told me I wasn't allowed to tell Mum and Dad anything about anything. Mum answered the door and professed her gratitude to Behnji.

'*Hanji, Hanji.* Thank you for bringing her.' Mum's face told a different story – we'd woken her up.

'I'm not stopping. You can't keep 'er. I'll be back tomorrow for 'er.' Obviously, Behnji just didn't get Mum. Inside, Mum was irritable.

'I told you not to come. He dead. There's no point you being here.'

In the morning, Dad was crying. We hugged. Various relatives came from Hounslow to pay their respects.

'Where's the daughter-in-law? Where's Shikta?' they asked.

Behnji picked me up at 10 a.m. We hadn't reached the end of my parents' road before she asked, 'What did they give you? I *want* my dowry.'

Chapter 25

HONEYMOON

Behnji's attitude to me was full of contradictions. She treated me like a servant, someone to perform all the household chores while she put her feet up. But, in her controlling way, she also wanted to show me off at family occasions, like a pet or a doll, so she would choose my clothes, Indian or western, and tell me what to wear and when. Frequently she changed her mind about my outfit, telling me to change out of one she'd chosen only shortly before. The Tojals lived in a nice, four bedroomed house in the suburbs, but many of their relatives and friends were far wealthier, with electric-gated mansions outside Liverpool and expensive sports cars. Some employed permanent domestic staff whilst Behnji had to make do with me. I think Behnji envied her crowd's riches and this fuelled her fantasy dowry demands. Apart from special occasions, social life included poker nights with plenty of cash and alcohol, with both men and women participating. My role was to serve rather than join in. When Behnji wasn't working on the market stall, there were also ladies' coffee mornings – Asian housewives of Liverpool swapping the latest gossip.

More importantly, perhaps, my function was to produce grandchildren. Whilst this obviously required me to have sex with Ajay, Behnji didn't want us to bond or have any kind of normal relationship apart from that, so she kept us apart as much as possible. During the arranged marriage negotiations, the Tojals had stated that I would be working with Ajay in the family business, but that never happened. I think Behnji was jealously protective of Ajay.

One time, Behnji sent me for a night out, clubbing with a young crowd of Indian girls – friends and relations. This seemed at odds with the rest of Behnji's behaviour towards me, but she was also one for keeping up appearances. It might have looked odd if she hadn't let me join the gang. For this outing, she selected a low-cut black mini-dress and stilettos for me to wear. The girls, some married, some not, went to a club on the Liverpool quayside area frequented by famous footballers. When I went outside for some fresh air, a white guy asked me if I'd like to go back to his place.

'No thanks, I'm married.'

'What you doin' 'ere then, like?'

What was I doing there?

I was finally dropped off at home at 2 a.m. Behnji had waited up for me and wanted to know all the details. She was cross with me for being sober. 'Why can't you drink alcohol like the others?' If only she knew!

* * *

The time had come for our honeymoon. Relatives were asking questions, so appearances needed to be kept up. I believe Behnji and Pavan got their money back for the cancelled Bali trip, and Behnji found a good deal for a week in Florida. Ajay and I flew from Liverpool John Lennon Airport to Orlando on Wednesday 23rd June 1999. For some reason, Behnji had reserved seats in such a way that we sat separately on the eight-hour flight there, and back. We stayed in a three-star hotel and were given seven day passes to *Wet 'n Wild Orlando*, a water park with plenty of activities to keep Ajay occupied. He was upset that we couldn't go to Disneyland, but that was more expensive and outside Behnji's budget.

There was a fly drive option at no extra cost, but Behnji didn't include this. Although Ajay could drive, I don't think his mother was comfortable with him driving overseas, on the wrong side of the road. I offered to drive but was, apparently, ineligible, being just under 21. So, we walked to local restaurants, took the bus to *Wet 'n Wild*, and coaches to various other attractions. We visited Universal Studios, where Ajay bought me a plastic talking *ET* toy, which said, 'ET, *go home*', and *Sea World* where we saw the killer whales. Ajay was easily bored – he would fidget or sulk, or want to play fight. It was a constant challenge to keep him amused. On one of the rides at *Wet 'n Wild,* Ajay particularly enjoyed playing with an inflatable doughnut. A boy aged about eight asked if he could have a go, but Ajay refused. The boy's mother gasped in astonishment as I tried to persuade Ajay to let the boy have a turn on the doughnut. He refused point blank – 'No!' It was like being with a child the whole time. At one of the theme parks – I forget which – a swan-shaped boat disappeared into a tunnel of love. We were refused admission because *I* wasn't yet an adult.

A coach trip to *Busch Gardens Tampa*, a theme park with rides and African animals, was especially trying. On the way, Ajay kept saying he was bored, asking, 'Are we there, yet?' He'd also seen a poster advertising a big firework party planned for the Fourth of July, but we were due to fly back on 30th June. 'I *wanna* see the fireworks,' he moaned. I explained that his mother had already made the arrangements, but I offered to pay by credit card to switch flights and stay another week. I thought it might be fun to be in the United States for Independence Day, which was also my 21st birthday, certainly more enjoyable than scrubbing floors for Behnji. Ajay rang Behnji to ask permission, but she refused. Ajay sulked – 'I *wanna* see the fireworks' – so I took him out for cake to cheer him up.

* * *

One night, when I was with Khan in Aldershot, there was a thunder storm. As a flash of lightning exploded from the angry sky, I clung onto Khan instinctively. He pushed me away and laughed. *CRACK!* A further flash lit up the bedroom and Khan's features; he was now angry, too. He put his hand around my throat. 'I've got a job for you.'

Khan got up and took me onto the landing. Going into the bathroom, he turned on the light, opened the window and threw something outside into the storm – I couldn't see what it was. Then he grabbed my wrist, telling me, 'Get downstairs.' I think we were alone in the house. Khan opened the back door. 'Go and find it.' I didn't know what I was looking for, but had to go outside, barefoot, into the pouring rain. Khan stayed behind the back door and switched the light off, presumably so I couldn't 'cheat' by using the light. The rain was relentless, but I didn't dare try to shelter. I tried looking for whatever it was as quickly as possible, to avoid the next flash of lightning, but I couldn't see anything in the dark.

Soaked to the skin, I went to the back door and threw myself at Khan's mercy. 'I'm sorry. I couldn't find it.'

I was expecting a beating, but Khan decided to give me a sporting chance. 'Alright, I'll give you another go. Stand under the bathroom window and watch. I'm going to throw a razor blade out. If you find it, you can come back in. If you don't, you'll have to stay outside. All night.' A little later, the bathroom light came on, but nothing happened. I stood helpless in the storm, waiting for the razor blade, battered by the cold rain. Perhaps Khan would leave me outside all night anyway. Thunder rumbled in the sky. I counted to four. *CRACK!*

Khan was still in the bathroom, watching me. I had to keep my head up in case he threw the blade after all, but this meant rain was pouring from my hair and face into my eyes and mouth. After about fifteen minutes and several more bursts of lightning, the window opened and something came flying out of the window. I tried to follow where the blade went and got down on my hands and knees, but couldn't find the razor blade in the earth.

The rain was lashing my back now as I scrambled in the dirt. *CRACK!* The sky lit up again and I saw the glint of the razor blade in the soil. Grabbing the blade carefully, I looked up and showed Khan, who was standing in the bathroom window. He disappeared. I waited. Presently, he opened the back door. Freezing and soaked to the skin, I was allowed back into the house but made to sleep on the bedroom floor in my wet night clothes. Khan explained the method behind his madness 'You will fear *me* more than *thunder*'.

* * *

Florida is known for its summer thunderstorms, experiencing more than any other US state. One time, we'd left our hotel a few minutes earlier and were walking along International Drive, when a storm broke out. As thunder rumbled menacingly, Ajay shrieked, 'Let's go back! Let's go back!'. He grabbed my hand for comfort. Then came an explosion from the heavens. *CRACK!* Terror-struck, Ajay covered his ears in dread, before taking my hand again. A streak of lightning blazed across the sky as we ran back to the hotel, drenched by the sub-tropical downpour. Back in the safety of our room, I tried to reassure Ajay, explaining how the distance between the flash and the bang showed how far away the lightning had struck.

As the week wore on, I worked out that Ajay became especially fidgety when he was hungry, so I knew when to steer him towards food. Meals were not included in the package, so we ate breakfast at *Denny's Diner*. At first, Ajay seemed reluctant to cross the busy road to get there, so I had to hold his hand. But it was more like being a parent with a child than a honeymoon couple. In the evenings, we ate Chinese food – eat as much as you like. Ajay loved his meat, but ate like an animal, regurgitating his food and spitting it back onto the plate whilst other diners looked on in disgust. Spare ribs were a particular challenge. Ajay would get sauce all over his face and drool while he gorged, so I would sit attentively with tissues to wipe his mouth and his face. It's a wonder we weren't banned from the restaurant.

Behnji had taken my gold bangles, but I still wore the ivory, chura bangles. I wasn't comfortable with the idea of ivory, taken from an elephant. The bangles made my arms itch, too, so I'd tried taking them off, but couldn't do so without cutting my hands again. On the third day of our honeymoon, we were standing at the bus stop and Ajay was bored again, so he started wrestling with me in public. Grabbing my arm roughly, he accidentally snapped one of the bangles. He laughed, like a child who knows he's been naughty. Then he snapped another bangle, this time deliberately. Ajay liked this game and carried on breaking off the bangles one by one. I didn't mind and felt a sense of relief as I let him do so, like shackles were being removed.

When he'd finished with one arm, I offered him the other so he could finish the job. From a passing bus, an Indian family gaped open-mouthed at the spectacle of Ajay destroying my wedding bangles. Like us, they were Hindus – the woman wore a *bindi* (red dot) on her forehead. Only later did I learn that the chura were sacred bangles and not supposed to be removed for at least forty days. Not knowing what else to do, I kept the broken chura in a plastic bag.

Throughout the week, Ajay kept asking, 'Are we married?' before giggling shyly. He saw my Shiva tattoo and thought it was cool. We had a twin room in the hotel, so slept in separate beds. Without Behnji encouraging him, Ajay didn't try and force himself on me. He did have a play fight with me one afternoon when I was sitting on the bed. I ended up falling onto the floor, along with *ET*. Another afternoon, we tried to have sex in a nice way. I wasn't physically attracted to Ajay, but realised I couldn't keep sex off the agenda for ever. But if it had to happen, I wanted it to be gentle, lovemaking, something we talked about first. In the end, it didn't happen. We were both too shy about taking our clothes off.

Ajay didn't wash throughout the week and, towards the end, his body odour became unbearable. Nevertheless, I began to care for Ajay during our honeymoon, I developed protective feelings. We started to bond without Behnji in the way, keeping us apart. There was no romantic interest on my part. It was more that Ajay seemed to need looking after, like a child or a pet and, at that stage, I believed I was in it for the duration.

Our flight back to England was delayed by five hours and patience was not one of Ajay's virtues. Waiting at the airport, we sat near an English family with a boy in a wheelchair, who was rocking backwards and forwards. Ajay smiled and began mimicking the boy's rocking action. 'Nnn! Nnn! Look at me! I'm brain damaged!'

My face burned with shame as the boy's parents looked at us with sadness.

'Be quiet, Ajay!'

'Nnn! Nnn! Retard!'

My anger boiled over. 'Ajay, if you don't stop that, I'm gonna slap you.'

Ajay wasn't listening and continued to mock the boy by rocking and laughing. I lost my patience.

As I slapped Ajay's face, an English tourist watching nearby spilt his coffee in shock. The boy's mother mouthed, 'Thank you.'

Ajay looked stunned and I felt terrible. 'I'm sorry. Please stop making fun of others, it's not nice.'

Ajay protested, 'But *I* have brain damage.' At first, I didn't take in what he'd said. I was too pumped up and walked off to calm down. Watching Ajay from afar, I realised how helpless he was and his revelation sank in – he, too, was mentally impaired. Feeling desperately sad, I returned to Ajay and apologised.

'I'm sorry, Ajay. I didn't know you had brain damage.' Ajay smiled sweetly.

Chapter 26

HAPPY BIRTHDAY, SUNITA

On my birthdays, when I was growing up, Dad would sing me a famous Indian happy birthday song, *Bar Bar, Din Yey Aaye*, which comes from a 1967 Bollywood spy thriller, *Farz*. In Hindi, the singer expresses the wishes that this day will return time and time again, and that the birthday girl, the film's heroine, Sunita, will live for a thousand years. In English, the chorus wishes Sunita a happy birthday.

* * *

Ajay and I had back to back birthdays on the 3rd and 4th of July – his 26th and my 21st – and parties were planned for both events. Since we'd returned from honeymoon, Behnji had done her best to keep us apart, except at night. The bond we'd started to build on our honeymoon had almost evaporated. Ajay barely spoke to me – I don't know whether that was his mother's doing – whilst Behnji was as spiteful towards me as ever. Ajay's birthday party was held in a large house in Liverpool with a large garden, which belonged to wealthy friends of the Tojals. Before we left, Behnji noticed I wasn't wearing the bridal chura bangles, which Ajay had broken in Florida, and warned, 'We'll deal with that later'. She kindly lent me my own gold set to wear, the ones she'd confiscated on my wedding night.

When we arrived at the party, Behnji took Ajay into the garden without me, so I was pretty much left to my own devices. I was surprised to see Mum and Dad there – I didn't know they'd been invited. After a while, Ajay's birthday cake appeared and was carried out to the garden. Other guests ushered me out to be with my husband. 'Don't let them leave you out,' said one. I went outside to watch from a distance as Ajay tucked into his beloved cake.

At the stroke of midnight, it was technically my birthday. I'd finally managed to speak to Ajay alone in the garden, away from Behnji. Dad staggered towards us, hugged me and wished me a happy birthday. Dad had realised something wasn't right and, with an evening full of lager inside him, his feelings towards his son-in-law now spilled over. 'Aren't you going to wish your wife a happy birthday?' Ajay blinked at Dad blankly – *angry grown-up talking*. Dad continued. 'Do you understand what I'm saying? Eh? No?' Behnji and Pavan must have heard Dad goading Ajay and joined us, as did Mum. In the absence of a response from Ajay, Dad took centre stage and sang me happy birthday, Indian style. '*Bar bar, din yey aaye …*' With his fingers, Dad conducted an imaginary orchestra while he sang. '*Happy birth-day to Sun-i-ta. Happy birth-day to you.*'

When Dad's performance was finished, Pavan played peacemaker, beaming as he put his arm around me. 'Happy birthday, Sunita! She's our daughter now!'

Behnji was in no mood for diplomacy and was snarling at Mum. 'We're doin' a party for 'er tomorrer. Whadda you gonna do?' Mum didn't speak but responded by turning her head towards Ajay, who was drooling. Then, turning back to Behnji, she smirked, as if to say, *That's your son, that is!* I went over to a forlorn looking Ajay and gave him a hug.

In the car on the way back, Behnji exploded. 'You're not allowed to talk to your parents tomorrow. Do you hear me? There'll be trouble if you do.'

Pavan joined in, asking, 'What kind of people are they?'

* * *

On the morning of my 21st birthday, I woke up next to a drooling Ajay. I went to hug him, but Behnji appeared at the door and called him away. He returned with a diamond cluster ring. 'Mum says it's for your 21st birthday. You 'ave to wear it.' I thanked Ajay. He replied, 'I didn't choose it, it was mam.'

I pointed at my engagement ring. 'Did you choose that, Ajay?'

'No, Mam did. I wanted a different one.' This didn't feel like a birthday.

After breakfast, the family drove around the corner to see Behnji's mother, known to all as *Naniji*. Naniji called me into her room, which was separate from the living room where everyone else was, and told me to close the door so we were alone. Furtively, Naniji whispered, 'I want to show you something.' Producing a pair of gold earrings, Naniji said she didn't want to give them to Behnji, her eldest, or her other daughters. 'They all have enough. But you are special. I like you, I want you to have my earrings,' before warning, 'don't let Behnji take them.' I put the earrings on to make Naniji happy. Naniji led me back to the lounge and announced, 'Look everyone, she looks so beautiful in my earrings.' Behnji glowered at me with envy. I thanked Naniji but sensed trouble and added, 'No. Thank you, *Naniji*. That's very kind of you, but maybe I'll just wear them for the day.'

But Naniji was adamant. 'No. My choice. I'm giving them

to you.'

Naniji's earrings were one of the few items of jewellery Behnji didn't take from me. She knew Naniji was watching.

Later, Mum and Dad came around to the Tojals' house. They'd been staying in Liverpool with Dad's doctor friend. Mum now presented me with my own gold set: earrings and a necklace. I paid for these when I was seventeen, but they were now presented as if they were a twenty-first birthday gift from Mum. Behnji intercepted, taking the gold set. 'I'll look after that.'

Behnji had warned me not to speak to Mum or sit next to her. I was told to be rude to her if she spoke to me. Dad walked outside to the garden with Pavan, whilst I stayed inside with Mum and Behnji, who scowled as Mum sat down next to me. Panicking, I said, 'Mum, you smell.' Well I had to live with Behnji, didn't I? Mum was outraged – she always wore expensive perfume. She stood up in a huff and stormed over to sit opposite me instead. I felt awful, while Behnji just laughed.

Conversation was stilted, dowry being the elephant in the room. Behnji now humiliated me in front of Mum. She made a pretend throat-clearing noise, 'Ha-hum', indicating that I'd forgotten something as she pointed to her feet. As I'd been trained to, I stood up, walked over to Behnji, knelt and touched her feet. Behnji smiled at Mum, who just thought it was bizarre. Mum asked me what had happened to the chura bangles. As a new bride, I was still supposed to be wearing them. Not wanting to get Ajay into trouble, I just shook my head and said nothing. When Behnji popped out of the room, I whispered to Mum that Ajay had broken them at the bus stop in Miami.

Mum laughed. 'Ha! Stupid boy!'

That evening, on the way to my 21st birthday party, Behnji

reminded me that I wasn't to open any presents. We arrived at an Indian restaurant, where about 60 guests joined us. I was told to greet the guests and collect the presents. The party wasn't being held for my benefit – I felt like a posh beggar collecting goodies for Behnji. At one point, tiring of the pretence, I suggested to one guest, 'Just give it to Behnji, she's taking them all, anyway.'

Towards the end of the evening, there was a heated discussion between Dad and Pavan, who was asking Dad to pay the bill. Dad refused. 'I thought you said she was your daughter now?'

Back home, Behnji screamed at the boys to go to bed. Even Ajay followed. I was apprehensive. Behnji and Pavan ranted and raved at me about my parents' behaviour and the lack of dowry so far. I expected nothing better from Behnji, but Pavan was now turning against me, too. Although it had been two months since the wedding, Behnji became more and more obsessed with the idea that she might still receive a dowry, despite all evidence to the contrary. Solely for this reason, she agreed to a suggestion Dad had made, that I go back to Woking for a few days. Behnji was hoping against hope that my parents would come up with the goods. Mum and Dad came around in the morning to collect me. Without Behnji's knowledge, Mum had asked Ajay for the wedding videos, which he gave her.

Behnji wasn't happy. 'No, I don't want them getting lost. Give 'em 'ere.'

'Oh, I only borrow them,' Mum reassured Behnji, as she secured the videos safely in her handbag.

'Didn't *you* get any videos done?' asked Behnji, knowing full well that Mum and Dad had not. Behnji wasn't finished. 'And what about the chura? She took 'em off and broke 'em. What are you giving us for them?' Mum's brother, Bantoo

Mama, had paid for the chura, but Behnji somehow felt *she* was entitled to compensation.

Mum glanced disdainfully at Ajay as she fired back at Behnji, 'Your son broke them! Ask him!'

Ajay happily owned up. 'Yeah, mam, I broke 'em at the bus stop. I was bored, like!'

Mum saw Ajay drooling, tutted and turned away in mock disgust.

On the drive down to Woking, I didn't feel like talking, but Mum had plenty to say about Behnji. 'Pfft! Who she think she is?' It was a long drive and Dad didn't want to hear it.

'Why don't you just shut up?'

* * *

On the Tuesday, Dilip and Shikta came around to Mum and Dad's to watch my wedding video. This was the first time I'd seen them since the wedding – we weren't exactly on speaking terms. Dilip broke the ice. 'Huh, I'm surprised they let you into America with your criminal record!' He asked me if I knew what my twelve months' conditional discharge meant. Enlightening me, Dilip explained. 'If you get caught doing anything, you'll go straight to prison. So, you'd better be nice to me!' Shikta chortled while Dad just shook his head.

We sat down to watch the show. 'Ooh, there's me!' shrieked Shikta as her face featured in still after still, leaving no illusion as to why they'd come around.

After about ten minutes, Mum went out to the kitchen to make tea – I followed to help. Shikta came in a little later to brag about her dancing on the video. 'You're missing it!'

Like me, Mum didn't seem too bothered by that, but asked Shikta's advice on the chura, which she was soaking in milk. Even though they were broken, Mum believed the ritual was to soak the chura after removal. 'Shikta, how long your mum soak them?'

Shikta looked at Mum scornfully. 'You're supposed to soak them *before* the wedding, *before* you put them on. *It's not difficult.*' That partly explained my difficulties with the bangles. Mum fumed silently at Shikta's condescension.

Back in the lounge, the wedding video moved from London to Liverpool and the party games at the Tojals' house. Shikta sulked. 'Dilip, why didn't *your* mum do party games for *us*?'

Mum exploded at Shikta's re-writing of history. 'We do games for you! We look for you! You and Dilip already done it together! Then you gone off and left dirty tissues!'

Shikta now showed Mum who was boss when it came to her Golden Boy. 'Dilip, how dare your mother speak to me like that? We're going!' Dad held his head in his hands as Dilip and Shikta stormed off, not for the first or last time.

When they'd gone, Mum turned on me. 'It's all your fault.' Yes, it usually was.

Ajay drove down from Liverpool on the Thursday to collect me. Upstairs, we saw Billy, whose Japanese girlfriend from University was staying over. Mum had given up arranging marriages, telling him, 'I muck up with other two. You do what you want.'

'Alright?' said Billy to Ajay as I re-introduced them.

Ajay grinned back at Billy. 'Guess what? Sunita slapped me!'

Later, Billy told Mum, who seemed rather pleased.

Chapter 27

EIGHT DAYS A WEEK

On 1ˢᵗ April 1999, the Labour Government introduced the first national minimum wage in the UK. The rate was set at £3.60 per hour for most adults, but only £3.00 for 18-22 year olds. In July 1999, I was put to work in the family business, but I wouldn't be joining Ajay, who drove every day to the family's warehouse in Manchester. Instead, I would be helping my mother-in-law at her indoor market stall just outside Liverpool. This enabled Behnji to sit on a chair, giving out orders, rather than serving customers herself. So, I would fetch clothes and bag them up while Behnji handled the money. On pay day, Pavan generously announced that I would be paid £20 for a week's work, but handed this to Ajay, along with his executive salary of £40 per week. I still had to carry out all my chores at home, including washing the family's underwear by hand.

In the continuing absence of a dowry from my parents, the Tojals had decided to get their money's worth from me one way or another. One day, Behnji gave me a shopping list and sent me and Ajay to buy the groceries for the family. In the supermarket, Ajay didn't have any money, so I paid on my credit card. Yes, I had a credit card despite being convicted of credit card fraud. This happened several times, as if Ajay had been told not to pay the shopping bill. My credit card bills were going to my parents' house in Woking and they were forwarding these to Liverpool. Before I got married, Mum had persuaded me to buy a television on hire purchase, which was being paid off on the credit card. Pavan saw the credit card statement and questioned me about the loan. 'But if you paid for the television, it's yours. You should bring it here.' Pavan was unconcerned by the grocery bills and the fact I didn't have any means to pay the credit card bill. Knowing I would have to pay off the credit card, I decided to get a job with a proper wage. I went to an employment agency and got a temporary job as a receptionist for Sun Chemical. It was just holiday cover for 11 days, but paid £5.00 an hour.

* * *

On the phone, before we married, Ajay sounded romantic, calling me his princess. But it was now clear that the Romeo on the other end of the phone had been an impostor. The closest Ajay got to romance was to ask, '*Do you love me more than cake?*' When I married Ajay, I was more or less resigned to the fact that sex would be part of the deal. This much was confirmed on our wedding night when Ajay raped me and, again, two nights later when he raped me at his mother's bidding. But after that, sex took a back seat in our marriage. Behnji didn't stand at the door any more, perhaps because of her other sons' reactions and the relatively calming presence of Pavan. I say relatively – he was now fully signed up to Behnji's dowry crusade. There were other attempts by Ajay to have his way with me. He would try and pull my pyjamas down, but I resisted and he didn't force me anymore. Ajay did wrestle with me a couple of times, but I think that was partly because he enjoyed wrestling for its own sake. Sex might have happened if it was proper lovemaking, something mutually enjoyable, which we talked about first. Believe it or not, I knew something about gentle lovemaking and foreplay from the porn videos Khan made me watch, although I'd never experienced it. But Ajay wasn't capable of initiating that kind of conversation. He knew the basics of sex, in and out, but not about pleasing a woman. To be honest, I didn't feel inclined to raise the subject of making love, either. Although, I had some tender feelings towards Ajay, I just didn't fancy him. He stank and he drooled, neither of which were his fault. Sometimes, I was sent to bed with Ajay and would climb under the duvet next to him. His bedroom wasn't quite big enough for a double bed, so without fail he would bang his knee on the dressing table, or stub his toe, before getting into bed. Other times, when Behnji kept me working to midnight or beyond, I would creep into the bedroom and sleep curled up on the floor. When things were particularly bleak, I would reminisce about Khan's cuddles – human warmth. But, I would also wake up with nightmares. Khan again, raping, biting or cutting me.

Ajay's body odour was not the only pungent aroma in our bedroom. One morning, I was lying on the floor when the bed began to shake. I thought Ajay was having a fit. He was shuddering violently and strange noises were coming from his mouth – '*Hnnnh, hnnnh*.' Concerned, I asked him if he was alright and quickly lifted the duvet, only to reveal Ajay masturbating into a condom. He knew condoms were associated with sexual activity, but wasn't exactly sure how or why. When he'd finished, he went to the bathroom, washed out the condom and brought it back, just like on our wedding night, before putting it into a drawer. This performance continued throughout our marriage. Ajay would either wash the condom immediately after use or, if he heard someone on the landing, he would store the used condom in the drawer and wash it later. Eventually, there were about thirty, not quite washed out condoms kept in the drawer, a stinking, semi-congealed mass of rubber.

One of Ajay's last attempts to have sex with me put him off for some time. Roughly grabbing the side of my pyjamas with his fat fingers, he pulled them down on one side – I didn't like to wear the sexy nighties Behnji had provided. I was having my period and shouted, 'Ajay, I'm bleeding!' With a confused expression, Ajay looked at my arm. 'Why are you looking at my arm, Ajay?'

Then Ajay looked in the right place and, seeing my blood-soaked sanitary towel, leapt to his feet, screaming as he ran downstairs like a man possessed. 'Help! Help! Sunny's bleeding! Sunny's bleeding!' Ajay's middle brother appeared at the door and asked if I was OK. Cringing with embarrassment, I lowered my head. Realising what the problem was, my brother-in-law went off to pacify Ajay.

One day, the whole Liverpool clan went to the Hindu temple on some festival day or special occasion. On the temple wall were gigantic paintings from the *Mahabharata*, the epic Indian tale. A pandit led prayers and singing, while the worshippers all sat on the floor, men on one side, women on the other. Behnji's sister made a point of sitting next to me. Either on her own initiative or Behnji's, she wanted to find out what, if anything, happened between me and Ajay at night time and asked in a whisper, 'What time do you go to bed? And what time do you go to sleep?' Then she giggled. I pretended not to understand and answered quite loudly.

'What do you mean, Aunty? You tell me. When do *you* go to bed? And when do *you* go to sleep?' Aunty seemed embarrassed as other worshippers turned to listen.

'Well, your uncle keeps me up for several hours.' Several people tutted – this was a temple, after all. I feigned confusion.

'Why doesn't he go to bed before you do, like Ajay does? *His* mum sends him to bed at seven-thirty.' There were gasps in the congregation. Looking straight ahead at the statues, I ignored further questions from Aunty and carried on praying.

A few days later, the question of my non-performance in the bedroom reared its head again. Behnji came into my bedroom one morning when Ajay wasn't around and told me she wasn't happy with my behaviour. I was taken to a family conference at her mother's house to discuss the problem. As well as Naniji, various aunties were in attendance, along with Uncle Robbie. Perhaps sensing that Behnji's presence might not be helpful, Naniji banished her to another room, while Ajay played with the children elsewhere in the house. Like Behnji, Naniji wanted me to have Ajay's children. All eyes were on me as Naniji came straight to the point.

'Why are you two not having sex? What's happening when you go to the bedroom?' Uncle Robbie looked away, embarrassed, as I replied.

'When we go to the bedroom, I get into bed, Ajay then turns the light off, bangs his knee, stubs his toe, and gets into bed.'

Naniji tried again. 'What time do you go to bed and what time do you go to sleep?'

I continued to play dumb. 'What happens, Naniji, is, we go to bed, Ajay turns the light off and stubs his toe. And then he goes to sleep. And then he snores.'

'Don't you have sex?'

'What's sex, Naniji?' I wanted it spelt out.

Naniji then used mime to explain herself. Holding out her forearms horizontally, she began moving them backwards and forwards like a piston in a steam engine or someone skiing.

Pulling a confused face, I asked Naniji, 'What's that?' and mimicked her *jiggy jiggy* mime.

'Has your mother not taught you about sex?'

'No.' That much was true.

'Does Ajay not try to have sex with you?'

'No,' I replied and decided they could hear the truth. 'Because he doesn't know how to make love and doesn't want me to see him naked. Or, he tries to wrestle with me and we play fight. Once we play fight, it turns really aggressive because he doesn't know when to stop. Or, his mother stands outside the door telling him to rape me.' This drew a stunned silence. Uncle Robbie looked down. For avoidance of doubt, I added, 'I don't want to have sex with him.'

Naniji was stunned, but recovered to deliver her verdict.

'Right. This is not good enough. We're calling your family.'

Shortly after this, the question of dowry reared its head again. Behnji's dowry obsession had reached manic proportions. She seemed to have abandoned all reason and taken Pavan with her. They decided to call Dad in front of me on speaker phone. Mum was at work. It was good to hear Dad's voice. 'Hanji, Behnji.'

Behnji got straight to the point. 'Right, we want dowry.' Then she proceeded to list her fantasy demands. 'We wanna washing machine. We wanna Mercedes with personalised number plates. We want £10k cash.'

The Mercedes was the most extravagant of Behnji's demands. Dad drove an E registration Nissan Bluebird. That means it was twelve years' old at the time. He told me that when he and Mum were visiting prospective husbands on my behalf, he would park it around the corner so it wouldn't be spotted. But the Tojals would have seen Dad's car when they first came to visit us in Woking. They would also have seen Mum's red Nissan Micra, which was even older, together with my white Micra, the newest car in our fleet, built ten years earlier in 1988. And yet, Behnji thought Mum and Dad would, or even could, buy her a Mercedes – with personalised number plates.

'Look, I've lost my job,' Dad explained. 'My wife works part-time in a card shop.' He sounded apologetic, but then he pointed out, 'We asked if you wanted dowry. You said no. You said our daughter was all you wanted.' Dad also mentioned that he'd told them I was a vegetarian. He was merely pointing out what was and was not covered in the pre-marital discussions, but this gave Behnji and Pavan an idea and events now took a sinister turn. After the phone call, they approached me together in the kitchen.

'Right. From now on you're gonna eat meat,' said Behnji.

'But I'm vegetarian.'

'If you don't eat meat, you can't eat,' she added.

'You're not serious?'

'Let's see how long she lasts,' said Pavan. This was the kind of behaviour I might expect from Behnji, but Pavan's involvement really shook me.

I still had to help Behnji prepare dinner. 'If you won't eat meat, you won't eat,' Behnji reminded me. And I wouldn't eat meat, so I didn't eat. Whilst she cooked meat for her family, Behnji watched me like a hawk to make sure I made only 15 chapatis instead of 16, since I was no longer allowed one. I was told to sit in a different room on the floor while the Tojal family ate.

As the days wore on, I became weaker and weaker. One night at around 2 a.m., I sneaked down to the kitchen and made myself a crisp sandwich. *Crunch!* As I took my first bite, I felt Behnji's hand on my shoulder. 'Put that down!'

Mentally, I'd become stronger since Khan and refused to back down and eat meat, but starvation took its toll and I became unwell, weak with kidney pains. I asked Ajay how to walk to the family doctors.

This was the Tojals' family doctor rather than Dad's friend. The doctor was visibly shocked as he read through my notes, the history of abuse, reports on my wounds and the psychiatric report for my court case. 'You poor soul. Everything you've been through, it's not right.' He warned, 'Behnji isn't very nice. If she finds out about any of this, she'll go mad.' The doctor destroyed my medical records there and then, tearing them up and putting them in the bin.

After examining me, the doctor told me I needed to go to hospital immediately and telephoned Ajay. 'Ajay, you must take your wife straight to the hospital. Now! Don't tell your mother. Take her straight there.' Ajay sprang into action and drove to the surgery.

Ajay looked worried. 'Mam doesn't know I'm 'ere.' I asked him to drop by the house first to pick up some pills and personal things – toothbrush and facial tweezers. Despite the pain, I was thinking of my daily regime of moustache plucking!

But Ajay was panicking. 'No. Doctor said you have to go to hospital now. He said now.' Ajay was scared for me. Although he was controlled by Behnji, he did care for me and I think he knew that what was happening at home, was wrong. Without his mother's permission, he raced the car to the Royal Victoria Liverpool Hospital, where I was taken to A&E with a letter from the GP.

Hospital notes state that I had malnutrition. I was put on a saline drip.

That afternoon, Behnji clomped into the ward while a nurse was taking my blood pressure. 'What's wrong with her? I wanna know everything that's wrong with her.'

The nurse answered politely but firmly. 'She's got pyelonephritis again.'

Behnji reacted as if I were faulty livestock. 'Whaddya mean "again"? They should have told us she was damaged.'

When the nurse left us briefly, Behnji warned me, 'Don't you tell 'em anything. Don't you dare! I *knew* there was something wrong with you.'

The nurse was clearly concerned about Behnji and hovered nearby. As Behnji continued to snipe at me, the nurse returned and asked, 'Are you alright, love?'

'She's stressing me out.'

The nurse turned to Behnji. 'I think you'd better leave, Madam.' Another nurse joined her and they ushered Behnji out of the ward. She was furious. My bed was next to the window. That night I gazed at the stars and thought of Dud Chacha.

Ajay came to visit the next day. 'Mam doesn't know I'm 'ere.' He looked concerned for me.

I asked Ajay to bring my contraceptive pills, explaining that otherwise I would bleed. 'They're in the drawer where you turn your condoms inside out.'

Later that day, Behnji stormed into the ward and waved the contraceptive pills in my face. 'What the hell are these?' I didn't answer. Behnji threw the packet of pills at me. 'We'll discuss this later. I'm gonna call your parents.' Behnji would also have found Ajay's collection of used condoms.

Behnji also brought some clothes for me, which she'd got off the market, and took my clothes, including my jacket and shoes. 'Why are you taking them?' I asked her.

'They'll need washing.' The jacket and shoes didn't need washing. Maybe she wanted to make sure I didn't run away.

I rang Dad from the hospital. I thought that if Behnji was

ringing my parents anyway, I might as well tell them my side of the story. I had no money so I had to reverse the charges.

'Dad, I'm at the Royal Victoria Hospital in Liverpool. The family have been abusing me. They keep asking me for dowry. They're forcing me to eat meat.'

'But I told them you were vegetarian.'

'Dad, can you please come and see me.'

'I can't. You belong to them now. They can do whatever they want.'

'But I'm your daughter.'

'I need to ask their permission to see you. I'll see what I can do.'

I couldn't believe Dad's response. 'You need their permission to see me?'

'Let me speak to your mum. She's got a headache. But let me see if we can come and see you.'

Behnji rang me at the hospital later. 'How *dare* you ring your fucking family without my permission? Who do you think you are, ringing them?'

I was discharged from hospital after a week. Back at the Tojals, I started eating again. This time no one stopped me – Behnji and Pavan probably realised they'd gone too far, but Behnji wasn't finished yet. I was put back to work on the market stall with my zero wages contract, but I obtained a two-week sick note from my doctor, which I handed to Behnji. She scowled but said nothing.

The next day, Behnji took me to her sister's hairdressing salon, where a young trainee started to cut my hair under Behnji's supervision. Behnji already told me what to wear, so if she now wanted to choose my hairstyle, I thought I might as well let her. Behnji took a clump of my hair in her hand to show how much she wanted cut off. The hairdresser cut my hair at the side to shoulder length as ordered. Then she went to cut the back, but Behnji intervened.

'Right, that's enough. Leave the back.'

The hairdresser didn't understand at first. 'But I haven't done the back yet.'

'Never mind, we'll leave it like that,' replied Behnji, grinning maliciously at me in the mirror. My hair now looked ridiculous, cut to shoulder length at the front but hanging to hip length at the back. The hairdresser was practically in tears at what she'd been made to do.

Behnji's sister came over and gasped when she saw my hair. 'What have you done?' she asked Behnji. 'There's a party next week. What *will* she look like?'

Behnji sent me down to Woking the next weekend with Ajay. I think she wanted me to show off my new haircut, her latest salvo in the dowry war with my parents. It was also Raksha Bandan, the brother and sister festival, the 'bond to protect'. 'Let's see what your brothers give you.' I'm not sure what she was expecting from Dilip and Billy. A Rolls Royce perhaps? Or an executive jet? Mum opened the door, saw my haircut and laughed. 'Ha! You even more ugly now!' Neither of my brothers were around that weekend, and there were no gifts to take back to Liverpool.

* * *

In August, Ajay took to me to an Everton match with his middle brother and a boy cousin. His youngest brother, being a Liverpool fan, didn't join us. This had almost certainly been arranged without Behnji's approval and I was looking forward to spending some time with Ajay, away from her malign influence. We drove to Goodison Park, Everton's ground, which is in Liverpool. Everton were playing Southampton and the boys wore the club colours, blue football shirts and blue and white scarves. The atmosphere inside the stadium was electric, with people singing and chanting, happy, like they belonged. I sat between Ajay and his brother behind the goal. Everton's players ran on to a tune, which, I'm told, is the theme from *Z-Cars*, an old TV police drama. The crowd roared as the match kicked off. Whenever Everton attacked, the crowd stood, causing the blue plastic seats to flap up in unison creating a chorus of sound – *dub-dub-dub-dub*. I quickly got the hang of standing up and joined in, but I couldn't do the chants because I didn't know the words. Ajay's brother explained what football was, what the goalkeeper did and so on. Actually, I already knew quite a bit. For his amusement, Khan had forced me to learn the offside rule, but Ajay's brother was being kind, so I thanked him. At half-time, the brother asked, 'Are you 'avin' a good time? Would you come again, like?' I said that I would love to come here with them all another time – I was really enjoying myself.

As we left the ground, it was crowded and noisy with people rushing to get out. Everton beat Southampton 4-1 that day and Ajay smiled as he put his arm around me. I snuggled up to him for safety – I didn't want to get lost in the crowd. He seemed embarrassed, but we looked at each other and shared a moment.

Back home, Ajay was on cloud nine. 'I'm taking my wife again!' he announced proudly.

Behnji asked me, 'Did you like going out with the boys?'

'Yes, thank you. I'd love to go again.'

'No, you won't be going again. Now, go and do the dishes.'

Ajay looked at me, crestfallen. The wind had been taken out of his sails and I felt desperately sad for him as his mother sent him to the toilet, whilst I trudged off to the kitchen. I suspect that if the football had bored me, Behnji would have bought me a season ticket. But, I will always remember my afternoon at Everton fondly.

Chapter 28

POISON PEN

In early September, Behnji took a phone call from Dad, who said he was coming up to Liverpool. Previously, Behnji had threatened to summon my parents to Liverpool to discuss my non-performance in the bedroom, and there was always the dowry to ask for, but this time Behnji didn't seem happy with their proposed visit. I don't know what Dad had said to her, but later, she approached me.

'I don't want them comin', d'you hear me? Call and tell 'em not to come,' she shouted. She'd obviously changed her tune and realised that Mum and Dad weren't going to buy her a Mercedes with personalised number plates, or a new washing machine, after all. But what was Behnji scared of? For once, I stood up to her and refused. We were in the front room with Ajay's brothers. She walked towards me menacingly. Tension was building up inside me – I'd had enough after months of Behnji's bullying. Clenching on a glass, which happened to be in my hand, I thought it might shatter as my mother-in-law squared up to me. 'Tell 'em not to come. Now!'

The lock in the front door clicked and Pavan and Ajay entered the house. Pavan came into the room, saw something was up and asked what the problem was.

'My parents are coming tomorrow and she doesn't want them to.'

Whatever Behnji's concerns were, Pavan clearly didn't share them.

'Nonsense! They're only taking her for a couple of days.'

Mum and Dad arrived the next morning. Pleasantries were in short supply on both sides and Mum told me, almost immediately, to go and get my jewellery. Walking upstairs to fetch what wasn't in Behnji's clutches, I wasn't entirely sure what was going on. I was already wearing the *mangalsutra,* but there were Naniji's earrings and a few other bits and pieces in a bag, which I handed to Mum. Ajay stood awkwardly by Mum and Dad near the front door as I struggled downstairs with a suitcase.

'Aren't you going to help your wife with that?' Dad asked Ajay, contemptuously.

Mum examined my jewellery bag with obvious disappointment. 'Where's the rest of it?'

I pointed at Behnji. 'She's got it all.' Mum glared at Behnji.

'Forget about that, we've got the girl,' said Dad.

'Never mind her, I want the gold!' Mum and Dad seemed to have a mixture of motives for coming to Liverpool.

I left Liverpool on Tuesday 7th September 1999, initially believing I would just be spending a few days in Woking. Dad suggested I find a temporary job so I could continue to pay off my loans and the court fines. I thought that was strange as I was only there for a visit, but supposed it wouldn't be for long.

When I'd been back in Woking about three days, Mum updated me with the news. She told me that Rinku was still carrying a torch for me. Perhaps she'd forgotten that she prevented us from marrying. This was the time I wrote to Rinku, asking him to move on with his life and forget about me. Then Mum told me some tragic news. Moonie's baby son had died. I don't know how Mum knew this. This was the child Moonie had been visiting in Great Ormond Street Hospital. I was trying to take this in, working out what to say to Moonie, as if words could be adequate.

Then Mum added, excitedly, 'Oh, and Khan got married!' I was puzzled at how Mum knew this. Maybe he'd rung her to taunt me, or perhaps Dad had heard from Khan's brother down at the Woking Liberal Club.

I got a temporary clerical job at Telewest in Woking, starting on the following Monday, 13th September. Ajay telephoned and I asked if he was coming down at the weekend, but he said he wasn't allowed to. Soon after this, I took a call on the house phone from my mother-in-law, who ordered me, 'Put your dad on.' Assuming the call related to me, I stayed with Dad and heard Behnji ask him in a raised voice, 'When are you bringin' 'er back. People are starting to talk.'

'I'm not bringing her back,' Dad replied. This was news to me at the time, although, with hindsight the writing was clearly on the wall.

'Bring 'er back now, you bastard!' screamed Behnji down the phone. Dad remained calm.

'*Hanji*, Behnji. You can swear at me all you like. I'm not bringing her back.'

After the call, Dad told me that he'd heard from friends in Liverpool that I was being mistreated, that they feared for my safety whilst I was living under the Tojals' roof. According to a sworn statement made later by Mum, Ajay had called Mum and Dad while I was in Liverpool to say that he couldn't look after me. I believe Ajay was trying to protect me from Behnji.

At this point, I still didn't realise my marriage was over. Although I wasn't attracted to Ajay, I did care for him and he was my husband. I thought we might live together, away from his parents, and felt I might somehow rescue him from Behnji. Things would be different away from her malign influence.

Through late September and into October, Ajay was calling me every day at work or home. He also called my parents and asked for help. Mum told him he'd have to come down and live in Woking. Dad wasn't impressed, asking, 'What kind of man is he?'

In October, Ajay rang to warn me that his mother would force us to divorce if I didn't return. Meanwhile, a rumour began circulating in Liverpool, which reached Mum and Dad on the Punjabi grapevine. Apparently, I was dying. Perhaps Behnji wished I *was* dying, but she needed to save face and explain how she appeared to have mislaid a daughter-in-law. Then, I received a phone call from Liverpool police. They'd received a complaint that I'd stolen some jewellery from the Tojals. The truth was, in my possession, I only had jewellery that belonged to me, either items my parents or I had bought, or wedding gifts from the Tojals. Behnji even claimed I'd stolen the *mangalsutra*, claiming it was a family heirloom. The *mangalsutra* is unique, like a wedding ring, and worn by Indian brides. In fact, the Tojals had far more of my jewellery than I did. The policeman who called me revealed that he knew about my criminal record. I don't know whether the Tojals were aware of this yet, or whether the police had run their own checks, but it didn't look good. The policeman threatened me with arrest if I didn't 'return' the jewellery. I denied the allegation.

Finally, I realised that my marriage was over. Dad didn't want me going back to Liverpool and Ajay wouldn't be allowed to join me. Her demands for dowry unsatisfied, Behnji also knew that my marriage to her son was finished, and had now gone to war over the jewellery. I contacted a solicitor, who wrote to Ajay on 21st October, informing him that I would be seeking a divorce on the grounds of unreasonable behaviour. My solicitor also asked for the return of my personal belongings, especially my passport and driving licence. Behnji raised the stakes. A solicitor, acting nominally for Ajay, responded to say that he was concerned I would leave the country with his property and, if I didn't return it immediately, they would contact police and take out an injunction, preventing me from disposing of these items.

The Tojals didn't respond to the request for my property, so I made a counter-complaint against the Tojals, stating that they'd stolen my possessions, including my passport and driving licence. Mum and Dad, who were outraged at the slur on the family, mobilised and came with me to Liverpool, where we stayed with friends. One thing I'd learnt from Khan was how to get the police involved. So, accompanied by a policeman, I rang the Tojals' doorbell. Pavan answered the door, then Behnji appeared. I was sad to see Pavan. I didn't want to see him dragged into this. He'd been fine with me in the beginning, before Behnji appealed to his dark side. The policeman explained I was here to collect my property and asked if my husband was in. Lurking behind Pavan, Behnji stuck her tongue out at me childishly. Pavan told the officer his son wasn't in. The policeman took out his notebook and asked Pavan his name.

'PP,' replied Pavan giving just his first two initials, whilst behind him, Behnji continued to stick her tongue out at me.

The officer sighed wearily before asking, 'Your name's Pee Pee?'

'Yes, PP.'

Ajay came down the stairs, dishevelled. On seeing me, he smiled shyly and began sighing and swaying. I felt sad that things had come to this and wished I could have talked to Ajay alone. Behnji snapped at Ajay to get back. He moved away only slightly and continued smiling at me. The policeman explained, again, the reason for our visit.

'We haven't got her property,' lied Pavan. 'It's at the solicitors.'

I saw my coat hanging at the bottom of the stairs. 'Look, there's my coat!'

Behnji then accused me again of stealing jewellery. Since most of my jewellery was in Behnji's possession, this fired me up.

'It's a lie. Tell her, Ajay. You saw me packing when I left. *She's* got *my* jewellery.' As a parting shot, I promised Behnji I would see her in court.

On Sunday, we paid a visit to the Hindu temple in Liverpool. This was around Diwali time. Several people were surprised to see me and asked after my health. Rumours of my impending death had clearly been exaggerated. We were told that the Tojals had driven to the temple, heard we were inside, and went home.

On Monday, we went to the Tojals' solicitor to collect my belongings. The solicitor didn't have my possessions and called Pavan and Behnji, who said Ajay had my passport and driving licence. Next, the solicitor called Ajay, who was driving, but said his parents had them. We went to the police station, where the Tojals were summoned to join us under the threat of arrest. In the police station, Behnji tried to turn the tables. 'She's got our jewellery. Look she's wearing her wedding ring and engagement ring. I want them back.'

The policeman attending to us was the one who'd accompanied me to the house. He wasn't impressed. 'So what? It's a wedding ring. Her husband's got his wedding ring, hasn't he?'

Behnji's performance at the police station is described in

a sworn statement later made by Mum. '*During the course of the interview with the police … Behnji changed her story on several occasions stating that either the jewellery had already been taken by my daughter, or that it was at the solicitors, or that is was in a safety deposit box, or that it was at home.*'

Eventually, the Tojals provided us with a locked suitcase with no key. When we prised it open, there were some of my clothes, stained with some oil, like they'd been in a garage. As for the counter accusations of theft between me and the Tojals, the police suggested this was a civil matter, which they would rather not get involved with.

My appearance at the temple had put paid to Behnji's story about my death, but then she struck gold. Mum heard from friends in Liverpool that Behnji was circulating copies of a document around the Punjabi community, which showed that I had a criminal record. Behnji could now save face by demonstrating that I was a thief and, therefore, Ajay was best rid of me. At first, Mum denied the story, saying that anyone could produce a piece of paper. It turned out that this was my certificate of conviction, issued by Guildford Crown Court, a document available both to convicted criminals and their victims.

One evening, I was with Mum when the house phone rang. She answered it. The volume on the phone was always loud so you could hear the other caller if you were nearby. A man with an Asian accent said, 'Hello. Is Sunita there?'

Mum frowned suspiciously, then, looking at me, put her finger to her mouth to indicate silence. '*Ek* minute' – One minute – she replied and then pretended to call me. 'Sunita, it's for you.' Mum now adopted a different voice, which really just sounded like a distorted version of her own. 'Hello? This is Sunita.'

'Sunita, why have you changed your voice?' The caller

clearly wasn't fooled by Mum's impression of me.

'Er, no, I haven't. Who is this?' asked Mum.

'It's Khan's uncle.' I froze – Mum glared at me as the voice added, 'I've been speaking to those nice Tojals in Liverpool.' Khan had never mentioned an uncle and, although my family have always referred to Khan by his surname, it seemed very odd for an uncle to introduce himself this way. I suspected this was one of Behnji's relatives, the one who pretended to be Ajay over the telephone when we were engaged. But how did he know about Khan?

'Sunita, you owe Khan lots of money.' Again, Khan's 'uncle' referred to him by surname only. Mum stopped pretending to be me.

'*She* owes *him* money! He take all her money!' Then she slammed the phone down. 'You stupid bitch. You tell them about him, didn't you?' Mum thought it was Khan on the phone. I was confused – it didn't sound like him, although he could change his voice and accent. I now feared for Ajay. If Khan knew about him, he would know we'd slept together as man and wife, and I thought he might go after him. Mum was panicking and shouting at me. Dad was out, so she called Dilip, told him about the phone call and asked him to come around, although history didn't suggest Dilip would be any use in dealing with Khan.

'I'm busy,' replied Dilip. That evening, Mum told Dad, who didn't see a problem.

'What does it matter? She's not going back up there.'

Although I'd started the ball rolling to divorce Ajay with a preliminary letter to him, his solicitors got their paperwork in beforehand, and Ajay moved to divorce me first, also on the grounds of unreasonable behaviour. These grounds included the fact that I wouldn't sleep with him and, astonishingly, the fact that my parents hadn't provided a dowry. They also wanted me to pay for the divorce. My counter allegation stated that Ajay raped me on our wedding night and that he wouldn't bathe unless his mother told him to. It was all rather sad. In the end, my solicitor recommended that, since both parties wanted a divorce anyway, I might as well let the Tojals' petition go through. This way they would pay more of the legal costs, and I would save about £2,000. I followed this advice and launched a separate action for the return of my jewellery. Perhaps I'm the only woman in the UK who has been successfully sued for divorce, partially on the grounds that no dowry was received by my husband's family – something that wouldn't be possible in India. It wasn't about money for me, and I returned the earrings Naniji had given me, via the solicitors.

Behnji had further tricks up her sleeve. Bizarrely, she sent the certificate of conviction to my solicitor, who produced it in her office when I was there with Mum. My solicitor said that Behnji had helpfully informed her that she'd received this from a family member. 'It must have been my brother, Dilip,' I said. The solicitor nodded. My first thought was that Dilip would have received a copy of the certificate as one of the victims, and may also have received my copy, since much of my post was being re-directed to his house because I shared an initial and surname with Shikta. But, then I looked closer at the date – 29th November 1999 (nine months after my conviction). Dilip had deliberately requested the document to help the Tojals against me. Big Brother's hatred was relentless.

Mum protested Dilip's innocence. 'Dilip never do that.' Years later, Dilip cheerfully admitted to providing Behnji with the certificate, breaking my parents' belief that it was either my haircut or black magic that had caused my marriage to fail.

Behnji provided further documents to my solicitor in a bungling attempt to discredit me. Perhaps she thought we would throw in the towel on seeing these, but a more brainless attempt to smear my reputation would be harder to imagine.

The first item was a page torn from a notebook I'd left behind in Liverpool, on which, in Behnji's handwriting, is written Khan's full name, misspelt as *Kaan*, along with the words Pakistan and Birmingham, and also the name of a female cousin of Dad's from Hounslow. The word *Yes* is written at the top of the note – as if Behnji thought she'd hit the jackpot with this information. Presumably, whoever had briefed Behnji about the credit cards, had also told her about Khan. The note almost certainly explains the strange phone call purporting to be from Khan's uncle. Why Behnji thought this mysterious scrap of paper would help her cause is anyone's guess. As for Dad's cousin, I hardly knew her, but I believe the inclusion of her name was an attempt by Behnji's real informants to cover their tracks.

The second offering was another page from my notebook, on which Behnji had written Ajay's middle brother's name and a sixteen digit credit card number. This seems to have been a crude, but ultimately half-hearted, effort to suggest I'd attempted to use my brother-in-law's card. In fact, when I was providing credit card details to Khan, I was able to memorise the numbers – I didn't need to write them down.

To allege that I'd tried to use the credit card would have been a lie – it didn't happen, and there was no evidence to support it. I don't believe Ajay's brother would have had anything to do with such a scheme. However, apart from this sly innuendo, the Tojals didn't explicitly make such an allegation, so this was all rather pointless.

Behnji's third document was a letter written by her

accomplice, a creature whose handwriting I recognised.

My Very Good Friend,

I have just heard of your very good fortune, and would like to congratulate You. I would just like to ask you, if you could find it in your heart to help a Friend out.

I have just saved enough money, to go to Spain for a week, but I would very much like to go to the Caribbean, just to see if it is suitable for you to go on holiday their. I don't mind travelling that far for a Friend as I'm sure you would do the same for me I should manage on about £2,000. but I will be very grateful for anything you can afford out of your big WIN.

P.S I might have to go to a health Farm First, to get in shape, and I will need to take a Friend with Me For company. I do hope you can oblige And I look forward to receiving your cheque.

May God Bless You.
and Harry Krishna
xxxxx

The letter was unsigned and undated, and appears to suggest, falsely, that I'd come into some good fortune. The writer goes on to ask me for some money to pay for a holiday. I have absolutely no idea where Behnji and her helper were going with this. Needless to say, Behnji's solicitor found no use for these papers and they didn't figure in the court case. As for the identity of the author of the begging letter, all I can say is, I'm pretty sure it wasn't Dilip. As an Oxford graduate, his English is much better than that.

When I married Ajay, I assumed it would be for life, and was willing to make a go of it. I think if we'd lived away from

Behnji, we might have stayed together. Whether that would have been good for either of us is another matter. I didn't love Ajay, although I did care for him and I believe he cared for me, too.

Behnji saw me purely in terms of what I could do for her. I was part skivvy, part doll. I was also there to provide grandchildren, but, above all, Behnji thought I would bring her riches in the form of dowry. In that quest, Ajay was as much a pawn as I was.

From experience, I know there are worse husbands than Ajay, and I wish him well.

Chapter 29

PIECES OF ME

I'm not a good sleeper. The world of dreams holds many terrors for me. A world where fragments of the past become all too real in the dead of night. Khan's face, his bloodshot eyes with their constricted pupils, his pitiless anger, which I can still feel. It's 1997 again. Khan's in the bedroom, about to rape me or violently assault me. There's no sound, but I hear him screaming at me. The threat of impending violence wakens me with a shudder. There's no one there. I lie awake, exhausted by the attack on my senses. Very slowly, my pulse returns to something like normal and, warily, I start to doze off. A memory – the first time, and many more times, of Khan pinning me against a wall, smashing my head against it. In my sleep, I feel something touching me. I jump with a start and gasp. Khan? No, there's no one else in the room. It's only our cat, Mo, purring, perhaps dreaming in black and white. Sometimes, when Maya's not well, she sleeps in my bed with me. I try and stay awake in case she touches me in my half-sleep, setting in train a nightmare. It's difficult. As far as I know, Khan doesn't feature in my dreams every night, but he's never far, ever present. The horrors of Khan haunt my waking hours, too. Incidents play in my mind's eye again and again, like a film reel on a loop – post-traumatic stress disorder, perhaps. The first rape. My head being held under water – I can't breathe. Khan, the surgeon, outlining my body parts with his marker pen. Khan locking me in the car boot. More rape, more violence. Khan outside my parents' house – he's come for me. I was barely out of childhood, naïve, when Khan got hold of me. He planned his approach, he groomed me and he took control of me. He owned me. Khan's influence, for better or worse, is with me for life. Small things. I drink out of a plastic glass at home. I don't like real glass – Khan used to smash and cut me with it. Bedtime. I brush my teeth the way Khan taught me, even after all these years. Conditioned. Everyday noises – a knife or a fork dropped accidentally, a can opening, a car backfiring in the street, and I flashback to one of Khan's rages. Then, at night in dreamland, I'm in his arms again. I can smell burning, a fresh scar smouldering on my flesh from Khan's lit cigarette, but it's all right now. Time for cuddles.

* * *

In 2014, whilst writing this book, I began dictating the details of my time with Khan onto tape, trying to put events in order. But, in doing so, my memories of Khan intensified and there were more frequent flashbacks. It almost seemed as if I were bringing Khan back into my life. My voice would shake with emotion as I struggled to describe his abuse. Torn between my desire to tell my story and the nightmares its telling conjured up, I decided to seek professional help. One afternoon, I went to see a hypnotherapist called Gary Turner near Aldershot, who asked, 'So, what are we here for today?' I explained that I was writing a book about my life, but that this was bringing back horrific memories, which I was struggling to deal with. Instead of breaking down when I spoke about Khan, I wanted to break through and make sense of my past. I also wondered whether some of the more frightening memories could be erased. Gary told me he would prefer not to erase my memories. He warned that, if he did so, I would no longer be the same person – my memories were a part of who I was. He said that what he could do was try and help me draw away some of the emotion, allowing me to leave the worst episodes in the past, not staying with me in the present or the future. Gary asked me to think of my life as a book, and to go back to the beginning, to my earliest bad memory. He said I didn't need to tell him all the details, but I decided I would. I felt I needed to explain what had happened. Gary told me to look at the end of a pen he was holding whilst I journeyed back in time in my mind. *I'm a three-year-old girl lying on the floor, terrified, struggling. On top is an older boy, V.* As I spoke of my childhood abuse, Gary was moving his pen from side to side, and then up and down. As I was telling my story, my eyes were jumping about, following the pen. It was kind of distracting, but I think that was the whole point. In therapy, I travelled though my life, visiting other traumatic events from the past, more of V's abuse, meeting Khan that fateful Saturday morning in 1997 in Woking, the first time Khan raped me, further instances of his cruelty, my rejection by my mother and the death of my husband, Ray. There were further episodes from after Khan, which I haven't covered in this book. Whilst I talked and remembered, I was also trying to concentrate on Gary's pen. I found that I was able to discuss my experiences with less emotion. I understand that this is something to do with the rapid eye movement caused by following the pen. The mind files the memories, defining them as past events, creating distance from the present. Years of anguish flooded out of me, as if a boil had been lanced. Speaking of V, I no longer felt like a three-year-old – I wasn't living in the moment any more. I was a thirty-six-year-old looking back at the three-year-old me. Remembering Khan, too, all the rape and the torture, I had some distance. I was looking back but not reliving the experience. My hypnotherapy session lasted two hours. Because of V, I've always been afraid of dogs. Gary has two blue-eyed huskies called Max and Harley, which welcomed me at the front door and stayed throughout the therapy. For some reason, I wasn't scared of them. Beautiful, intuitive animals, they seemed to know I needed healing and would gently place their paws on my feet, transferring their warmth.

After the session, I decided to see if I could confront some of my demons by visiting the house where Khan and I lived for most of our time together, and drove to Morland Road in Aldershot, which is a short drive from Gary's place. Previously, driving through Aldershot would trigger memories of Khan, causing me to shake. This time, I drove there without the same reaction. Parking outside the house, I got out calmly and took photos of it from the front. The house is on a corner, so I walked around into the adjacent street to look at the back, and saw the windows of our bedroom. This was our home, my prison, the room I was locked in, where Khan threatened to carve me up and much more. The memories came flooding back, but I was no longer there, living in that time. Standing, looking at the house for a while, I was able to endure the memories. I still felt anger at what Khan had done, but I now had the strength to control the emotion. Driving back to Woking, I felt a sense of liberation. After the therapy, I found I could talk about Khan and other painful memories more dispassionately.

Victims of abuse often experience feelings of guilt. *It's my fault he hurts me.* The Stockholm Syndrome, first used in relation to kidnapping victims, describes how abuse victims become sympathetic towards their captors and blame themselves. Captive and captor bond as temporary lulls in mistreatment are interpreted as kindness. Reading about the Stockholm Syndrome, this struck a chord with me. This was me and Khan. Our relationship. For years, I felt guilty for ever having feelings towards Khan. With my low self-esteem and expectations back then, he was the man who gave me cuddles and told me he loved me. Understanding the condition better has helped me to move on.

People often ask why the victims stay. Instead, perhaps they should ask why people abuse in the first place. Small time Birmingham gangster, petty drug dealer, junkie, wife beater and rapist; perhaps Khan saw himself as a big fish in Woking. But in his way, Khan was as broken as me. Calculating and controlling, I now believe Khan stalked me from the moment he saw Mum and Dilip treat me with contempt at work the time they came for my passport. Seeing my vulnerability – damaged goods – he read me like a book.

Everywhere I go, I see pieces of me – reflections of my past. The child with sad eyes, the lady who flinches, the homeless man living on the margins, the broken and the rejected. Each of them has a story to tell. Where possible, I try and reach out to them, tell them they're not alone. I help out with former young offenders at *The Academy of Hard Knocks* at *Fight Science* in Aldershot. Many of the young people come from troubled backgrounds. Some have been drug addicts, some were abused as children. The Academy aims to break the cycle of re-offending.

I used to want to change my past, or erase it. For years, I felt ashamed. Ashamed of the abuse, ashamed for being the victim. I was told I was 'dirty' for sleeping with Khan.

I'd brought shame on my family for being with a man from a different community. I know my parents did what they thought was best.

But now I've come to terms with who I am. A Survivor. I've accepted each piece of me, made peace with my past. By removing the bad chapters, my story wouldn't have made sense. I'm proud of who I am today. My journey was filled with detours, but I'm happy with the destination.

Twenty years on from that fateful meeting with Khan, I've tried to tell my story. I first planned to write about my life back in 2003, when Ray was still alive, but I never got going for various reasons. The memories were too painful and events got in the way. Then, in 2012, I began making recordings using a Dictaphone, recalling the events of my life. In total, there are hundreds of hours' of tape recordings of my voice, no longer silent as, slowly but surely, my story poured out. The process was harrowing as I relived traumatic events and began to remember more and more. But it was therapeutic at the same time. I was telling *my* story at last.

I also hope to encourage other victims of abuse to come forward and tell *their* stories, seek *their* peace and *their* justice, and become survivors. There is no 'honour' when honour and shame prevent victims of abuse from receiving help, or when abusers walk free. Love starts at home.

* * *

Epilogue

A TALE OF TWO HUSBANDS

An Englishman and an Irishman walked into a pub. I ended up marrying them both. In 2001, to pay for the legal cost of suing the Tojals over the jewellery, I took an evening job working in *The Sports Bar* opposite *The Planets* in Woking. Mum and Dad were already talking of another arranged marriage. One evening, an Englishman called James asked me out for dinner and an Irishman named Ray invited me for a drink. I wasn't hungry, so I opted for the drink with Ray.

Ray and I didn't properly get together until 2002, when we fell in love. We spoke of our dreams. Ray said I'd saved him. He gave my life a purpose, too. It was a whirlwind romance. Ray proposed to me and I said, 'Yes.' We married in Fiji in 2003. It seemed like my fairy tale came true.

* * *

On 10th June 2004 at 5.30 a.m., I was lying awake when there was a knock at the front door. I was staying with my parents because Ray and I had argued the night before. Dad was already up for his prayers and answered. He called for me. 'Sunita, there's two policemen at the door.' I hurried down the stairs. One policeman looked at the floor while the other spoke solemnly.

'Mrs Murphy, we're sorry to inform you … your husband's dead.'

I broke down and collapsed on the floor, unable to accept what the policeman had said. I looked at Dad like the frightened little girl I was. 'Dad, who are these people? These aren't real police. My Ray's not dead. They've made a mistake – he's sleeping. Tell them, Dad! Tell them, please!' Dad cried as he tried to pick me up off the floor.

* * *

When Ray lost his job as a recruitment consultant, he decided to try his hand as a cocaine dealer. Ray had admitted to me that he'd been a heavy cocaine user since he was 21, and he knew a lot of people who did coke. But he began associating with a different crowd, including other drug dealers. He found himself out of his league and managed to run up large debts to some of these dealers. I had to take out loans to pay these off. Part of the problem was, a lot of Ray's stock would find its way up his nose. Ray promised me he'd stopped dealing and he started a window cleaning round. We put out fliers in the name of the business – *Sun Ray*. But Ray carried on drug dealing in secret. Ray also suffered from depression, for which he took medication. Out of work and in debt to some dangerous people, Ray plunged into despair and he began to threaten suicide. Nevertheless, the circumstances of Ray's death didn't add up.

Some months before, there'd been a stabbing in our flat during a fight over cocaine. All the men in the flat at the time were arrested and questioned on suspicion of attempted murder. Subsequently, Ray was threatened and warned not to co-operate with the police investigating the incident. He also owed money big time.

On the day Ray was found dead, once the 'crime scene' had been made safe, I returned to the ground floor flat where Ray and I lived. A friend who was passing had discovered Ray sitting motionless on the windowsill with a metal tow rope around his neck. I was accompanied by a policewoman. This was Gemma, the same officer who'd attended to me back in 1997 and 1998, in connection with Khan.

I felt physically sick as we approached the flat. My mind was at bursting point, overwhelmed by a wave of emotions and questions. I couldn't take in what was happening. Part of me asked whether I could have saved Ray. I wanted to speak to Ray. I wanted to hear his voice. Mentally, I was breaking down, but I needed to know the truth. What happened? How did my husband die? I was nervous as we entered the flat, fearful that there would be no last-minute reprieve. We entered the flat and I didn't wake up from a bad dream. Things were out of place and the stench of vomit greeted us. This was for real – Ray was dead.

Gemma said, 'Sunny, you poor love. After all you've been through, you really should write that book before anything else happens.'

Alone in the flat after Gemma had left, I thought about Ray. I thought about those last few days and all that had happened. Then I noticed Ray's trainers. Something didn't look right about them. I was trying to make sense of what had happened and there were Ray's trainers, sticking out like a sore thumb. They were tidy, with the shoelaces tied in a knot. That was it – the laces! Who would tie the laces up? Ray had enormous feet with a large instep and just couldn't remove his trainers without untying the laces, as some people do. He would always have to not only untie the knot, but also loosen the laces in all the holes. Sometimes, I would help him put his trainers on or take them off. But here were his trainers, removed, with the laces tied. It struck me that Ray's trainers may have been pulled off him forcibly, perhaps after his death. This June day was the longest of my life. When darkness eventually came, I discovered the lights didn't work because the electricity cable had been cut outside the house.

Ray's death certificate later stated that he was hanged, although his neck wasn't broken. This didn't make sense. Ray was found sitting down. Hanging takes place from a height, but the tow rope wasn't high enough above the floor. So, Ray was supposedly hanged sitting down, with no suspension either to break his neck or strangle him. It takes about two minutes to strangle someone and, even with suicide, the body's natural instinct is to fight for survival. Since he wasn't dangling from a height, Ray would just have needed to stand up to save his life. What stopped him? Was Ray already dead *before* his supposed hanging?

In the months following Ray's death, not convinced that he'd taken his own life, I began making my own enquiries. Ray drank in a pub in Woking called *The Goldsworth Arms* – 'The Goldy' – since demolished. Drugs were dealt in the The Goldy and Ray was there on the night of his death, reportedly drinking with a mystery stranger. I asked to see the security tapes from that night. But the tapes for that evening – 9th June – were missing. Tapes for all other nights were available.

At Ray's inquest on 24th March 2005, the coroner returned an open verdict stating, 'In the circumstances, I am not satisfied the high level of proof that is needed is present for me to conclude that he took his own life.'

There was a painful 71 day wait for Ray's funeral – but that's another story. The police file on Ray's death has now been destroyed on the grounds that it was classified merely as a 'suspicious incident'. My quest to discover the truth about Ray's death continues.

* * *

I started dating James in 2006, while I was still grieving for Ray. We married in 2007, when I fell pregnant with Maya. I was torn. I felt I couldn't fall in love again after Ray. But James was different, he felt like 'the real thing' and being Maya's Dad, I really hoped it would work. Sadly, we divorced in 2010. Giving birth to Maya in 2008 changed my life completely. Having been told I was unlikely to have children, I was overjoyed. Maya is my miracle, the best thing in my life. Every day is a joy. I feel I can have a second childhood with my daughter, Maya, and have the gift of giving and receiving unconditional love, too. I feel truly blessed as we make our list of happy moments grow.

Love starts at home.

Helplines

Please don't suffer in silence. There are help groups and laws to help you. You are not alone xx

The Samaritans – You don't have to be suicidal to call Samaritans. Whatever you're going through, call us free any time from any phone on 116 123 (this number is free to call and will not appear on your phone bill), email jo@samaritans.org or visit www.samaritans.org to find details of your nearest branch.

Karma Nirvana is a UK registered charity that supports victims and survivors of Forced Marriage and Honour Based Abuse.
Honour Network Helpline: 0800 5999 247 (National)
www.karmanirvana.org.uk

True Honour – Help and support all victims of Honour Based Violence (HBV), Forced Marriage (FM) and Female Genital Mutilation (FGM) victims of abuse.
Contact: 07480 621711 (Surrey)
Website: www.truehonour.org.uk

The Crown Prosecution Service aims to ensure those who commit crime in the UK are brought to justice. They also support the victims of crime. Recent legislation has toughened laws regarding harassment, stalking, domestic violence and forced marriages. www.cps.gov.uk

Harassment – It is illegal to 'cause alarm or distress' and to 'put people in fear of violence'. The legal definition of harassment includes 'repeated attempts' to contact someone against their will.

Stalking – This can cover: following a person, watching or spying on them or enforcing contact through any means, including social media. In the most serious offences, where the offender causes 'fear of violence', the maximum prison sentence is five years.

Domestic violence – As well as violence and abuse, legislation now outlaws 'controlling or coercive behaviour in an intimate or family relationship'. Controlling behaviour is making a person subordinate or dependent. The definition includes 'isolating the victim, exploiting their resources, depriving them of the means for independence ... and regulating their everyday behaviour'. Coercive behaviour entails 'assault, threats, humiliation and intimidation ... used to harm, punish or frighten the victim'. As well as more obvious forms of coercion, the definition of domestic violence now includes 'stopping or changing the way someone socialises' and 'changes in routine', including the imposition of domestic chores.

Forced marriage – It is illegal to 'use violence, threats or any other form of coercion' to force another person to marry someone. The legal definition of forced marriage includes emotional pressure, as well as more obvious forms of persuasion.

Dedications and Acknowledgements

For anyone who has ever felt suicidal, betrayed, lonely, abused, not believed or too scared to tell ... you're not alone. Some get justice, some don't – but karma always delivers. Never lose hope. Step into the light with me ... this is for you. X

For the abusers, there were too many of you to count over the years. I didn't want to wait until you all died. I'm brave enough now to handle the truth – hope you are, too. Victim shaming is a thing of the past, not the future. I don't carry the shame anymore. You all tried to waste my life in some way. Even if I help 'just one' with my story, my life was not wasted. Peace comes from within. Truth always finds a way to the light.

With special thanks to:

Paul King

Patricia Edwards

Michael Phipps

Sarbjit Kaur Athwal, Author of *Shamed* and Founder of True Honour. You are my inspiration for sharing your story, thank you for your permission to share your helpline.

Jasvinder Sanghera CBE, Author of *Shame* and Founder of Karma Nirvana. You are my inspiration for sharing your story. Thank you for your permission to share your helpline.

Lisa Von H – Singer/Song writer Twitter @LittleLost_Soul. *Holding onto Life* song on https://www.youtube.com/watch?v=-H25H0VU5j0

Gary Turner – www.garyturner.co.uk

Cressida Downing – www.thebookanalyst.co.uk

SpiffingCovers – www.spiffingcovers.com

Ben Cameron at Cameron Publicity and Marketing Ltd – www.cameronpm.co.uk

Hannah at Doxzoo – www.doxzoo.com

Jane at XS Typing – www.xstyping.com

Sam Rowe and Nick 'Headhunter' Chapman from the Academy of Hard Knocks at Fight Science (Aldershot) – www.academyofhardknocks.com

Rachel Fowler Keene – www.rachelkeene.net

Woking News and Mail – www.wokingnewsandmail.co.uk

Samaritans – www.samaritans.org

True Honour – www.truehonour.org.uk

Karma Nirvana- www.karmanirvana.org.uk

Crown Prosecution Service – www.cps.gov.uk

Surrey Police – Every Officer over the last 20 years who helped me.

Mike Bland, Paula Thompson, Lisa Lloyd, Sam Rowe, Charly Green, Aditi Kapur, Chris Bowes, Marie Hedegaard Holm, Lisa Johnson, Sam Johnson, Sarahjane Tuckey & Paul Turgoose

Thank you all. Much love,
Sunny Angel x

www.sunny-angel.com
www.onelove-healing.com

10399788R00173

Made in the USA
Monee, IL
28 August 2019